RESORT & HOTEL CHEF
Top Secrets

A Cookbook & Travel Guide

by Laura W. Rosen

Graphic Design by Debi Wright

L.R. Publications
Phoenix, Maryland

L.R. Publications
16 Fairwood View Court
Phoenix, Maryland 21131

Resort & Hotel Chefs' Top Secrets
A Cookbook and Travel Guide
was organized and published by L.R. Publications

Author: Laura W. Rosen
Graphic Designer: Debi Wright
Illustrator: Mark Wert
Contributing Writer: Anne Childress
Copy Editor: Mickie Workman

All photographs were provided by the various hotels, resorts,
and gourmet food retailers, except where otherwise noted.
Cover photograph of Philippe Boulot: Jim Lommasson, photographer
Cover photograph of Chinese-Style Lobster, property of Windsor Court Hotel.

Color Separations by Bright Arts Hong Kong
Printed in Singapore

While every attempt has been made to provide accurate information,
the author and publisher may not be held liable for errors and omissions.

10   9   8   7   6   5   4   3   2   1

ISBN: 0-9649163-0-4

Library of Congress Catalog Card Number: 95-95366

Introduction

The enjoyment of great food is a very personal experience—everyone just knows what he or she likes. The resort and hotel chefs featured throughout this book not only have a great sense of their own personal tastes in cuisine, but they have also learned what travelers want from dining. Aromatic ingredients. Inventive combinations of textures. Exotic flavors. Warm foods that feel good when it's cold outside. These culinary professionals have spent years testing and developing dishes that taste divine and look beautiful.

All featured recipes are foods that the chefs prepare on a regular basis. They have been modified for household use, and carefully reviewed (by myself and the chefs) for accuracy. Unless otherwise noted, dinner portions are given for each recipe. Time-saver recipes are illustrated with a clock, and healthy recipes that skimp on fat without sacrificing flavor are identified as "light." Some of the recipes jump to the next page, so be sure to review a recipe in its entirety before buying what you need to prepare the dish.

Don't be intimidated by recipes that look too difficult or time consuming. When I get a craving for Chuck Wiley's Corn Dough Pizza, I double the dough recipe, and pop half of it into the freezer for next time. The delicious cilantro pesto can also be doubled and stored for later use. You will also discover ways to cut steps by purchasing prepared pesto sauces, dried tomatoes, smoked meats, and more.

Many pages include highlights called **Chef's Secret, Ingredient Footnote, or About this Dish.** These highlights show you how to create a sauce or some other food the four-star way; introduce a rare or exotic ingredient; or simply give an insight that should help you make the dish better and quicker. The **Glossary of Chef's Techniques** provides a handy list of the various food preparation and cooking procedures mentioned throughout the book.

The chefs' collective words of wisdom to all of us mortal cooks is this: use the finest ingredients available, buying only the freshest, highest-quality foods you can find. With that in mind, I added a **Resource Section** to the back of this book. Resources for tropical fruits and other specialty produce, farm-raised meats and poultry, and spices from around the world are just some of the specialty foods listed in the section. These merchants will take your order by phone, and ship the goods to your home.

And a final word about the travel information. The large, beautiful photographs and travel tips for each property may be used as a convenient reference to the nation's top resorts and hotels. For each property, there are descriptions of: the private and public areas; activities for adults and children; and overviews of the region or locale. Only the highest-rated hotels, lodges, inns, and resorts were invited to submit recipes for *Resort & Hotel Chefs' Top Secrets.*

I hope you enjoy them as much as I have!

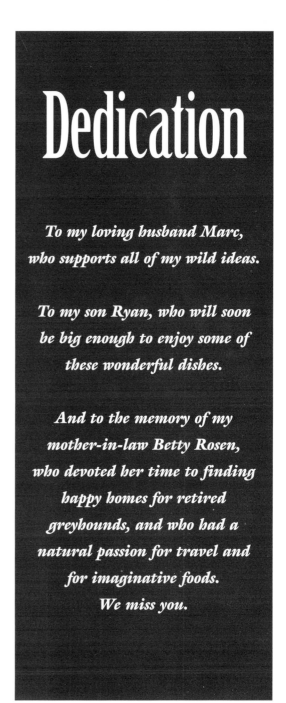

Dedication

To my loving husband Marc, who supports all of my wild ideas.

To my son Ryan, who will soon be big enough to enjoy some of these wonderful dishes.

And to the memory of my mother-in-law Betty Rosen, who devoted her time to finding happy homes for retired greyhounds, and who had a natural passion for travel and for imaginative foods. We miss you.

Table of Contents

Glossary of Chef's Techniques

6

Chapter 1
The American Southwest

Introduction   *10*

Central Arizona

THE BOULDERS
Resort Highlights   12
Chef Charles Wiley's Recipes   18

THE PHOENICIAN
Resort Highlights   14
Chef Robert McGrath's Recipes   23

HYATT REGENCY GRAND CYPRESS

THE WIGWAM
Resort Highlights   16
Chef Jon Hill's Recipes   27

Around Sedona

ENCHANTMENT RESORT
Resort Highlights   32
Chef Kevin Maguire's Recipes   36

L'AUBERGE DE SEDONA
Inn Highlights   34
Chef John Harings' Recipes   40

Colorado

THE BROADMOOR
Resort Highlights   44
Chef Siegfried Eisenberger's Recipes   48

TALL TIMBER
Resort Highlights   46
Chef Anthony Moleterno's Recipes   51

Chapter 2
The American South

Introduction   *56*

Eastern Mountains

THE GREENBRIER
Resort Highlights   58
Chef Robert Wong's Recipes   62

ENCHANTMENT RESORT

GROVE PARK INN
Resort Highlights   60
Chef Jeffrey Piccirillo's Recipes   66

Bayou & Northern Florida

WINDSOR COURT HOTEL
Hotel Highlights   68
Chef Jeff Tunks' Recipes   74

AMELIA ISLAND PLANTATION
Resort Highlights   70
Chef Jacky Burette's Recipes   78

THE RITZ-CARLTON, AMELIA
Resort Highlights   72
Chef Steven Schaefer's Recipes   80

Central & Southern Florida

BOCA RATON RESORT & CLUB
Resort Highlights   84
Chef Brian O'Neil's Recipes   90

THE RITZ-CARLTON, NAPLES
Resort Highlights   86
Chef Pierre Dousson's Recipes   94

HYATT REGENCY GRAND CYPRESS
Resort Highlights   88
Chef Kenneth Juran's Recipes   97

Chapter 3
Northern California

Introduction   *102*

Napa Valley

MEADOWOOD
Resort Highlights   104
Chef Roy Breiman's Recipes   108

AUBERGE DU SOLEIL
Resort Highlights   106
Chef Andrew Sutton's Recipes   111

San Francisco & Monterey

CAMPTON PLACE HOTEL
Hotel Highlights   114
Chef Todd Humphries' Recipes   120

QUAIL LODGE
Resort Highlights   116
Chef Robert Williamson's Recipes   122

THE LODGE AT PEBBLE BEACH
Resort Highlights   118
Chef Beat Giger's Recipes   125

Chapter 4
The American West

Introduction   *132*

Unspoiled Hawaii

HYATT REGENCY KAUAI
Resort Highlights   134
Chef David W. Boucher's Recipes   140

THE LODGE AT KOELE
Resort Highlights   136
Chef Edwin Goto's Recipes   143

MANELE BAY HOTEL
Hotel Highlights   138
Chef Philippe Padovani's Recipes   146

Oregon & Utah

THE HEATHMAN HOTEL
Hotel Highlights   150
Chef Philippe Boulot's Recipes   156

SALISHAN LODGE
Resort Highlights   152
Chef Rob Pounding's Recipes   159

STEIN ERIKSEN LODGE
Resort Highlights   154
Chef Mikel Trapp's Recipes   162

Chapter 5
The East & New England

Introduction   *166*

The Cities

FOUR SEASONS, CHICAGO
Hotel Highlights   168
Chef Mark Baker's Recipes   174

THE RITZ-CARLTON, NEW YORK
Hotel Highlights   170
Chef Craig Henne's Recipes   178

FOUR SEASONS, PHILADELPHIA
Hotel Highlights   172
Chef Jean-Marie Lacroix's Recipes   183

The Getaways

THE POINT
Resort Highlights   186
Chef Sam Mahoney's Recipes   192

THE BALSAMS GRAND RESORT HOTEL
Resort Highlights   188
Chef Charles Carroll's Recipes   195

WHEATLEIGH HOTEL
Hotel Highlights   190
Chef Lesley Iacobacci's Recipes   198

THE POINT

Resource Section
Gourmet meats, spices, chocolate, herbs, and more, available by mail order   *207*

Index
    210

Credits and Acknowledgments
    214

Glossary of Chef's Techniques

This handy glossary explains the various procedures for food preparation and cooking techniques used throughout Resort & Hotel Chefs' Top Secrets. While there are many more procedures used in four- and five-star cooking, these zero in on what you need to know, plain and simple.

Adjust Seasonings: The addition of salt, pepper, and/or herbs to enhance the flavor of a prepared food. Most of the chefs featured in this book suggest you taste the food first, and then adjust seasonings according to your own personal preferences before service.

Aioli: A classic Italian mayonnaise using olive oil that chefs often adapt with the addition of herbs, chile peppers, and other flavorful ingredients.

Al Dente: To briefly blanch a food (generally pasta and fresh vegetables) in hot water until it is firm to the bite. Broccoli and many of the leafy green vegetables turn a brilliant green when cooked al dente.

Blind Bake: To pre-bake a food before adding a filling. This generally refers to baking a pie shell or tart, pricked or lined with beans to prevent rising.

Brunoise: To cut food into a fine dice, usually 1/8" square.

Buerre Manie: A mixture made with equal parts of flour and whole butter, which is then kneaded and added into sauces as a thickener.

Caramelize: To sprinkle sugar on a food (usually a dessert such as crème brulée) and then burn lightly under the broiler to make a caramel topping. Generally speaking, to caramelize is the process of browning sugar in the presence of high heat.

Caramelized Onions: To slow-cook chopped onion in a sauce pan, allowing the onion to brown and release its sweet juices. Try caramelized onions on chef Wiley's Corn Dough Pizza (The Boulders).

Chop: To cut food into small, rough pieces, either by hand or in a food processor.

Chutney: A slow-cooked condiment, generally made with fruit, spices, and vinegar.

Clarified Butter: Butter that is melted and skimmed, leaving only the clear liquid.

Concassé: To pound or chop coursely; usually refers to peeled, seeded, and chopped tomatoes.

Coulis: A purée which generally consists of a cooked vegetable or fruit.

Crème Fraîche: A topping made using 3 parts whipping cream and one part buttermilk.

Deglaze: To add a liquid (often wine or stock) while cooking something in a sauce pan.

Demi Glace: A rich sauce made by reducing veal or beef stock, or by roasting soup bones in the oven. A mirepoix (fine mince) of soup vegetables such as carrots, onion, and celery are often added for flavor. *See the Resource section for mail order sources of Demi Glace.*

Dice: To chop food into small, square pieces (about 1/4" on each side).

Dredge: To lightly coat food (generally chicken, veal, & seafood) with flour or another ingredient.

Egg Wash: Lightly beaten eggs used to coat foods before sautéing or pan-frying. (The egg wash precedes a coating of flour or cornmeal.)

Grill: To cook food over a barbecue, in a hearth oven, or some other means by which food is cooked over burning wood or coals.

Ice Bath: To rest one dish inside another filled with ice, so as to immediately stop the cooking process.

Julienne: To cut food into strips, about 1/8" square by 1"-2" long.

Jus: The reduction of a stock, usually veal or chicken, over medium-high heat in a sauce pan.

Marinate: To allow food to soak in a sauce or vinaigrette.

Mince: To chop food into very small pieces.

Mirepoix: A combination of chopped, aromatic vegetables (usually 2 parts onion, one part celery, and one part carrot) used to flavor stocks, soups, stews, and sauces.

Napoleon: A food that is layered before its final presentation. In this book, there are appetizer, entrée, and dessert napoleons.

Non-Reactive Cookware: Cookware that cannot impart an unwanted metallic taste due to acids. (Aluminum is a reactive metal.)

Purée: To make something completely smooth (almost like a loose paste), generally done using a food processor.

Rehydrate: To hydrate a dried food, such as dried tomatoes or corn husks, using a steamer or other means, such as pouring on scalding water.

Roux: A mixture of fat (usually butter) plus a thickener, such as corn, wheat, or rice flour. The mixture is thoroughly blended by hand and cooked, and is then used in various recipes.

Reduce: To thicken a mixture by cooking it down by a certain percentage.

Sauté: To cook food quickly over a burner, generally using medium-high heat and a little olive oil or butter.

Sear: To brown the surface of food over high heat in a shallow amount of fat, before finishing the cooking process by another means.

Sweat: To slow cook a food in a sauce pan, releasing its juices and flavors, without browning.

Whisk: To blend two or more ingredients together, lightly beating by hand, using a wire or balloon whisk.

Cook's Tools & Pantry Items

The following cook's tools and pantry items are called for in many of the featured recipes. However, it is often possible to make a reasonable substitution, such as the use of a wax paper coronet instead of a piping bag. Try some of the recipes to get a feel for what your kitchen may be lacking before investing in too many new gadgets and accessories.

Cheesecloth

Colander

Cookie Cutters & Molds

Dutch Oven

Electric Mixer

Food Processor

Grater

Grinder *(for peppercorns and spices)*

Herbs, Dried & Fresh

Knives *(including high-quality knives for butchering and deboning meat)*

Measuring Cups *(with liquid and dry measurements)*

Measuring Spoons

Mixing Bowls

Non-Reactive Cookware

Piping Bag *(for "painting" sauces & glazes)*

Pizza Stone *(useful whenever you have to bake a pizza, rather than grilling it)*

Soufflé Cookware

Spices & Seasonings

Steamer or Steaming Basket

Strainer or China Cap

Whisk

Many thanks to Robert Wong, Executive Chef of the Greenbrier in White Sulphur Springs, West Virginia for his assistance with this section.

chapter 1

The American Southwest

Central Arizona
The Boulders
The Phoenician
The Wigwam

Around Sedona
Enchantment Resort
L'Auberge de Sedona

Colorado
The Broadmoor
Tall Timber

The American

Few regions of the United States can compete with the lure of the American Southwest. The southwest is very diverse geographically, with vast deserts and evergreen-covered mountains. Dramatic sights such as Monument Valley, the Grand Canyon, and various Anasazi Indian dwellings provide days (or weeks) of education and enjoyment for the whole family. The region boasts warm, sunny destinations for winter travelers in search of a respite from icy weather, but it is also a cultural melting pot, with strong Spanish and Native American influences. Because of this rich eth-nic diversity, many travelers find the American southwest to be an Epicurean's delight.

The cuisine of the American Southwest is a rich and varied as the land itself. There are sizzling hot salsas and cool dishes blend-ing the fruits and vegetables of the region. Prickly pears and other exotic resources flourish in the dry soil and arid climate. Spanish, Mexican, and Anglo influences are evident in many of the foods prepared by notable chefs throughout the southwest. Perhaps there is no finer example of how southwestern cuisine has matured as an art and as a science than at many of the finest resorts. In the shad-ow of Phoenix, Arizona, there's The Boulders, The Phoenician, and The Wigwam Resort. Next to lovely Sedona, Arizona, is quaint L'Auberge de Sedona and the Enchantment Resort, a

Southwest

ARIZONA OFFICE OF TOURISM

beautiful hideaway nestled in Boynton Canyon. Finally, Colorado is home to two five-star favorites: Tall Timber and The Broadmoor.

On the following pages, chefs at these top resorts help you create their extraordinary dishes so that you can explore the tastes and textures in your own home. The Phoenician's chef de cuisine, Robert McGrath is known for his healthy, reduced-fat dishes that feature all of the flavors typically found in southwestern cooking. His Tamale of Shredded Wild Turkey with Molé Rojo and Salsa of Grilled Pineapple and Habañero is a festival of colors, textures, and flavors. For guests visiting The Wigwam Resort, chef Jon Hill whips up innovative delicacies such as Pacific Rim Tamales (winner of a pork recipe contest in 1993), and Black Bean Soup with Cilantro Lime Sour Cream.

But the gamut of fine cuisine doesn't end there. You'll discover how to make Painted Desert Corn Chowder with the Broadmoor's executive chef, Corn Dough Pizza from the Boulders, Chicken Piccata with Tall Timber's chef, Margarita Mousse with Tuile Tacos from Enchantment Resort, and Medallions of Venison with a Sun-Dried Cranberry Sauce from L'Auberge de Sedona.

Whether you need a simple appetizer or a dazzling main course, the range of flavors and the broad scope of dishes presented here opens up a great new way to dine. 🍃

The Boulders

A high-style refuge in Arizona's Sonoran landscape

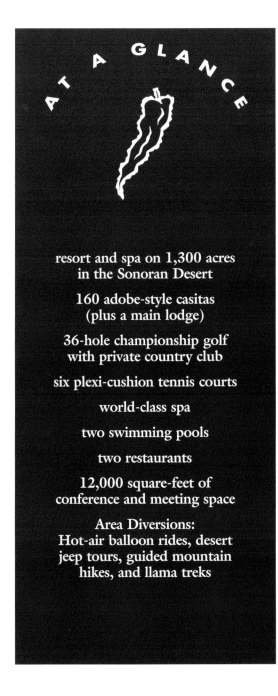

AT A GLANCE

resort and spa on 1,300 acres
in the Sonoran Desert

160 adobe-style casitas
(plus a main lodge)

36-hole championship golf
with private country club

six plexi-cushion tennis courts

world-class spa

two swimming pools

two restaurants

12,000 square-feet of
conference and meeting space

Area Diversions:
Hot-air balloon rides, desert
jeep tours, guided mountain
hikes, and llama treks

EACH YEAR, travelers flock to the little town of Carefree, Arizona, in search of The Boulders, a resort sprawled out among dramatic rock formations under the warm desert sun. The Boulders promises, "No place on Earth is as relaxing, inspiring, and as enchanting as the high Sonoran Desert that surrounds our property." Some are drawn to the resort's peaceful setting among the desert flora and fauna. Others come for the bountiful recreation and for the sunny climate.

The recently refurbished and expanded Sonoran Spa at The Boulders enables guests to rejuvenate their minds and bodies. In addition to full spa treatments, there is a fully equipped Workout Center with treadmills, step machines, exercise bikes, and a rowing machine. LifeCircuit™ equipment and free weights are also available. And, as a regular winner of *Golf Magazine's* Gold Medal Award, The Boulders' championship golf—on two 18-hole courses—ranks as one of the best in America. Guests can also enjoy a workout in the majestic desert mountains, by opting for a scenic guided hike up a mountain path to ancient Indian ruins. Guided mountain bike tours of the area, hot-air balloon rides, and jeep treks are offered as well.

However, many guests come for the award-winning southwestern cuisine orchestrated by executive chef Charles Wiley, whose devotion to intensely-flavored dishes utilizing the foods of the region has consistently won acclaim.

Wiley and his culinary staff keep the resort's dishes "light and fresh, with robust flavors" in the property's five restaurants. Consequently, a meticulous balance of colors, flavors, and contrasting textures is the goal met with each new creation added to The Boulder's menus. ✆

P.O. Box 2090 ✆ Carefree, Arizona 85377 ✆ (602)488-9009

The Phoenician

A desert playground at the base of Camelback Mountain

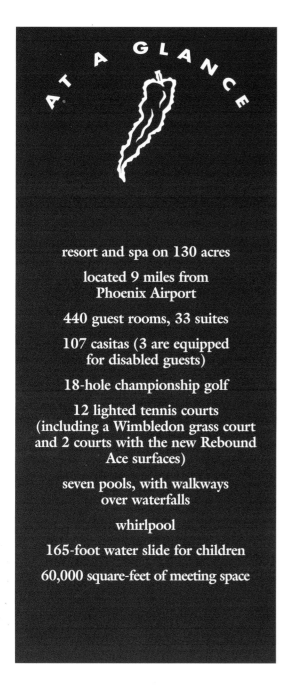

TUCKED INTO the Valley of the Sun, surrounded by majestic Arizona scenery, The Phoenician gives travelers whatever they want from a vacation—unbeatable recreation, exquisite dining, top-rate accommodations, and more sun per hour than many destinations. Strolling the beautifully landscaped grounds, guests discover life-size sculptures by notable southwestern artists, including an eleven-foot tall bronze figure by the late Allan Houser entitled, "May We Have Peace." The sculpture depicts a native American offering a peace pipe up to the Great Spirit. These special touches provide the resort's guests with an important link to the spirited culture of the American Southwest.

Attention to detail carries through to The Phoenician's guest rooms as well. Those in search of private accommodations within arm's length of resort amenities opt for one of the luxury casitas, nestled along the edge of a lake. Each casita has parking, fireplaces, walk-in closets, and breathtaking views of the surrounding landscape. Rooms in the main hotel are noteworthy, too, with Italian marble bathrooms, private lanais, Berber carpeting, McGuire furniture, and decorative artworks selected to coordinate with the room's muted southwestern colors.

This region of Arizona has so many pleasant diversions: hiking Camelback Mountain, browsing shops and galleries, plus sightseeing in nearby Phoenix. Or, enjoy The Phoenician's sports and fitness facilities. At the resort's Centre for Well-being, guests can partake of cardiovascular and weight-training programs, aerobics, meditation, and a variety of spa treatments—all designed to "unify body, mind, and spirit."

The Wigwam

Great golf and fine dining in the shadow of Phoenix

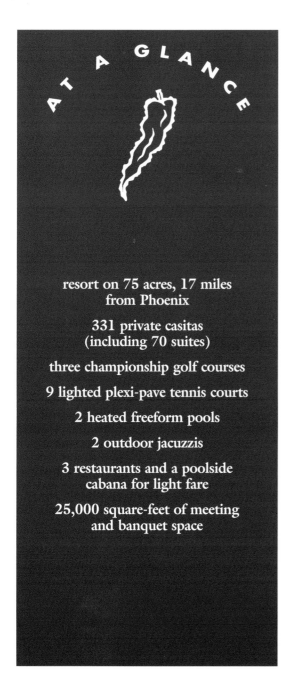

AT A GLANCE

resort on 75 acres, 17 miles from Phoenix

331 private casitas (including 70 suites)

three championship golf courses

9 lighted plexi-pave tennis courts

2 heated freeform pools

2 outdoor jacuzzis

3 restaurants and a poolside cabana for light fare

25,000 square-feet of meeting and banquet space

SIXTY-FIVE years ago, The Wigwam opened as a 13-room guest ranch tucked in between Phoenix and the peaceful Sonoran Desert. While guests still enjoy the towering saguaros and colorful southwestern sunsets, much has changed at the Wigwam since those early years. The resort has earned nineteen five-star ratings by *Mobil Travel Guide* plus the AAA Four Diamond award, and it continues to strive for perfection. Today, The Wigwam is a top-rated golf resort, with three championship courses, including one designed by Robert Trent Jones, Sr. But activities at the Wigwam don't end there. Guests can play on any of the resort's nine lighted tennis courts, work out in the health club, or relax in a bubbling whirlpool.

Guests stay in private casitas, many appointed with massive stone fireplaces for mesquite wood fires. Each casita's furniture, art, and decorative accessories reflect the many cultural influences of the southwest—including Spanish and native American. The casitas look out onto a thoughtfully manicured landscape, with clusters of towering palms, fragrant orange trees, and flowers in full bloom.

The Wigwam promises guests an "authentic Arizona" experience. Adults and kids can saddle up at the Wigwam Stables for a trail ride out through the desert terrain. Groups can arrange for a western cook-out, complete with a wild west town and hay-wagon rides. For a more modern Arizona experience, many guests opt to spend their days basking in the sun beside The Wigwam's beautiful free-form pool, or playing a round of tennis on the property's plexi-pave courts.

Travelers beware—spend a week at The Wigwam and you may never want to go home! ꙮ

P.O. Box 278 ꙮ *Litchfield Park, Arizona 85340* ꙮ *(602)935-3811*

Charles Wiley

THE BOULDERS

Before coming to The Boulders, Charles Wiley worked as a chef at various resorts and luxury hotels in Alaska, Utah, and northern California, gaining experience in the preparation of fresh seafood and other delicacies. Today, Wiley is a member of the American Institute of Wine and Food, and he serves on the advisory board of the Scottsdale Culinary Institute, where he sometimes teaches cooking courses.

At The Boulders, chef Wiley supervises a 96-member staff at the property's five restaurants. He also acts as Executive Chef for Carefree Resorts' other properties in Carmel, California, and Telluride, Colorado.

He often demonstrates the art of healthy cuisine for guests at The Boulders. Perhaps it comes as no surprise that Food & Wine *magazine named him one of "The Ten Best New Chefs in America" in 1994.*

Shrimp Salad With Spicy Golden Tomato Vinaigrette and Crisp Phyllo *Pictured on p.22*

Makes 4 servings

20 shrimp (approximately 1 oz. each)
2 tsp. olive oil
2 cloves garlic, peeled and minced
2 Tbs. red onion, finely diced
2 Roma tomatoes, peeled and diced
1/4 cup yellow bell pepper*
2 tomatillos*
3 Anaheim chiles (roasted, peeled, seeded and diced)
2 Tbs. cilantro, chopped
8 oz. mixed lettuce

* Cut in a dice

Golden Tomato Vinaigrette
1 large golden tomato, cored and seeded
1 shallot
2 cloves garlic
2 Tbs. vegetable oil
1 lemon, juice only
kosher salt to taste

Crisp Phyllo
1/2 sheet of phyllo pastry

Method for Salad: Peel and devein shrimp, then cut eight into chunks for the salsa, leaving the remaining 12 whole. Heat oil in a skillet over medium heat and cook all shrimp briefly, transfering the shrimp pieces into a mixing and reserving the 12 whole shrimp loosely covered on plate. Add garlic and onion to the skillet, and sauté until tender. Add remaining ingredients (except lettuce) and heat slightly.

Method for Vinaigrette: Combine all in a blender and emulsify.

Method for Phyllo: Spread out a little shredded phyllo on a baking sheet and fashion into a little circle approximately 3" in diameter. Bake in a 350° oven for about 10 minutes until the phyllo is a light golden brown.

Presentation: Toss lettuce in the yellow tomato vinaigrette and divide among four plates. Place a small pile of the shrimp mixture in the center of each lettuce pile, and top with some crispy phyllo. Drizzle golden tomato vinaigrette around plate and arrange whole shrimp around lettuce.

This is a southwestern version of the Chinese chicken salad. It's a wonderful blend of tastes and textures. We designed this shrimp salad as one of our spa selections.

Skillet-Seared Squab With Apples, Sweet Potato, and Red Onion

Makes 4 servings

Seared Squab
2 squab (approx. 1 lb. each, cut into 1/4s)
1 recipe squab marinade (recipe follows)
4 strips bacon, cut into 1" squares
kosher salt
black pepper, freshly ground
1 sweet potato, cut into 1/2" cubes
1 red onion*
1 granny smith apple**
fresh cilantro leaves to taste

* Peel and cut into thin wedges
** Core and cut into wedges

Squab Marinade (yields 3 cups)
2 Tbs. olive oil
12 cloves garlic, chopped
4 chipotle chiles (chopped fine and added to 1 Tbs. adobo sauce)*
3 Tbs. cilantro, chopped
4 Roma tomatoes, chopped
4 lemons, zest only
1/2 cup apple cider
1/2 cup molasses
1 cup tequila
1/4 cup white wine vinegar
2 tsp. kosher salt

*Available in gourmet grocers and at Hispanic food markets; or, see Resources section

Method for Marinade: Combine all in a glass or stainless steel bowl and whisk together.

Method for Squab & Vegetables: Place the squab in a glass dish, stainless steel bowl, or plastic bag. Cover with 1 cup of the marinade (reserving the remaining 1 1/2 cups for the sauce), and marinate for at least 6 hours, or overnight.

Prepare a wood or charcoal fire and heat a 12" cast iron skillet over the glowing embers. Add the bacon and cook until rendered and crispy; remove from pan. Season the squab with salt and pepper, and place in the hot bacon fat, skin-side down. Brown squab very well (on the skin side only) over high heat. This should take only a couple of minutes, as the squab should be served medium-rare. Remove from skillet.

Add potato and onion to the skillet and cook, stirring with a wooden spoon until browned and caramelized. Add apple and cook slightly. Deglaze pan with the remaining 1 1/2 cups of marinade, scraping the bottom with the wooden spoon.

Return squab and bacon to the skillet; cover and cook and additional 5 minutes until the squab is heated through.

Presentation: *Plate individual portions of squab, arranged beside the browned apples, onions, and sweet potatoes. Sprinkle with cilantro leaves and serve immediately.*

Dutch Oven Green Chile Cornbread

Makes 8 servings

1 cup butter
3/4 cup sugar
4 eggs
1/2 cup green chiles, diced (or substitute canned)
1 1/2 cups cream-style corn
1/2 cup jack cheese, shredded
1 cup flour
1 cup yellow corn meal
2 Tbs. baking powder
1 tsp. salt

Method for Cornbread: To prepare your fire: Light 18 charcoal briquettes or use glowing embers from a wood fire which will have to be replaced halfway through baking. Meanwhile, make the bread.

Beat together butter and sugar. Add eggs slowly, one at a time. Add remaining ingredients and mix until well incorporated. Sift together dry ingredients, then add moist ingredients, and mix all until smooth.

Pour into a well-buttered 10" dutch oven fitted with a lid. Place oven on top of 9 of the briquettes and place the remaining 9 coals (or the embers) on top of the lid. Bake approximately 1 hour.

> This has become so popular that guests might start a riot if he ever took it off the menu.

Corn Dough Pizza With Smoked Chicken, Plum Tomatoes, Cilantro Pesto, and Pepper Jack Cheese

Makes 2 pizzas

Pizza

pizza dough (recipe follows)
cilantro pesto (recipe follows)
2 plum tomatoes, sliced 1/4" thick
1 breast of chicken, smoked*
1/2 cup pepper jack cheese
1 whole onion for caramelized onions
(recipe follows)
1/2 red bell pepper**
1/2 yellow bell pepper**

* Purchase a smoked breast of chicken or duck from a specialty food store (or see Resources section)
** Roast and cut into strips

Dough

1 package dry yeast (approx. 1/4 oz., or 2 tsp.)
3/4 cup warm water (80°-90°)
2 tsp. sugar
1/4 cup yellow cornmeal
1 Tbs. milk
1 3/4-2 cups all-purpose flour
2 Tbs. olive oil
1/4 tsp. salt

Cilantro Pesto

1 large bunch cilantro, leaves only*
1/4 cup aged Monterey Jack cheese, grated
2 Tbs. toasted pumpkinseeds
3 garlic cloves
1/4 cup olive oil
salt and pepper to taste

* Approximately 1/2 cup, tightly packed

There are so many flavors in this pizza—ranging from spicy to smoky to sweet—you'll want to savor each and every bite. We use smoked duck for this recipe, but it's also good with chicken.

Chef's Secret

HOW TO CARAMELIZE AN ONION

Chop the onion and slow-cook it over low heat, allowing the onion to become golden-brown, and the juices to cook out into the pan. Reduce the onion down to about 3-4 Tbs. with this process. "This slow simmering process really develops the sugar in the onion, hence the name 'caramelizing,'" says chef Wiley. These soft, sweet onions make a great topping for southwestern pizzas.

Method for Dough: In a bowl, combine yeast, water, sugar, and cornmeal; mix to incorporate. Set aside 10 minutes until bubbling and foamy. Add the rest of the dough ingredients, holding out 1/4 cup of the flour for kneading, and mix well. Turn out onto a floured work surface and knead about 2 minutes, adding only the absolute minimum of flour to the work surface. Place in a lightly oiled bowl; cover and let rise in a warm place. Punch down and divide in half.

Author's Note: This dough is rather sticky to work with, but it makes for a light, tender crust. Just add more flour (conservatively) as needed.

Method for Pesto: Combine all ingredients in the work bowl of a food processor and process into a paste.

Assembling and Baking the Pizza: Preheat an oven fitted with a pizza stone to 475° about 30 minutes before baking. Flatten dough on a lightly floured work surface, rolling out into a circle about 6" in diameter, keeping the dough 1/8-1/4" thick. Transfer to a pizza peel or to the back of a baking pan that has been sprinkled with a little cornmeal. Spread 3 Tbs. of the cilantro pesto on each pizza, leaving a 1/2" border.

Place the slices of tomato on top of the pesto and arrange the chicken on the tomatoes. Sprinkle with cheese and top with the onion and pepper. Move the peel back and forth to make sure the dough is loose and slide onto the pizza stone. Bake until crisp, browned, and the cheese is bubbling (about 12 minutes).

Chocolate Macadamia Nut Praline Torte

Makes 2 9 1/2" tortes (enough to serve 16-20 people)

Pastry
4 cups all-purpose flour
2/3 cup sugar
10 oz. sweet butter, unsalted*
2 egg yolks
3 Tbs. heavy cream

* Cold, cut into cubes

Macadamia Nut Filling
1/4 cup light corn syrup
1 1/2 cups sugar
6 oz. sweet butter, unsalted
3/4 cup heavy cream
2 1/2 cups unsalted macadamia nuts*

* Toast and chop into large pieces

Chocolate Topping
1 cup sour cream
1 cup heavy cream
2 whole eggs
4 egg yolks
3/4 Tbs. corn starch
6 oz. semi-sweet chocolate, finely chopped

To Assemble and Finish the Torte:
1 qt. heavy cream, stiffly whipped
dark chocolate shavings
white chocolate shavings

Special Thanks
Thanks to former Boulders chef Jeff Gustie, who helped create some of these great dishes.

> **This torte was developed six years ago by one of our top pastry chefs. Take it out of the refrigerator and let the torte warm slightly to room temperature before serving for optimal taste and consistency.**

Method for Pastry: Preheat oven to 375°. Combine flour and sugar. With pasty cutter or two knives, cut cold butter into flour and sugar until the mixture has the appearance of cornmeal. In a separate bowl, stir together eggs and cream; add to flour mixture. Mix until dough comes together and forms a big ball. Wrap in plastic wrap and chill. (Will keep up to one week in the refrigerator or one month in the freezer.)

When dough is chilled and firm, roll out to between 1/8-1/4" thickness to fit the bottom of a false bottom tart pan. Line pan with foil and pie weights. Bake the shell in preheated oven for 20 minutes or until golden brown.

Method for Macadamia Filling: Have all ingredients measured and close at hand. In a heavy-bottom sauce pan, combine corn syrup and sugar. Cook over low-medium heat until sugar is completely dissolved. Turn heat to medium-high. Stir mixture constantly until it reaches a deep golden color. Reduce heat to low and carefully add the butter, as it can splatter. Stir the mixture slowly with a whisk until butter is melted and partially blended in.

Slowly add the cream, stirring with a whisk until butter and cream are completely combined. Remove from heat. Stir in macadamia nuts. Pour caramel nut mixture into the two cooled pastry shells. Chill at least 1 hour. (This recipe can be prepared up to this point three days in advance.)

Method for Topping: In the bottom section of a double boiler, bring water to simmering. In the top section of boiler, combine all ingredients except chocolate. Cook over the simmering water until mixture is the consistency of mayonnaise, stirring with a whisk constantly for about 5-10 minutes.

Remove from heat. Add chocolate and stir until chocolate is completely melted and mixture is smooth. Pour evenly over the macadamia caramel in pastry shell. Chill at least two hours or until torte is set and firm.

Presentation: Remove the torte from the tart pan and place on a serving plate. Cover the top of the torte with whipped cream, using a pastry bag or spatula. Cut the tart with a hot knife before finishing with chocolate shavings. Cover with dark chocolate shavings; pile white chocolate shavings in the center.

*Shrimp Salad
With Spicy Golden
Tomato Vinaigrette
and Crisp Phyllo.
Recipe on p.18*

Robert McGrath

THE PHOENICIAN

Resident chefs Robert McGrath and Alessandro Stratta create award-winning foods that embody the culture and exotic flavors of the Valley of the Sun. "After only two visits to Scottsdale, I knew this was where I wanted to be," says McGrath, whose training at the Culinary Institute of America and at the Cordon Bleu in Paris prepared him for a career in the culinary arts.

As chef de cuisine at The Phoenician's Windows on the Green, McGrath serves up unbeatable combinations of flavors, such as Tamales of Wild Turkey with Molé Rojo and Pineapple Salsa. In 1988, McGrath was voted among the "Ten Best New Chefs in America" by Food & Wine *magazine, and he continues to earn national acclaim for his creations. As executive chef, Alessandro Stratta makes sure that all of the dishes prepared at The Phoenician are innovative, delicious, and artistically presented.*

Rustic Soup of Butternut Squash, Chile Pasilla, Roasted Garlic, and Pepitas

Makes 4 servings (yields 3 cups)

Rustic Soup
1 1/2 cups butternut squash*
1 1/2 cups chicken stock
1/8 cup heavy cream
1/4 cup yellow onion, chopped
1 tsp. shallots, chopped
1 Tbs. garlic, chopped
1 tsp. chile pasilla, minced
1/8 tsp. cayenne pepper
1/8 tsp. cumin
kosher salt to taste

* Peel, seed, roast, and purée

Garnish
1/2 cup roasted garlic cloves, coarsely chopped
1/2 cup pumpkin seeds, toasted
1/4 cup chile pasilla, finely chopped*
4 cilantro sprigs
4 brioche croutons (or pita crisps)
2 Tbs. garlic purée
1 garlic clove**

* Can substitute dried New Mexican chiles
** Slice lengthwise and fry quickly as chips

About this Dish
"Chile peppers are high in vitamins A, C, and D," says McGrath.
He also notes that there is less salt needed when cooking with chiles.

Method for the Rustic Soup: Sauté the onions, garlic, chile pasilla, and shallots until soft. Add the chicken stock and bring to a boil; add the butternut squash, and reduce by 1/4. Next, purée the soup in a food processor.

Season soup with the cumin, cayenne pepper, and kosher salt. Add the cream.

Presentation: Place empty soup bowls atop wide-rimmed soup plates. Put a crouton in each bowl, extending out of the bowl at 2:00. Pipe the garlic purée onto the crouton and place a couple of garlic chips in the purée. Next, ladle the soup in and garnish with the roasted garlic cloves, chopped chile pasilla, pepitas, and a cilantro sprig.

This is a nice autumn country-style soup with baked squash and a few chiles added while it cooks. It can be creamed and garnished with toasted seeds, too.

Spinach Leaves with Texas Peanut Dressing and Buttermilk-Fried Sweet Onions

Makes 4 servings

Garnish
1 medium white onion*
1 cup buttermilk
1 cup flour
1 Tbs. salt
1 tsp. cayenne pepper
corn oil for frying
1/2 cup raspberries
1/2 cup green onions, chopped

* Cut in halves and slice 1/4" thick

Dressing
(yields 1 1/8 cups)
1/4 cup peanut butter
1/4 cup honey
1/4 cup raspberry vinegar
1/4 cup water
1 Tbs. marigold mint, chopped
1 Tbs. cilantro, chopped

Spinach Salad
3 cups spinach leaves
4 raddichio leaves for cups

Method for the Garnish: Mix the flour and seasonings together. Soak the cut onions in the buttermilk. Take the onions out of the buttermilk with your hands and let them drip dry, gently shaking off the excess. Toss these in the seasoned flour and fry them in oil heated to about 350° F. until golden brown and crisp.

Method for the Dressing: Heat the peanut butter in a microwave for 10-15 seconds. Mix the peanut butter, honey, and corn oil together; then add the raspberry vinegar and the water. Add the chopped cilantro and marigold mint. Set aside at room temperature.

Salad Preparation & Presentation: Place the raddichio cups in the upper left hand quarter of the plate. Wash and stem the spinach leaves and toss them with the dressing; place the salad coming out of the raddichio cups onto the plate. Garnish the salad with the raspberries and green onions. Place the fried sweet onions on top of the spinach leaves and serve immediately. ✺

> **This salad has very compatible flavors and is very easy to make. Substitute fried sweet potatoes for the buttermilk onions for a change of pace.**

Steamed and Seared Scallops with Cilantro Leaves, Tamarind, & Ginger

Makes 4 servings

12 jumbo scallops (about 1 1/2 oz. each)

Garnish
1 Tbs. tamarind paste
1/4 cup plus 2 Tbs. soy sauce
1/4 cup ginger, julienned
1/4 cup cilantro leaves
1/4 cup leeks, julienned (white parts only)
1/4 cup peanut oil
12 scallop shell halves
1 pound assorted dried beans*
12 arbol chiles*
1 1/2 cups seaweed salad (or substitute wilted spinach)

*Reusable garnish

Method for Scallops: Steam the scallops until just cooked, approximately 5 minutes. Set aside. Mix the tamarind paste and the soy sauce. Heat the peanut oil on a hot griddle until smoking hot. Sear the scallops on the hot griddle, or in a non-stick skillet over high heat.

Presentation: Place the beans and chiles on a plate and rest the scallop shells on the beans. Place the seaweed salad on the bottom of each shell; spoon the soy sauce mixture over the salad and then top with the scallops. Place the cilantro, leek and ginger on top of scallops. Spoon the hot oil over all and serve. ✺

Tamales of Shredded Wild Turkey, Molé Rojo, and Salsa of Grilled Pineapple and Habanero

Makes 4 servings

Tamales

(4) 8 oz. turkey breast cutlets
1 tsp. dark chile powder
1/4 cup chicken stock
1/8 cup veal demi-glace (see recipe or see Resources section)
1/8 cup apple juice
1/4 cup onion, chopped
2 Tbs. garlic, chopped
1/2 tsp. New Mexico dried chile, minced*
1/2 tsp. chile poblano, chopped**
kosher salt and freshly ground black pepper to taste
1 Tbs. lard
1/4 cup masa harina (corn flour)
1 tsp. southwest seasoning
1/8 cup chicken stock
4 dried corn husks***
2 ears of corn (each cut in half at a 45° angle)

* Readily available, packaged mild or hot
** From your gourmet grocer, or substitute jalapeño chiles
*** Dry in oven, or purchase tamale wrappers from a gourmet grocer (or see Resources section)

Salsa Garnish

3/4 cup pineapple, grilled and diced
1 Tbs. cilantro*
1 Tbs. red onion*
1 Tbs. chile poblano*
1 Tbs. chile habanero, minced
1 Tbs. red bell pepper*
1 Tbs. lime juice
4 cilantro sprigs

* Chop

Sauce Molé Rojo

(yields 1 cup)
1 tsp. achiote paste*
1 Tbs. chile ancho, minced
1 Tbs. dried New Mexico chile, minced*
2 Tbs. tomato, chopped
3/4 cup chicken stock
1 tsp. garlic, chopped
1 tsp. pickling spice
1 Tbs. Ibarra Mexican chocolate*
1 Tbs. sugar
kosher salt and fresh ground black pepper to taste

* See Resources section

How to Make a Demi-Glace

Demi-glace is a sauce made by reducing veal or beef stock. At The Phoenician, this is done by roasting veal bones with a mirepoix (very fine dice) of carrots, onions, and celery. The mixture is then put into a saucepan, and allowed to thicken over medium-high heat to a desired consistency.

When time is tight, chef McGrath suggests using a good quality packaged brown sauce, such as Knorr-Swiss®, as a substitute.

Method for Tamales: Sear the turkey on both sides until brown. Slow roast the turkey about 45 minutes, or until the meat can be shredded. Sauté the onion, garlic, and chiles until soft. Add the shredded turkey meat. Add the stock, demi-glace, and apple juice. Reduce over medium heat until all of the liquid has evaporated. Season to taste.

Mix the lard in mixing bowl until it is fluffy in consistency. Add the masa harina and seasoning mix, blending thoroughly. Add the broth slowly and mix until dough is soft, but not sticking to your hand.

Separate the dough into 1 1/2 oz. portions and flatten in a tortilla press to the thickness of 1/4". Lay in the rehydrated corn husk (rehydrate the husks using water to moisten.) Place ☞

1 1/2 Tbs. of the turkey mixture in the center of the masa and fold the edges of the dough around the tamale, then fold the top of the corn husk down over the tamale. In a non-pressurized steamer, steam the tamales, placing them folded-ends down, for approximately 2 hours (or until they don't stick to the husk).

Method for the Salsa Garnish: Mix the pineapple, cilantro, red onion, habañero, and lime juice. Set aside in a cool place.

Method for the Sauce: Sauté the garlic, chiles, and tomato until they are soft. Add the remaining ingredients and bring to a boil. Simmer 30-40 minutes and then purée. Run through a food mill or a coarse strainer. Set aside in a warm place.

Presentation: Roast the half ears of corn until just darkening. Rest the tamale against the angled-out end of the corn. Ladle the sauce over the tamale and let it run down the plate. Garnish the top of the tamale with the salsa and decorate the tamale with a cilantro sprig.

> You can substitute any sauce you prefer for the molé, but it is fun to make, and the flavors are so rich and earthy that the effort is worthwhile.

An assortment of southwestern foods on display at The Phoenician

Jon Hill

THE WIGWAM

The Wigwam's attention to detail continues through to its culinary staff as well. Executive chef Jon Hill grows many of his own herbs and vegetables in order to provide guests with the freshest ingredients possible.

A former White House chef during the Reagan Administration, Hill is well-versed in culinary artistry. When 28 Arizona chefs were invited to prepare a benefit banquet sponsored by American Express™, Absolut Vodka™ and Share Our Strength for hunger relief, Hill rolled up his sleeves and whipped up some of his top creations.

Chef Hill creates award-winning meals for guests at the Terrace Dining Room, featuring classical cuisine pared down with lighter ingredients, and the Arizona Kitchen, where guests enjoy fireside dining by candlelight. The chefs promise "artistic expressions of contemporary southwest cuisine" in the adobe-style Arizona Kitchen.

Smoked Corn Chowder *Pictured on p.9*

Makes 18 servings (yields 1 gallon)

1/2 cup onion
1/2 cup celery
1/2 cup leeks
1/2 cup carrots
1/4 cup red bell pepper
4 cloves garlic, minced
8 ears corn on the cob
1 cup peeled potatoes (red or baking, such as Idaho russetts)
1/2 Tbs. thyme
1/2 Tbs. oregano
1/2 Tbs. basil
2 tsp. chili powder
1 tsp. cumin
1/2 tsp. cinnamon
1 qt. chicken stock (or use cold water and add bouillion)
8 oz. roux (4 oz. each: butter and flour, blended)
1 gallon heavy cream
1/4 cup olive oil
dash tabasco
kosher salt and black pepper to taste

Method for Chowder: Chop first 5 ingredients. Clean ears of corn, place in smoker and smoke for 30 minutes, or until dark brown. Boil the chicken stock. Remove kernels from cob, and then add cobs to boiling stock. In a large bowl, cover kernels with water, and break apart with hands—skim off excess pulp from top. Set aside.

In a large, well-heated sauce pot, add olive oil and sauté vegetables (except corn and potatoes.) Add thyme, oregano, basil, garlic, cinnamon, chili powder, and cumin.

While the vegetables are cooking, add roux to chicken stock to make a velouté; then remove from heat. Add corn, potatoes, and half of the water (no more than 2 cups) to the vegetables; then, strain the velouté.

Heat heavy cream to a boil and reduce by 1/4. Stir reduced cream into the vegetable mixture, and allow to simmer for about 20 minutes (stirring frequently). Season soup with salt, pepper, and a dash of tabasco.

> This chowder has become a signature dish in our Arizona Kitchen restaurant. I grow Arizona sweet corn on 20 acres of property here, and then mesquite-smoke the kernels for this flavorful soup.

Grilled Dungeness Crab and Bay Shrimp Cakes with Fresh Strawberry Salsa

Makes 4 servings (8 cakes, 3 oz. each)

Crab Cakes

1/2 cup red onion (cut in a fine mince)
1/2 cup celery (cut in a fine dice)
1 tsp. dry mustard
1/8 tsp. cayenne pepper
1/2 lb. jumbo lump crab meat
(Dungeness crab is best)
1/2 lb. bay shrimp
1 egg
2/3 cup bread crumbs (white, without crust)
1/4 cup mayonnaise
2 Tbs. fresh basil
2 Tbs. cilantro, chopped
1 tsp. salt
1 tsp. zest of Valencia orange
2 Tbs. corn oil

Strawberry Salsa
You've never tasted strawberries like this!

1/4 medium red onion, finely diced
1/4 medium green pepper
3/4 pint fresh strawberries
    (seed, cap, and dice)
3/4 cup fresh pineapple juice
1 Tbs. corn oil
1/4 medium yellow pepper
1/4 medium jalapeño pepper, diced & seeded
1 tsp. clover honey
salt to taste

Method for Crab Cakes: Sauté onion and celery in corn oil over medium heat until slightly brown. Allow to cool and stir in mustard, cayenne pepper, and orange zest. In a medium bowl, combine all remaining ingredients with the cooled onion and celery mixture.

Spoon out approximately 1/3 cup of mixture and shape into patties. When mixture is proportioned out, grill each cake over a mesquite fire, until golden brown on each side.

Method for Strawberry Salsa: Sauté onions and peppers in corn oil and add all other ingredients. Refrigerate until chilled and then serve at room temperature.

Presentation: *Serve 2 cakes accompanied by strawberry salsa to each guest.*

Ingredient Footnote
Chef Hill uses fresh opal basil in this recipe, but you can substitute any fresh basil.

> Be sure to use the best quality lump crab available for this recipe.
> The strawberry salsa makes the dish seasonal and light.

Jalapeño Fry Bread

Makes 24 pieces, each about 1 1/2 ounce

1 cup whole wheat flour
1/2 cup white enriched bread flour
3 Tbs. Rio Grande honey (or a substitute brand)
2 Tbs. olive oil
1/2 tsp. salt
1/2 oz. dried yeast
3/4 cup warm milk
2 fresh jalapeño peppers, diced
4 Tbs. whole kernel corn

Method for Fry Bread: In a 3-qt. mixing bowl, place the flours, honey, oil, salt, jalapeños, and corn. Set aside. Warm milk to 90° F. Add yeast and stir mixture until lumps disappear. Pour milk/yeast mixture into flour mixture, and continue to stir for 5 minutes. Cover the dough and let rise for 15 minutes. Remove dough from bowl and, using a knife, cut dough into strips approximately 12" long and 1 1/2" wide.

At this point, dough can be frozen for a week. Just thaw and continue cooking process.

Deep fry individual pieces of the bread at 375° until golden brown.

Presentation: *Serve in a bread basket, alone or with other freshly-baked breads. Or, use the fry bread as you would a pizza crust. Chef Hill often tops his fry bread with cardamon honey.*

> This dish came from one of the area's Indian reservations. I recommend using peanut oil, which has a high boiling point, and is healthy.

Black Bean Soup with Cilantro Lime Sour Cream

Makes 20 servings (yields approximately 5 quarts)

Soup
1 lb. black beans (if using dried beans—
pick over and soak overnight)
2 qts. chicken stock
2 qts. ham stock

dice the following into 1/4" pieces:
    4 oz. bacon strips (about 4 pieces)
    1/3 cup celery
    1/3 cup carrots
    1/4 onion
1 cup tomato purée
2 tsp. garlic, minced
1 bunch cilantro
1/2 Tbs. thyme leaves

1/2 Tbs. ground black pepper
1/2 Tbs. dry mustard
4 Tbs. port wine
3/4 tsp. cumin
1 chipotle chile, minced
salt to taste

Sour Cream Topping
1/4 cup fresh sour cream
cilantro (use 3 broad leaves per portion)
juice of one lime

Optional Garnish
tri-colored corn tortillas (red, yellow, blue,
or green)

Method for Soup: Rinse black beans thoroughly and cover with cold water; soak overnight. Sauté bacon with onion, garlic, celery, and carrots until nicely browned. Add port wine, then add all remaining ingredients. Simmer until beans are tender. Taste and adjust seasoning.

Presentation: Blend the 3 ingredients listed for sour cream topping. Garnish top of each soup portion with 1/4 tsp. dollop of topping, and place the cilantro leaves atop cream. Cut the tri-colored corn tortillas into julienne strips. Fry them quickly just before serving, and arrange on the plates, resting under each soup bowl. The colorful tortillas make a festive presentation. ✺

This is a very popular appetizer here at the Wigwam. The soup has a dramatic look, with lots of color and fresh cilantro that we grow here on the property.

Pacific Rim Tamales

Makes 12 tamales

1 lb. fresh boneless pork loin
1/2 cup peanut oil
1/8 cup achiote seed (see Resources section)
1/2 cup onion
3 cloves garlic
1/2 tsp. oregano
1 Tbs. salt
12 green bananas
12 banana leaves (12")
1/4 cup tomato sauce
1/8 tsp. fresh ground pepper
15 calamata olives
1 oz. parsley, chopped

Ingredient Footnote

Achiote (or annatto) are the dried seeds of a small flowering tree native to Tropical Geneva, and they are widely used in Latin American and Pacific Rim cooking. The outer orange pulp surrounding the seeds is also used as a natural food dye.

Method for Tamales: Cut pork into 1/2" cubes, add tomato sauce, grated garlic, oregano, salt, pepper, olives, and parsley. Take achiote seed and fry in hot peanut oil until it turns dark yellow. Strain and remove seeds. Add half of this oil to the pork. Simmer until pork is tender (braise), about ☞

1 hour and then allow to cool.

Prepare 2 qts. of cold water in a bowl with 2 Tbs. salt. Peel bananas and scrape inside string off with knife, then drop each into the salt water. Retrieve and scrape bananas with a fine grater.

Add remaining yellow oil, salt, and half of the oil to the pork; stir evenly. Drop banana leaves into a pot of hot water for about 5 minutes to soften them. Wipe leaves dry and lay flat on work surface. With a spoon, evenly spread oil from the pork mixture. Now take 2 Tbs. banana mixture and place on oiled leaf. Flatten to about 6" by 3". Take 2 Tbs. pork mixture and line across middle of the leaf on top of the banana mixture.

Roll and tie each tamale with butcher string, then simmer in just enough water to cover.

Presentation: Center each tamale on a serving plate. Cut it in half, lengthwise and on the diagonal, and prop one half up against the other. Garnish as desired and serve.

This dish won a pork recipe contest in 1993. It is a blend of 'east meets west.' I worked in Hawaii as a chef for six years and like to combine tropical ingredients, such as bananas, with southwestern ingredients. Our clientele are seasoned travelers, and enjoy innovative cuisine.

Appetizer Pizza
LIGHT

Makes 8-10 servings (four 10" pizzas)

Pizza Dough
1 envelope (1/4 oz.) active dry yeast
1 cup water heated to 110° F.
1 tsp. kosher salt
1 1/4 cups whole wheat flour
1 1/4 cups unbleached all-purpose flour

Method for Pizza Dough: Add yeast to water in a bowl. Allow to rest for 20 minutes. Then, stir in whole wheat flour gradually with a wooden spoon until dough is fairly stiff.

Turn dough onto a work surface and knead until smooth and elastic. Add remaining all-purpose flour as necessary to keep dough from sticking. Return dough to bowl and allow it to rise double its size (should take 1 1/2-2 hours.) Punch down the dough, and now work it into the pizza pans, or

Toppings
1 1/2-2 cups low-fat parmesan cheese, grated
3/4 cup portabello mushrooms
1 small eggplant
1 cup sun-dried tomatoes

shape pizzas to go directly onto your grill.

Cooking & Presentation: This basic recipe has a wonderful flavor and texture when grilled over mesquite. In menu planning, consider a starter course pizza, with any combination of the toppings listed above, and low-fat grated parmesan cheese. These pizzas are very heart-healthy and simple to make. Instead of grilling, you may bake the pizzas in an oven preheated to 375° for 18-20 minutes.

These pizzas are very light and not overly complex to prepare. Chef Hill uses hearth ovens loaded with mesquite wood to bake them, providing lots of rich taste and texture.

Chef's Secret

SPECIAL USES FOR FRESH HERBS
Jon Hill offers the following uses for fresh herbs, plucked right out of your windowsill or backyard garden—

COOKING WITH FRESH HERBS

Because fresh herbs aren't as potent as dried herbs, you'll need to use more of them in your cooking. "Put in the fresh herbs while cooking to get the predominent flavor. Then if you strain the item being prepared, add a handful of that same herb, chopped fresh, back in before serving the dish," he says.

FRESH MINT OR DILL WEED

Make homemade sun tea by thoroughly washing fresh mint or dill, and then placing it in a gallon jar with tap water. Cover the jar tightly and put it out in the sun. "It works just like sun tea," says Hill, who has grown to love working with a wide variety of fresh herbs. The next day, pour some of the herb-essence water into a pan and allow it to reduce slowly over a medium burner. You'll end up with a wonderful mint (or dill) sauce.

TO PRESERVE HOMEGROWN HERBS

Chef Hill recommends using a small herb dryer to preserve your home-grown herbs for year-round use. As a result, you'll have a stock of flavorful herbs that are higher-quality than commercial dried herbs.

Filet Mignon and other house specialties of The Wigwam's Arizona Kitchen

Enchantment Resort

A unique southwestern experience, in its own private canyon

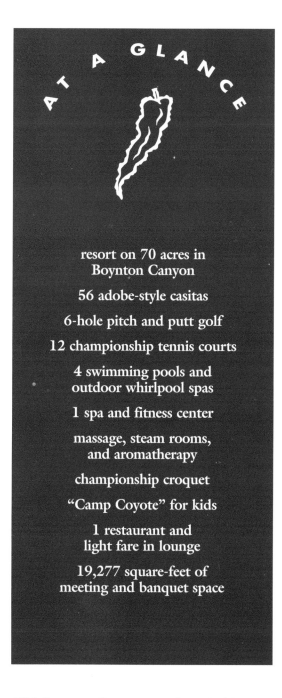

RED ROCK mountains, bright nighttime stars, and a dramatic blue sky paint a perfect backdrop for the Enchantment Resort, located in Boynton Canyon, just five miles outside Sedona, Arizona. While many resorts boast that they commune with nature, Enchantment's main lodge and scattered casitas respectfully blend with the neighboring forests and canyon. The dwellings are low and inconspicuous, with very little lighting used at night. (Guests are provided flashlights to use at night, so as not to disturb the coyotes, rabbits, and foxes that thrive in this beautiful area.)

The Enchantment's adobe-style casitas afford more space and amenities than most resort lodgings. Each casita has its own balcony with sliding glass doors opening up to breathtaking views. Some of the casitas have living rooms and kitchenettes, offering villa-style accommodations. Everyone gets a complimentary daily newspaper and pitcher of fresh-squeezed orange juice delivered to their door each morning. Or, guests may enjoy a delicious full breakfast in the Enchantment's dining room.

There are so many diversions here for active couples and families: a full-service spa, swimming, championship tennis, mountain biking, and guided hikes through Boynton Canyon. A couple of easy hikes near the resort provide scenic views of the valley below. According to Mark Grenoble, Resident Manager for Enchantment, "Our guests are outdoor-oriented, hiking enthusiasts, and looking for something different in a vacation. We offer a beautiful environment at their doorsteps, with nearby Native American ruins, several popular canyons, and a number of New Age vortexes."

525 Boynton Canyon Road ☙ Sedona, Arizona 86336 ☙ (800)522-2282 or (520)282-2900

L'Auberge de Sedona

Located near one of Arizona's loveliest towns,
L'Auberge is the ultimate hideaway

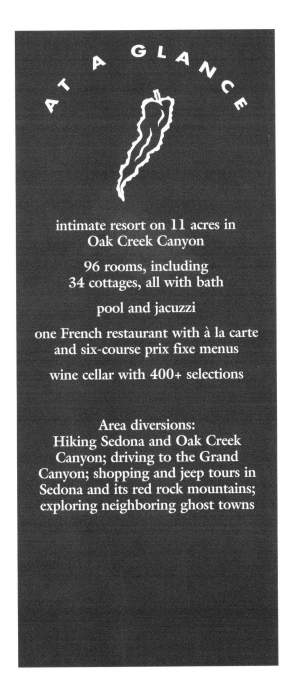

AT A GLANCE

intimate resort on 11 acres in
Oak Creek Canyon

96 rooms, including
34 cottages, all with bath

pool and jacuzzi

one French restaurant with à la carte
and six-course prix fixe menus

wine cellar with 400+ selections

Area diversions:
Hiking Sedona and Oak Creek
Canyon; driving to the Grand
Canyon; shopping and jeep tours in
Sedona and its red rock mountains;
exploring neighboring ghost towns

IMAGINE ALL of the monuments in Monument Valley being pushed together to form a giant circle. Now picture the circle of rock with a glittering little town inside of it, and you'll have a pretty good image of Sedona, a growing little city within towering red rock formations. Jeep tours give adventurous visitors an up-close look at the red rocks, the valleys below, and the various Anasazi Indian ruins in the area. For the less adventurous, there are miles of shops and galleries to explore, many with western trading-post exteriors.

Nestled in a lovely wooded setting in Oak Creek Canyon, L'Auberge de Sedona is considered the perfect hideaway from the pressures of life in the fast lane. From Flagstaff, the drive to L'Auberge is spectacular, as the road cuts through deep forests and wanders by creeks and lovely valleys. The Inn includes a central lodge that resembles a European chalet, plus private cottages with fireplaces located beside the creek. Guest rooms are decorated in country-French fabrics, and some rooms feature queen or king canopied beds. L'Auberge guests can swim in the heated pool by day, and gaze up at the brilliant Sedona stars at night.

At dinnertime, the magic here begins. The tuxedo-clad staff is friendly, professional, and trained to provide guests with a sensational dining experience. The Restaurant's creekside setting and country French decor lend even more romance, but the real focal point here is the food—fresh, gourmet, unpretentious, and, of course, French. ᔕ

P.O. Box B, L'Auberge Lane ᔕ Sedona, Arizona 86339 ᔕ (520)282-1661 or (800)272-6777 outside Arizona

Kevin Maguire

ENCHANTMENT RESORT

When you've had your fill of hiking, tennis, and vortex adventures, wander down to the Enchantment's Yavapai Dining Room to savor the adventurous cuisine orchestrated by chef Kevin Maguire and staff.

A native of Boston, Maguire studied at the Johnson and Wales Culinary School in Rhode Island while applying his talents in the kitchen at Boston's Copley Plaza Hotel. During those early years, Maguire trained with top chefs Lydia Shire, a renowned restaurateur, and Jasper White, who wrote Cooking from New England. *Today, chef Maguire creates foods that are both superlative and fun. Popular dishes such as Rack of Colorado Lamb, punctuated with dijon mustard and ground pistachios, feature all of the bold flavors and fanciful ingredients that diners expect in a top-rated restaurant.*

If you're feeling especially adventurous, try the rattlesnake chili!

Baked Swordfish with Ancho Chile Aioli and Cornbread Herb Crust

Makes 8 servings

Swordfish
(8) 6 oz. swordfish fillets
12 oz. cornbread crumbs*
2 oz. clarified butter
fresh sage and chives, chopped
salt and black pepper to taste
1-2 oz. butter (for sautéing)

* Use leftover cornbread or make by combining equal amounts of cornmeal and dry bread crumbs

Ancho Chile Aioli
3 egg yolks
2 tsp. dijon mustard
1/4 tsp. kosher salt
2 cloves garlic, minced
1/2-3/4 cup olive oil
6 Tbs. Ancho chile purée (see recipe)
1 Tbs. balsamic vinegar
1 tsp. fresh lemon juice
black pepper, freshly ground

> This entrée is an inspired combination of seafood and hot chiles, plus the addition of a tasty crust that surprises the palate with each bite.

Method for Swordfish: Combine the crumbs, clarified butter, herbs, salt, and pepper by hand or in a food processor. Using this mixture, coat the fish fillets and set aside. Add the remaining butter to a skillet, and heat it over a medium-high burner. Add the coated swordfish, and brown evenly on both sides. Finish the fillets by placing them in a 400° oven for 7-8 minutes.

Method for Aioli: Purée yolks, mustard, salt and garlic in a blender or food processor until thick. With blender on low, drizzle in oil until a thick mayonnaise forms. Pulse in ancho chile purée, vinegar, and lemon juice until smooth. Season with black pepper; refrigerate until needed.

Chef's Secret

HOW TO MAKE A CHILE PURÉE
Remove and discard stems and seeds from 1-2 cups of ancho chiles. Soak them in 1/2 cup hot water until softened; purée in a food processor and reserve until needed.

HOW TO COOK FISH THE FOUR-STAR WAY
Rich Pasich, Enchantment's Chef de Cuisine suggests using a probe thermometer to test fish for doneness. When the inside of the fillet reaches 120°, it will be a perfect medium-rare when put on the table a minute or two later.

Baked Onion Soup Yavapai

Makes 12 servings

10 black peppercorns
3 bay leaves
1 1/2 tsp. whole thyme
1 1/2 tsp. whole marjoram
1/2 cup clarified butter
3 lbs. onions, sliced thin
1 1/2 cups red wine
3 qts. veal or beef stock

1 large green bell pepper
1 large red bell pepper
1 large Poblano chile
12 tsp. applejack brandy
24 slices Monterey jack cheese
24 French bread croutons, as needed
chili powder as needed
salt and pepper to taste

Chef's Secret

For a novel presentation that we use in our Yavapai dining room, hollow out colossal yellow onions without making a hole in the bottom or sides. Place about 1/2 cup rock salt in serving bowls and place onion on top; proceed with recipe.

Method for Onion Soup: Wrap first 4 ingredients in cheesecloth and tie (making a bouquet garni.) Heat butter in large heavy pan over high heat. Add onions and cook until they begin to brown, stirring frequently. Reduce heat to medium and cook until well-browned (about 20 minutes.) Add wine and bring to a boil, scraping up any browned bits. Reduce heat and simmer for 10 minutes. Add stock and herb bag and simmer for another 30 minutes. Season to taste with salt and pepper. Discard herb bag.

Char bell peppers and Poblano chile over an open flame on a barbeque grill or under a broiler. Let the skins burn a little, and then remove peppers and place them in a bowl sealed with plastic wrap. (This allows the peppers to steam.) Remove peppers and peel skins, remove seeds, and cut into a small dice.

Presentation: Preheat oven to 500° Fahrenheit. Measure 1 tsp. applejack into each of 12 oven-proof bowls. Fill to brim with onion soup. Place croutons in soup and cover each bowl with 2 slices of Monterey jack cheese. Top with peppers and Poblano chile. Bake in oven until cheese is brown and bubbly, about 6 minutes. Sprinkle with chili powder and serve. ᯤ

> **Prepare this classic onion soup and then serve it "Enchantment-style"—
> in a colossal yellow onion bowl, topped with roasted peppers.**

Rack of Colorado Lamb
Pictured on p.38

Makes 6 servings

Sage and Sun-dried Tomato Sauce

1 Tbs. butter
1/3 cup mushroom pieces
1 small carrot*
1/2 small onion**
1 stalk celery*
1 shallot**
2 Tbs. parsley**
2 tsp. thyme leaves**
2 tsp. sage leaves**
2 bay leaves, crushed
2 cups Zinfandel wine
2 Tbs. tomato paste
1/2 cup sun-dried tomatoes
1 qt. lamb stock (see Resources section)
roux as needed
salt and black pepper to taste

* Cut into a dice
** Chop

Lamb

3 racks of lamb, trimmed and boned
salt and pepper to taste
6 Tbs. dijon mustard
1/2 cup pistachios, ground
1/2 cup bread crumbs
1 tsp. Herbes de Provence
1/2 cup butter ☞

Method for Sauce: Melt butter in a skillet and sauté the mushroom pieces, diced carrot, celery, onion, shallot, and garlic with the herbs until vegetables are softened. Deglaze with the Zinfandel and simmer for 3 minutes. Add the tomato paste, sun-dried tomatoes, and stock; reduce heat and simmer until reduced by 1/2.

Method for Lamb: Season filets with salt and pepper and sear them in a large hot skillet. Mix the ground pistachios, bread crumbs, and Herbes de Provence together. Brush the seared lamb with the dijon mustard and roll them in the ground pistachio mixture. Melt the butter in skillet, place the pistachio-coated lamb filets in the skillet and roast them in a 350° oven for 8-10 minutes, until the pistachio crust is toasted and the lamb is cooked to medium-rare.

Presentation: Slice each nut-encrusted lamb filet into three pieces. Ladle three small pools of the sauce onto each plate and arrange the lamb with accompaniments. ✎

An acclaimed house specialty, this dish combines succulent lamb with the flavors of mustard and pistachio. An herb- and tomato-infused sauce finishes it off nicely.

Rack of Colorado Lamb, Enchantment style

Margarita Mousse with Tuile Tacos

Makes 6-8 servings

Mousse
1/4 cup cold water
1 envelope unflavored gelatin
1/4 tsp. salt
1/2 cup lime juice
1 1/2 tsp. lime zest, minced*
3 Tbs. triple sec
1/3 cup tequila
4 eggs, separated
2/3 cup sugar

* Blanch in boiling water for 30 seconds

Tuile Tacos
1 cup (4 oz.) almonds, sliced & blanched
1/4 cup + 2 Tbs. sugar
egg whites, room temperature (using the eggs listed under Mousse)
1/4 cup all-purpose flour
2 Tbs. butter, melted and cooled

Crème Fraîche
(yields about 1 cup)
1 cup whipping cream
5 Tbs. buttermilk, room temperature

Enchantment's Margarita Mousse is a cool, refreshing southwestern dessert with just the right kick. And, the Tuile Tacos are light and fun to make.

Special Thanks
Thanks to former chef Gerald Peters for his help in compiling these favorite recipes.

Method for Crème Fraîche: Heat cream in a small, heavy sauce pan to lukewarm (85° Fahrenheit). Remove from heat and mix in buttermilk. Cover and let stand in warm, draft-free area until slightly thickened, 24-48 hours, depending on room temperature. Refrigerate until ready to use.

Method for Mousse: Put the water in a bowl and sprinkle gelatin over it. Let stand until spongy, 4-5 minutes. Place the bowl over simmering water until gelatin dissolves, about 2 minutes.

Whisk salt, lime juice, blanched lime zest, triple-sec, and tequila into gelatin. Place the bowl over ice-water and stir until mixture is the consistency of unbeaten egg whites, about 10 minutes.

In another bowl, beat egg yolks with 1/3 cup sugar until the yolks thicken and form a ribbon when trailed from a whisk, 4 to 5 minutes. Stir thoroughly into the gelatin mixture.

In a third bowl, beat the egg whites until they form soft peaks. Slowly add the remaining 1/3 cup sugar. Beat until the whites form stiff peaks. Fold into the gelatin mixture. Place into glass serving bowl, cover and refrigerate for at least 2 hours.

Method for the Tuile Tacos: Mix almonds, sugar, egg whites and flour in small bowl. Blend in melted butter. Let stand at room temperature 30 minutes. Preheat oven to 350° F. Generously butter a heavy baking sheet. Spoons the batter up 2 Tbs. at a time, and place onto a prepared sheet pan, spacing each tuile 5" apart. Using the back of a fork, spread each mound of batter into a 4" round.

Bake until edges of cookies are golden and centers are pale gold, about 12 minutes. Working quickly, remove with spatula and mold around 1-inch thick dowel or broom handle, forming taco shapes. (If tuiles become too hard to mold, re-warm in oven 30-60 seconds.) Let each tuile stand until firm, about 3 minutes. Transfer to rack and cool completely. Repeat with remaining batter. (Can be prepared 2 days ahead: store in airtight container.)

Presentation: Carefully spoon 2-3 Tbs. of mousse into bottom of each tuile. Top with dollop of crème fraîche and garnish with mint. Or, if desired, place bowl of mousse and platter of tuiles on the table and let guests serve themselves.

John Harings

L'AUBERGE DE SEDONA

L'Auberge de Sedona is known for its first-class French cuisine, prepared under the direction of John Harings, Executive Chef. Harings worked under Michel Bourdin, President de l'Academie Culinaire de France for Great Britain at the Connaught Hotel in London. While in Lyon, France, Harings trained with some of the region's top culinary professionals, learning how to create exceptional dishes for the most discerning gourmands.

At the L'Auberge Restaurant, diners are treated to an elegant multi-course meal. French-country cuisine that combines sensual textures and flavors, such as Sautéed Medallions of Venison with Braised Cabbage and a Sun-Dried Cranberry Sauce, earn chef Harings and the L'Auberge Restaurant high marks.

Roasted Cornish Game Hens with a Supreme Sauce

Makes 4 servings

Cornish Game Hens
(4) 1 1/2 lb. cornish game hens
4 cloves garlic
4 sprigs thyme

Supreme Sauce
1 oz. olive oil
1 carrot*
1 onion*
1 stalk celery, diced
1 cup dry chardonnay
1 shallot*
3 cups heavy cream
salt and white pepper

* Peel and dice

> When I was in London, I prepared lots of game birds. The game hens are sized perfectly for individual servings.

Method for Cornish Hens: Rinse the game hens thoroughly inside and out. Pat dry with paper towels and season inside and out with salt and pepper. Inside each bird, place one crushed garlic clove and one sprig of fresh thyme. Tie the legs together for even cooking, and place in a 400° oven for approximately 20-25 minutes.

Method for Sauce: While the hens are cooking, sweat the carrots, shallots, onions, and celery in 1 oz. olive oil for about 10 minutes. When the birds are done, remove the backbones by making two cuts on either side of the backbone from the neck to the tail and remove. Pull the ribcage bones from each hen, and make an incision between the breasts to separate the bird into two pieces. Add all of the bones, garlic, and thyme to the vegetables; turn up heat. Add the dry white wine and reduce mixture by 80%.

Add the heavy cream and slowly reduce until the sauce coats the back of a spoon—about 20 minutes. Also note that the cream sauces need to be skimmed occasionally to remove impurities. When the sauce has reached desired consistency, strain it through a fine china cap.

Presentation: This dish goes extremely well with steamed asparagus and sautéed potatoes. You can serve the hens cut in halves, or section again into quarters. Chef Harings keeps the birds as whole as possible, and then ladles on the sauce.

Pan-Seared Jumbo Sea Scallops Provençale

Makes 4 servings

1 lb. sea scallops, cleaned
2 Tbs. virgin olive oil
2 oz. dry white wine
2 diced Roma tomatoes, peeled and seeds removed
1 tsp. niçoise olives, chopped
1 clove garlic, chopped

1 Tbs. chives, chopped
2 Tbs. unsalted butter
4 French bread croutons (see recipe)
salt and white pepper

Method for Scallops & Sauce: Heat olive oil in a large sauté pan. Season scallops and cook in olive oil for approximately 30 seconds on each side and remove. Add chopped garlic to the olive oil used to cook the scallops, and sweat for 30 seconds. Add olives, tomatoes, and white wine. Reduce by 80% and whisk in unsalted butter.

Season to taste with salt and white pepper, and add chopped chives.

Presentation: Place scallops on croutons and finish with sauce. Garnish each serving with snipped chives or fresh thyme.

This is a five-minute dish, prepared all in one pan
(which is typical of Provençal cookery.) And, it's light and healthy.

Chef's Secret

HOMESTYLE CROUTONS

Butter and toast bias-cut slices of french bread. You may rub on a raw, peeled clove of garlic for a more pungent flavor. Toast the croutons in a 350° oven for 5-10 minutes.

Sautéed Medallions of Venison with Braised Cabbage and a Sun-Dried Cranberry Sauce

Makes 4 servings

24 oz. venison loin; or (8) 3 oz. medallions (see Resources section)
1 medium head green cabbage
1 lb. fresh cranberries
2 Granny Smith apples
2 oz. sun-dried cranberries (see Resources section)
8 oz. orange juice
2 oz. olive oil
1 Tbs. sugar
1/4 tsp. fresh caraway seeds, crushed
salt and white pepper

Method for Braised Cabbage: Prepare the braised cabbage by first removing the core. Section into four pieces and cut into a medium julienne. Heat 1 oz. olive oil in a medium skillet and sauté the cabbage on high heat for 5 minutes. Peel and core the apples, and cut into slices. Add apples to the cabbage and season with salt and pepper. Cover and place in a 400° oven for approximately 20 minutes, or until soft. Add the fresh crushed caraway and set aside.

Method for Cranberries: Wash and drain the fresh cranberries. In a medium saucepan, add the cranberries, orange juice, and 24 oz. of water. Add salt and pepper. Boil for 20 minutes on medium ☞

heat until berries are soft. Purée in food processor and strain through a fine china cap. Add the sun-dried cranberries and sugar; boil for 5 minutes over low heat. Next, adjust the seasonings to taste with sugar.

Method for Venison: Place 1 oz. olive oil in a large sauté pan and sauté the venison medallions on high heat, keeping them medium-rare.

Presentation: Place the cabbage on a plate and add the venison medallions. Finish with the sauce and garnish with fresh snipped chives. ✍

> For a perfect wintertime entrée, serve this game dish, which calls for good-quality venison and sun-dried cranberries.

Sauteed Striped Sea Bass with a Wild Mushroom Fricassee

Makes 4 servings

2 lbs. fresh striped sea bass
1 oz. olive oil
6 oz. fresh shiitake mushrooms
6 oz. fresh chanterelle mushrooms
1 Roma tomato*
1/2 tsp. chives, chopped
1/2 tsp. fresh thyme, chopped

1 1/2 oz. sherry vinegar
1 oz. extra virgin olive oil
salt and white pepper to taste
2 tsp. unsalted butter

* Peel, remove seeds, and cut in a dice

Method for Sea Bass: Remove bones and scales from the sea bass. Cut fillets on an angle to give a diamond-shaped appearance. Place 1 oz. olive oil in a large sauté pan and season the sea bass to taste with salt and pepper. When the pan is hot, place the sea bass, skin-side down, and cook for 1 minute. Turn each fillet and continue cooking for 1 more minute. Remove from pan and keep warm.

Method for Mushrooms: Wash and slice the mushrooms. Sauté them in 1 oz. of olive oil for approximately 2 minutes; season with salt and pepper. Next, add the sherry vinegar and reduce by half. Add the Roma tomatoes and fresh herbs, and cook for 1 minute. Then whisk in the unsalted butter.

Presentation: Place the sea bass skin-side up on plates and arrange the fricassee mushrooms on top. Garnish with more herbs, if desired. ✍

> Sherry vinegar provides the foundation for this sauce; its sharp flavor wakes up the mild-tasting sea bass. Substitute your own favorite mushrooms, if you prefer.

Terrace dining at picturesque L'Auberge de Sedona

The Broadmoor

European elegance and five-star cuisine at the foothills of Colorado's Rocky Mountains

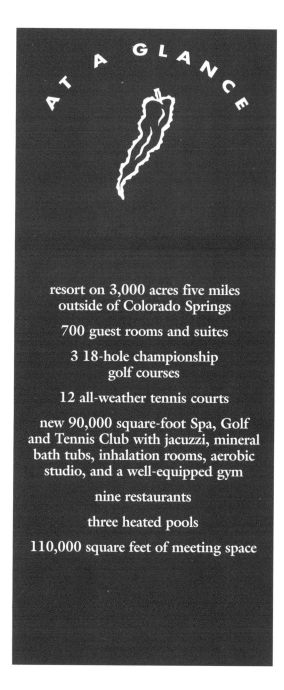

AT A GLANCE

resort on 3,000 acres five miles outside of Colorado Springs

700 guest rooms and suites

3 18-hole championship golf courses

12 all-weather tennis courts

new 90,000 square-foot Spa, Golf and Tennis Club with jacuzzi, mineral bath tubs, inhalation rooms, aerobic studio, and a well-equipped gym

nine restaurants

three heated pools

110,000 square feet of meeting space

THIS RESORT'S pristine setting between the Colorado Rocky Mountains and a glistening lake is hard to beat. Add on a wealth of activities, five-star dining, and European charm, and there is even more reason to stay at least one week. Last year, when organizers of the U.S. Women's Open Golf Championship™ had to choose a location for their fiftieth annual tournament, the Broadmoor's challenging golf courses were selected. But even if your game doesn't match that of the pros, you can still enjoy playing a round on either of the Broadmoor's three famous courses.

The Broadmoor offers 700 guest rooms and suites, located in two complexes. Each room is furnished with one king-size bed or two double beds, and cable television. At The Broadmoor's lavish 90,000 square-foot Spa, Golf and Tennis Club, guests can enjoy recreational facilities designed with every fitness detail in mind. The Spa houses a lap pool and indoor recreation pool, a whirlpool, an aerobics studio, and a fully-equipped gym. Travelers may choose their favorite indulgence in the multi-level Spa: a whirlpool soak, mineral bath, inhalation therapy, or steam shower. Facials and full body massages (indoors or on a secluded balcony) are other options for sports enthusiasts.

Resembling a grand European spa with its towering Italian Renaissance hub, The Broadmoor's muted pink exterior and red tile roof are in striking contrast to sapphire-blue Lake Cheyenne, seen just in the distance. If you didn't know better, you might think that The Broadmoor's developers carved a little piece of Bavaria into the Colorado Rockies. ⚬

P.O. Box 1439 ⚬ *Colorado Springs, Colorado 80901* ⚬ *(800)634-7711 or (719)634-7711*

Tall Timber

This resort's isolated location in the southwestern Rocky Mountains offers unspoiled wilderness

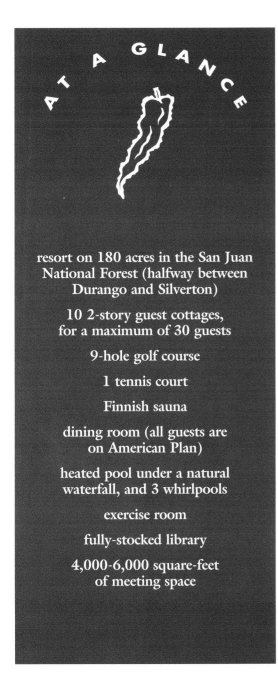

AT A GLANCE

resort on 180 acres in the San Juan National Forest (halfway between Durango and Silverton)

10 2-story guest cottages, for a maximum of 30 guests

9-hole golf course

1 tennis court

Finnish sauna

dining room (all guests are on American Plan)

heated pool under a natural waterfall, and 3 whirlpools

exercise room

fully-stocked library

4,000-6,000 square-feet of meeting space

THERE ARE only two ways to get to Tall Timber—via the resort's private helicopter or on the "Silverton", America's only narrow-gauge train running on a regular schedule. Travelers on the Silverton ride along narrow rocky ledges, and pass through dramatic evergreen forests (part of the San Juan National Forest) and deep canyons punctuated by rivers. Long ago, this land was occupied by the Ute Indians. At the turn of the century, Wyatt Earp, Doc Holliday, and others rode the historic train, which carried valuable cargoes of precious metals. The helicopter ride from Durango also offers sweeping views of the mountains and wilderness surrounding Tall Timber.

Don't come here looking for the ordinary. Instead of the typical hotel room, Tall Timber guests stay in private, two-story apartments, each with a living room, wet bar, and stone fireplace. Because the resort has no televisions or newspapers, media fanatics and workaholics might have to do some serious detoxification at Tall Timber, but I can think of no better place. Active guests can choose golf, tennis, fishing, or swimming, before plunging into one of the resort's three outdoor whirlpools, each with its own breathtaking view. Quieter activities might include a visit to the resort's large, well-stocked library, or a stroll down one of the paths on the property.

At Tall Timber, five-star cooking is as unfettered as the scenery surrounding the resort. The resort's helicopter ride and gastronomic picnic excursion to a nearby mountain lake is a favorite junket.

At dinnertime, guests enjoy a multi-course feast while they take in one last glimpse of the valley below before the sun slips past the horizon. ✦

Box 90 ✦ Silverton Star Route ✦ Durango, Colorado 81301 ✦ (970)259-4813

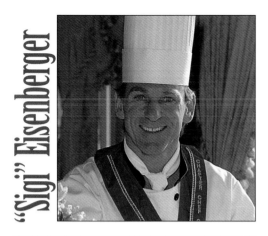

"Sigi" Eisenberger

THE BROADMOOR

In keeping with The Boardmoor's grand European style, its executive chef hails from Tyrol, Austria. In the Edwardian-style restaurant called the Penrose Room, chef Siegfried "Sigi" Eisenberger prepares modern twists on classic foods. The Resort's cuisine—offered in nine restaurants and cafés—ranges from contemporary American to authentic pub fare.

From 1963 to 1991, chef Eisenberger worked at prestigious hotels in Holland, Switzerland, and Jamaica, before coming to the United States. After honing his craft at a couple of top American hotels, Eisenberger became the proprietor of Chef Sigi's Restaurant in Nashville, Tennessee. He is a member of the American Culinary Federation, and the National Restaurant Association, among other prestigious organizations; and, he has served on the U.S. Culinary Teams in 1984 and in 1988.

Couscous-Crusted Salmon with Cumin Carrot Sauce

Makes 6 servings

Salmon
(1) 2 lb. salmon fillet, skinless
2 whole eggs, lightly beaten
1/2 cup milk
1 cup flour
coucous crust, moistened slightly (see recipe)

Couscous Crust
1/2 box couscous
24 oz. chicken stock
1/2 tsp. saffron threads
salt, white pepper, cumin, and tumeric

Cumin Carrot Sauce
1/4 yellow onion, rough cut
1/2 carrot, rough cut
1/2 pint chicken stock
1/2 pint orange juice
salt, white pepper, cumin, and tumeric

Method for Coucous Crust: Spread couscous out on a 1/4" deep baking pan. Warm chicken stock and add the saffron threads; let simmer until stock is warm and has a bright color. Pour 16 oz. of the stock over the couscous, and rub with your hands to prevent lumps. Repeat the process twice. Coucous should be tender after third addition of the stock. Season to taste with salt, pepper, cumin, and tumeric.

Method for Crusting Salmon: Neatly trim salmon and remove all the grey fat. Roll a small amount of couscous out between two sheets of plastic to the size of the fish, and pat it down thinly. When the size is correct, remove the top piece of plastic. Season the salmon with salt and pepper and set aside. Make an egg wash using the eggs and milk. Lightly dredge the skin side of the salmon with flour, and then dip it in the egg wash. Lay the skin side on the couscous and fold the plastic around the salmon. Let it get close to freezing, and then slice the crusted salmon into six 5 oz. portions.

Just before serving, bake fillets to desired doneness in an oven heated to 400°.

Method for Sauce: Sweat the onions and carrots in a saucepan using a small amount of butter, but do not allow them to change color. Add a little salt. Add the orange juice and bring to a simmer; reduce the liquids slightly. Add chicken stock and return to a simmer. Cook until vegetables are very tender. Season to taste with salt, white pepper, cumin, and tumeric. Purée in blender, strain through cheesecloth (optional), and chill.

Presentation: Place a portion of salmon in center of each serving plate, and ladle on the carrot cumin sauce. Paint the plate with more sauce. You can serve this with carrots, red pepper, and zucchini, cut confetti-style. Risotto is another good accompaniment.

Our Crusted Salmon is a heart-healthy, light dish. The orange carrot sauce and the crunchy texture of the crust makes a wonderful combination.

Savorin with Grand Marnier®

Makes 6 servings

Savorin
2 1/2 cups flour, sifted
1 tsp. dry yeast
4 eggs
10 Tbs. unsalted butter
1/2 Tbs. salt
1 1/4 Tbs. sugar

Apricot Glaze
1 qt. water
1 cup Grand Marnier
1 1/2 cups sugar

Orange Sauce
1/2 cup water
3/4 cup sugar
8 oranges, peeled with all the white
membrane removed

Garnish
Use as much or as little of the following as you like

orange segments
orange peels
whipped cream
raspberries
mint

> Cake serves as the base for this traditional dessert. For variety, bake the savorin in a round ring mold, and fill the center with seasonal berries just before serving. Vary the fillings, glazes, and garnishes with your seasonal favorites.

Method for the Savorin: Combine the flour, yeast (dissolved in a little lukewarm water), and 4 eggs in a mixing bowl. Knead and cover with the unsalted butter. Do not mix the butter into the dough. Let the dough rise for 2 hours. Then, mix in the salt, butter, and sugar. Grease 8 individual savorin molds and fill. Let rise for 1 hour. Cook in a 325° oven for 12-15 minutes. Unmold and let cool.

Method for Glaze: Combine water, sugar, and Grand Marnier in a saucepan and bring to a boil. Reduce heat and letter simmer for 10 minutes. Soak the savorin in the syrup and drain them on a rack. Heat the apricot glaze and brush the savorins with the glaze.

Method for Orange Sauce: Combine the sugar and water in a saucepan, and bring to a boil for 5 minutes. Then add the orange pieces (cut in eighths) and stir well. Cook over low heat for 10 minutes; then remove from heat, purée in a blender, and strain.

Presentation: To serve, place a pool of sauce on each plate. Top with the savorin. Garnish each with orange sections, orange peels, raspberries, mint, and whipped cream. ᵔ

Painted Desert Corn Chowder

Makes 6 servings

2 cups corn kernels
1 oz. corn oil
1 Tbs. onions, finely diced
2 Tbs. flour
1/2 cup jicama, diced
1/2 red bell pepper*
1/2 green bell pepper*
1/2 yellow bell pepper*
2 cups chicken stock
2 Tbs. black beans
1 1/2 cups milk
salt and white pepper to taste
2 sprigs coriander
1 sprig oregano leaves
1 clove garlic
6 oz. frying oil
2 Tbs. sour cream

* Cut 1/3 of each pepper piece in a dice, and leave the remaining pieces whole

> This southwestern-style soup looks like a sand painting, with layers of different colors artistically arranged on top of each serving.

Method for Chowder: Sauté the following in corn oil: onions, 1/3 of the red, green, and yellow bell peppers, jicama, garlic, and herbs. Add the flour and stir for a few minutes. Then add the milk and chicken stock, salt, and pepper. Cook all until the jicama is almost tender. ☞

Fry the remaining bell peppers in hot oil, allow to cool, and peel them. Boil the black beans in salt water until well done. Place in a blender with some liquid and purée until smooth. Keep warm. Purée each pepper individually as done with the black beans.

Presentation: Ladle soup into serving bowls and "paint" with the frothed peppers and beans in layers on top of the chowder. Do the same with the sour cream. For the best effect, you may wish to use a piping bag or wax paper coronet for the painting process. 🍃

Tournedos of Beef "Perigourdine"

Makes 4 servings

Tenderloin
(8) 3 oz. tenderloin of beef filets
8 oz. goose paté, sliced into 1 oz. pieces (see Resources section)
salt and white pepper to taste

Brown Truffle Sauce
(yields 1 quart)
2 cups demi glace (see Resources section)
2 tsp. shallots, diced
1 tsp. garlic, diced
1 cup Zinfandel wine
1 tsp. whole butter
1 Tbs. truffles (truffle peelings may be substituted)
salt and pepper to taste *(cont. next col.)*

Method for Tenderloin: Season and sear the tenderloins in a lightly-oiled skillet and cook to desired temperature. Place paté on top of tenderloin (two 1 oz. slices per filet). Place in oven until paté is slightly warm.

Method for Sauce: Place a lightly-oiled sauce pan over a medium burner, add the shallots, and cook until translucent. Next, add the garlic, truffles, and red wine to the shallots. Reduce the mixture to almost dry. Add demi glace and bring to a simmer over low-medium heat until just barely bubbling. Season to taste. Add butter to finish the sauce, and keep hot until ready to serve.

Presentation: Serve two tournedos atop truffle sauce on each serving plate, along with roasted potatoes and seasonal fresh vegetables. 🍃

There is a great emphasis on flavor in this entrée. Be sure to slow-cook the sauce for best results.

Stewed Anasazi Beans with Morel Mushrooms

Makes 8-10 servings

2 cups dried Anasazi beans (see Resources section)
4 sprigs scallions
2 cloves garlic, minced
1 tsp. chervil, chopped
salt to taste
1/2 cup onions, chopped
4 oz. morel mushrooms, diced medium
1 oz. mesquite oil

1 tsp. mesquite seasoning
2 bay leaves
2 sprigs thyme
3 leaves fresh basil, chopped
1 Tbs. hot tomato jam (see Resources section)
2 smoked jalapeño peppers
1 1/2 pints beef stock

Method for Soup: Soak beans in cold water overnight. Simmer the beans slowly over low heat with the beef stock, garlic, chervil, half of the onions, thyme, bay leaves, basil, and smoked peppers until the beans are done. Add more stock if necessary.

In mesquite oil, sauté the remaining onions, scallions, and mushrooms in a larger pot until glazy. Then add the beans with reduced stock. Gently fold under the sautéed ingredients. Simmer until it looks like a stew.

Presentation: Remove from the heat, season to taste, and serve in stone crocks. 🍃

I use buffalo stock for this stew, but you can substitute beef or chicken stock. We use native Anasazi Indian beans, which may be found in health food stores and at gourmet grocers.

Anthony Moleterno

TALL TIMBER

Tall Timber's executive chef, Anthony Moleterno, whips up chicken piccata, homemade breads, radicchio salads, and flaming desserts (on a set menu) for guests while they relax in the candlelit dining room. Chef Moleterno and his staff make sure that each meal is memorable, with many international dishes. His lavish use of fresh vegetables and herbs—many of which are grown in Moleterno's own gardens—makes for fresh, healthy cuisine. Extra care is taken when Tall Timber chefs bake breads and desserts, using the finest grains and top-quality fruits and other ingredients.

Moleterno has been a professional chef for 10 years, and he is primarily self-taught. Before coming to Tall Timber, chef Moleterno worked at the Camelback Inn and at other prestigious properties in Scottsdale, Arizona.

Pineapple Banana Salad

Makes 6 servings

20 oz. pineapple tidbits* (approx. 1/4 cup)
2 bananas**
1 egg, beaten
1/4 cup granulated sugar
2 tsp. cornstarch

* Use fresh pineapple with its juice or canned pineapple, and cut a little smaller than chunks
** Peel and cut into 1/4" rings

This refreshing, chilled salad has a custard made from the fruit juice and folded back in.

Method for Salad: Drain the pineapple, reserving about 1/4 cup of juice. In a sauce pan, mix the egg and the reserved juice together. Stir in the sugar and cornstarch, and heat the sauce over a medium-high burner until it thickens. Continue stirring to make sure the mixture is smooth. Remove from burner and allow the mixture to cool slightly. Next, add the pineapple and bananas and mix thoroughly. Refrigerate for 2 hours before serving.

Presentation: Serve individual portions of the chilled salad in tulip glasses, each with a small garnish of fresh fruit.

Radicchio and Butter Lettuce with Orange Vinaigrette

Makes 4-6 servings

4 large oranges
1/3 cup salad oil
1/3 cup olive oil
3 Tbs. white wine vinegar
1 tsp. salt
dash of white pepper
2 heads butter lettuce (wash and drain)
2 heads radicchio (wash and drain)
1 Tbs. fresh orange peel (optional garnish)

This is a pretty salad, with lots of color from the radicchio and the light-green butter lettuce.

Method for Salad: Grate enough orange peel and set aside. Juice the oranges and set aside.
Method for Salad Dressing: In a medium-size bowl, combine oils, vinegar, salt, pepper, and all the juice (approx. 2 Tbs.) from the oranges. (If needed, add more orange juice to equal 2 Tbs.) Mix until well-blended and set aside.

Presentation: Tear lettuce as desired and place equal-size portions onto salad plates. Arrange orange segments on top of lettuce. (At this point, you may hold in the refrigerator until ready to serve.) Mix dressing again, and pour about 1 oz. of dressing over the lettuce. Garnish with orange peel.

Sunflower and Millet Seed Bread

Makes 1 loaf

1/4 cup warm water
2 1/2 tsp. yeast
2 1/2 Tbs. honey
2 1/2 Tbs. olive oil
1 1/2 tsp. salt
3/4 cup warm water
2-3 cups wheat flour
1/4 cup millet seeds
1/4 cup sunflower seeds
1/4-1/2 cup white flour

Method for Sunflower Bread: Proof yeast in first measurement of water. Add honey, salt, second measure of water, and enough wheat flour (approx. half of the total) to make a thin batter. Add millet and sunflower seeds and mix well. Then add remaining wheat flour to make a stiff dough. Knead for 10 minutes. Place dough in a greased bowl and cover. Allow it to rise until doubled, approximately 1 1/2-2 hours. Punch down and shape the dough to fit a greased 9x5x3" loaf pan. Cover the pan and let dough rise again until it tops the pan.

Bake in a 350° oven for 40-45 minutes, or until the loaf sounds hollow when tapped. Remove from pan and let cool on a rack. ◖◗

Time Needed

First Rising	1 1/2 to 2 hours
Second Rising	3/4 to 1 hour
Baking Time	3 to 3 3/4 hours
Total Time	3 to 3 3/4 hours

Chicken Piccata

Makes 6 servings

6 whole chicken breasts*
1 cup flour**
1/3 cup butter, separated
1/3 cup lemon juice
1/3 cup dry white wine
2 Tbs. capers

Method for Piccata: Thaw chicken breasts, if necessary, and refrigerate them until needed. Before guests arrive, lightly flour the breasts and sauté them in the butter until they are tender, approximately 8-10 minutes. Hold the cooked breasts in a warm oven.

Deglaze the pan used to cook breasts with lemon juice and add the white wine, mushrooms,

Chicken Divan Crêpes

Makes 6 servings

1/4 cup butter
1/4 cup flour
2 cups chicken stock
2 tsp. worcestershire
6 1/2 oz. cheddar cheese (grated)
2 cups sour cream

Method for Sauce: Make a roux by combining the butter and flour and cooking it over medium heat for 2-3 minutes. Using a separate sauce pan, boil the chicken stock and worcestershire sauce together; then, add the roux and heat the mixture until it thickens slightly. Add the first measurement of cheddar cheese and heat the sauce until it is melted, stirring constantly. Remove the sauce from the heat, and stir in the sour cream.

Method for Crêpes: Lay each crêpe flat and

> This dish should be prepared quickly, just before serving to guests, for best results.

1 Tbs. parsley
1/3 lb. mushrooms (slicc and sauté)
approx. 5 whole lemons for garnish

* De-bone, remove skin, and cut into halves
** Season with salt, white pepper, & paprika

and parsley. Reduce the mixture by 1/4. Add the cooked breasts to the sauce mixture and heat briefly. Add capers at this point.

Presentation: Place the breasts on serving plates and spoon some of the sauce (with capers) over the chicken. Cut whole lemons into wheels and place 3 wheels on each serving. Serve immediately. ◖◗

3 cups chicken*
1¹/³ bunches broccoli spears (cook & drain)
12 crêpes
1/4 lb. cheddar cheese*
* Remove skin, de-bone, cook, and cut into 3/4" cubes

place two broccoli spears in the center. Place 1/4 cup of the chicken next to the broccoli and top it with 1/8 cup of the sauce. Roll the crêpe by folding the edges to the center, leaving the ends open and the broccoli ends exposed.

Presentation: Place two rolled crêpes into each greased serving dish. Top the serving with 1/2 cup of the sauce and 1/8 cup of the remaining cheese. Bake in a 325° oven for 20 minutes and serve immediately. ◖◗

Helicopter picnic site
near Tall Timber

chapter 2
The American South

The Greenbrier
Grove Park Inn

Bayou & N. Fla.
Windsor Court Hotel

Amelia Island
Plantation

The Ritz-Carlton,
Amelia

Central & S. Fla.
Boca Raton Resort
& Club

The Ritz-Carlton,
Naples

Hyatt Regency
Grand Cypress

The American

From a travel perspective, this chapter features several of the nation's most popular and prestigious resorts and hotels. We begin with the Greenbrier, an American landmark resort located in the southeast corner of West Virginia. Nestled in the Great Smoky Mountains of North Carolina is The Grove Park Inn Resort, another favorite destination for non-stop recreation and memorable dining. At the top-rated Windsor Court Hotel in New Orleans, guests enjoy five-star pampering and unbeatable cuisine in a city known for offering the best of everything.

Next, we go to two special properties in northern Florida— Amelia Island Plantation and the Ritz-Carlton Amelia Island—two outstanding resorts on the sunshine state's lovely unspoiled island, a place where time stands still. In central and southern Florida, we begin with the elegant Boca Raton Resort & Club, a fanciful resort on Florida's Gold Coast. Next, there is the Ritz-Carlton Naples, located near the gateway to Everglades National Park, and the Hyatt Regency Grand Cypress, a beautiful central Florida destination with one of the world's largest swimming pools, with 12 waterfalls and a grotto bar.

The innovative cuisine offered at these resorts and hotels is as distinctive as the properties themselves. Perhaps a common thread throughout the New Orleans and Florida destinations is

South

FLORIDA DEPT. OF TOURISM & PROMOTION

the lavish use of fresh seafood. Many of these properties also offer spa selections, for guests who insist on fresh, flavorful foods that have major reductions in fat and calorie contents.

Fresh adaptations of southern cuisine include Robert Wong's Salmon Medallions with Saffron Grits, and Jeffrey Piccirillo's Sweet Potato and Jalapeño Pepper Soup. Smart, flavorful dishes with Asian flair include: Jeff Tunks' Chinese-Style Smoked Lobster and Seared Sashimi of Tuna; Brian O'Neil's Steamed Dumplings with Miso Sauce, and Kenneth Juran's Lobster and Cabbage Spring Roll. And, fresh fish gets lightly grilled (or sautéed) and delicately sauced, enhancing the food's natural flavors, by many of the south-

ern chefs. Jacky Burette's Sautéed Red Snapper Fettuccine is a crowd-pleaser, while Steve Schaefer's Amelia Seafood Risotto is full of the area's natural bounty. Pierre Dousson's Grilled Tournedos of Swordfish, and Sautéed Red Snapper with Mamey Sauce show his flair for producing simple, yet sensational results with fresh seafood and delicately balanced sauces.

If your idea of a great vacation includes sparkling beaches, majestic mountains, luxurious facilities, and access to great foods prepared by award-winning chefs, the south might already be your favorite getaway. ᔕ

The Greenbrier

America's favorite resort caters to the gourmand with grand cuisine and a cooking school

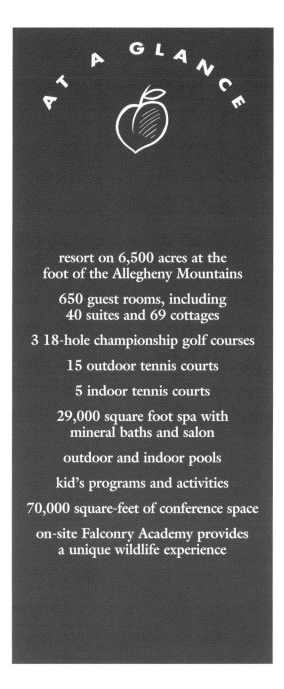

THERE AREN'T many resorts where guests can learn how to make a soufflé in the morning, raft whitewater midday, and then train wild falcons just before dusk. At the Greenbrier, guests delight in all these activities and more. Spread out upon 6,500 acres at the foot of the Allegheny Mountains in the southeast corner of West Virginia, the Greenbrier opened more than a century ago as a grand resort for socialites and wealthy American business owners. Today, the Greenbrier is still considered to be a landmark American resort.

The resort is devoted to sports and rejuvenation. Guests can spend their days at golf, tennis, fishing, and much more. The Greenbrier's spa with mineral baths uses sulphur water from the area's White Sulphur Springs and mineral water from Alvon Springs. Guests can luxuriate and renew tired bodies in the spa's whirlpool baths, soaking tubs, sauna, steam and Swiss showers, and Scotch spray facilities. A complete range of spa services, such as herbal wraps and European pressure-point facials are also available.

There is no mistaking the resort's southern heritage when guests sit down to breakfast each morning. Hominy grits, pan-seared brook trout, cornbread, and Virginia ham and biscuits are served in the Main Dining Room. Guests may opt for "Greenbrier Light Cuisine," which contains only about one-third of the calories in a typical restaurant meal, with drastic reductions in fat and sodium. Whatever you choose to eat, Greenbrier dinners are elegant, romantic, and truly memorable.

White Sulphur Springs ✆ *West Virginia 24986* ✆ *(800)624-6070 or (304)536-1110*

The Grove Park Inn

Splendid views in the heart of the Blue Ridge Mountains

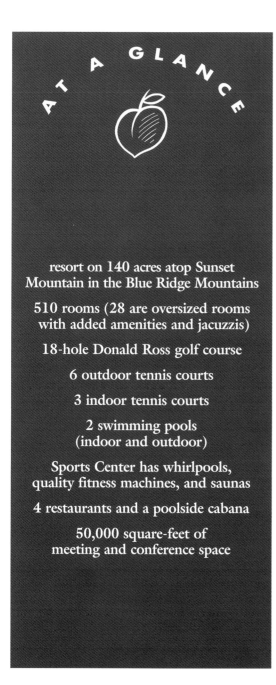

SINCE THE Grove Park Inn's opening in 1913 by Edwin Wiley Grove as a grand resort in North Carolina's Blue Ridge Mountains, there have been numerous upgrades and expansions, crafting the resort into an award-winning travel destination. The adjoining Country Club of Asheville was purchased in 1976 and added to the Inn, and a multi-million dollar expansion (including the opening of a Sports Center with racquet courts, whirlpools, and fitness equipment) and room renovation occurred during the 1980s. Today, active guests come to play on the Resort's challenging golf course and tennis courts, or to explore the scenic vistas spread out in all directions from the property.

Between events and special weekends held at The Grove Park Inn Resort and in nearby Asheville, there is much to do throughout the year. But autumn through the holiday season is an especially festive time to visit the area. The mountains turn brilliant hues of red, yellow, and gold, the area comes alive with Oktoberfest celebrations, and, close to Christmas, Asheville's renowned Biltmore Estate hosts candlelight tours of its decorated mansion. And back at the Inn, 30 Christmas trees, 171 bows, and nearly 40,000 lights are commonly used to make a spectacular display throughout the public areas.

Take advantage of the Inn's many weekend packages, or plan your own special vacation here, and sample the best the region has to offer. ☙

290 Macon Avenue ☙ Asheville, North Carolina 28804-3799 ☙ (800)438-5800 or (704)252-2711

Robert Wong

THE GREENBRIER

Executive chef Robert Wong keeps the Greenbrier's continental cuisine up to the resort's standards for excellence. Wong's Grilled Salmon Medallions and Sea Scallops is topped with creamy stone-ground grits, served atop a bed of wilted watercress, and surrounded with a delicate lemon chive butter sauce. The dish combines modern culinary expertise with a nod to southern cooking. "My philosophy is to use fresh ingredients and simple presentations, combining interesting yet compatible flavors," he says.

The Greenbrier employs 120 culinarians (including 58 chefs), many of whom have received training on-site at the resort's Culinary Apprenticeship Program.

Guests who would like to study any number of five-star culinary techniques, including pasta-making, cooking light, or making appetizers and hors d'oeuvres, are welcome to reserve a space in the Greenbrier's gourmet cooking classes, held at the La Varenne Cooking School.

Grilled Salmon Medallions and Sea Scallops with Saffron Grits, Wilted Watercress, and Lemon Chive Butter Sauce

Pictured on p.55

Makes 6 servings

Salmon & Scallops
(6) 2 1/2 oz. salmon medallions, skinless and boneless
6 large sea scallops (10-12 count)
salt and white pepper to taste

Creamy Stone-Ground Saffron Grits
2 Tbs. olive oil
2 tsp. minced shallots
1/2 cup stone-ground white grits (see Resources section)
1 pinch saffron
1 1/2 oz. dry vermouth
2 cups chicken stock
1/4 cup heavy cream
3 Tbs. grated asiago cheese
salt and white pepper to taste

Lemon Chive Butter Sauce
(yields one quart)
4 oz. shallots, minced
8 oz. white wine
3 oz. lemon juice
3 oz. white wine vinegar
1 pint heavy cream
1 1/2 lbs. unsalted butter, softened
1/4 cup chives, chopped

Method for Salmon: Season salmon with salt and white pepper. In a non-stick skillet, add 2 Tbs. of olive oil and cook over medium heat. Sear salmon for approximately one minute per side until cooked.

Cut each scallop in half (cross slices). Repeat same process used for salmon, except cook the scallops only 30-45 seconds on each side.

Method for Grits: In a sauce pot, heat olive oil over medium heat. Add shallots and sauté (do not brown) approximately 1 1/2 minutes. Next, add the saffron threads and vermouth; reduce mixture by 1/2. Add grits and mix well. Add in chicken stock and stir continuously for 10 minutes until cooked. When cooked, add heavy cream. Remove from heat and stir in cheese. Season to taste.

Method for Sauce: Combine shallots, wine, lemon juice, and vinegar. Reduce mixture over medium heat by about 1/3. Add heavy cream ☞

> The saffron grits in this dish add traditional southern flair to the salmon and scallops.

About this Dish
The lemon chive sauce can be adapted many ways. Try adding other herbs, and/or using red wine, chopped tomatoes, and mushrooms.

and reduce again by 1/2. Gradually whisk in butter. Adjust the seasoning to taste with salt and pepper. Add chives just before serving.

Presentation: Place sautéed watercress in center of a small serving plate (be sure to drain excess liquid before serving). Place salmon atop watercress, and top salmon with about 1 1/2 oz. of saffron grits. Next, top grits with scallops, and sauce the plate with 1 1/2-2 oz. of lemon chive butter sauce. ✑

Rosemary Pinot Noir Sorbet

Makes 12 servings (yields 6 cups)

1/2 cup pink grapefruit juice
3/4 cup water
1/2 cup sugar
1 1/2 cups Pinot Noir
1 sprig fresh rosemary
3 Tbs. fresh lemon juice

Method for Sorbet: Simmer water, sugar, rosemary, grapefruit juice, and 3/4 cup of the Pinot Noir over low heat for 10 minutes. Strain and add to remaining Pinot Noir and lemon juice. Chill in the refrigerator until cold. Freeze according to the instructions on your ice cream maker. ✑

> Serve this sorbet as a nice segue from a seafood dish to lamb or veal—it's an intermezzo with an interesting, herbaceous quality.

Roast Veal Tenderloin with Wild Mushroom Crepinette, Root Vegetable and Butternut Squash Hash, and Madeira Sauce

Pictured on p.65

Makes 6 servings

2 veal tenderloins*
salt and white pepper to taste
2 Tbs. olive oil
4 oz. caul fat (purchase from your local butcher)

* Each about 12 oz., skinless, boneless, and completely trimmed

Wild Mushroom Crepinette
Makes 1 1/2 pounds

6 oz. ground veal
6 oz. ground pork
1 whole egg
8 oz. chilled heavy cream
salt and white pepper to taste
2 Tbs. fresh chopped herbs (parsley, thyme, and chervil)
10 oz. wild mushrooms*

* Sauté and then chill

Madeira Sauce

1 gallon veal stock (recipe follows; or, see Resources section)
2 cups mirepoix, finely chopped*
3 cups Madeira wine
* A common sauce and soup base; combine carrots, onions, and celery (finely chopped

Veal Stock

10 lbs. veal bones
2 lbs. vegetable mirepoix
2 gallons cold water
1 herb sachet bag*
1 cup tomato purée
1 cup red wine

* Tie bay leaf, peppercorns, thyme, and parsley sprigs up in a cheesecloth pouch

Root Vegetable and Butternut Squash Hash

4 Tbs. unsalted butter
4 cups root vegetables, diced medium*
2 cups butternut squash, diced medium
1 1/2 cups onion, finely chopped
6 strips bacon, diced
1 Tbs. fresh thyme, chopped
1 tsp. garlic, chopped
salt and cracked black pepper to taste

* Carrots, celery root, turnips, and rutabagas

Garnish

8-10 Brussel sprouts (optional) ☞

Method for Tenderloin: Season loins with salt and white pepper. In a sauté pan, heat 2 Tbs. olive oil over medium heat and sear loins for approx. 1 1/2 minutes per side.

Method for Veal Stock: Brown bones in a large roasting pan for 1 1/2 hours at 350° until caramelized. Remove bones from pan and sauté mirepoix in same pan. Once the mirepoix is caramelized, deglaze pan with wine and reduce to 1/3. Place mirepoix in a stock pot and add bones. Add 2 gallons of water, and slowly bring to a simmer (do not boil). Continue to simmer for approximately 6 hours.

Strain the stock through a cheesecloth. Reduce mixture by 1/2 over low heat, and simmer until it has a slightly thickened consistency (the sauce should coat the back of a spoon).

Note: Stock can be made up to 3 days ahead of time and refrigerated until needed.

Method for Madeira Sauce: Sauté mirepoix until caramelized. Add the 3 cups madeira wine and reduce by 1/2. Add 1 gallon of veal stock and reduce by 1/2 again at a slow simmer (do not boil). Strain and adjust seasoning with salt and pepper to taste.

Method for Crepinette: Place ground veal and pork in a chilled bowl of a food processor.

Process the veal, pork, and egg until it is smooth, but do not let the formeat get overcooked. Add heavy cream, salt, pepper, and herbs to the mixture. Add in sautéed mushrooms and blend all together well.

Method for Vegetable Hash: In a large sauté pan, cook the diced bacon over medium heat until brown and crisp. Remove bacon and set aside. Add butter to bacon fat, then add root vegetables, onions, and garlic. Sauté over medium-high heat for 5 minutes. Add butternut squash and thyme, and continue to sauté for 10-15 minutes until cooked. Season with salt and pepper.

Finish & Presentation: Using a small spatula, cover the top of each veal tenderloin with 2 oz. of forcemeat (crepinette). Wrap in caul fat to ensure the veal and forcemeat stay secure.

Roast in a 375° oven for 15-18 minutes until cooked (internal temperature should be 140°). Let rest at room temperature for 10 minutes before slicing.

Place 2 oz. of root vegetable hash in the center of a serving plate. Top hash with 3 slices of veal crepinette, overlapped a bit. Garnish plate with blanched outer leaves of brussel sprouts. Ladle 2 oz. of sauce around perimeter of plate. ᥣ

> ## Chef Wong serves local wild mushrooms and crepinette (a light paté) over tender veal in this cool-weather favorite.

Brier Run Chèvre Cheese Soufflé

Makes 12 servings

1/2 qt. milk
1/2 qt. heavy cream
1/2 lb. bread flour
1/2 lb. butter
1/2 lb. chèvre cheese
5 egg yolks
salt and pepper to taste
nutmeg and paprika to taste
10 egg whites

Method for Soufflé: Heat milk and cream. Pre-mix flour and butter, keeping mixture loose in consistency. Bring milk and cream to a boil and add butter/flour mixture, making a roux.

Place roux in a mixing bowl and start cooling by adding the cheese in small pieces. Next add the egg yolks. Add nutmeg, paprika, salt, and pepper to taste. Make a meringue with the egg whites by beating them to a stiff consistency with a mixer. Fold the stiffened whites into the base mixture.

Divide mixture among six small buttered soufflé baking bowls. Sprinkle thyme lightly over top and bake in a 350° oven until golden-brown (about 18-22 minutes). ᥣ

> ## This hearty soufflé makes a lovely side dish at dinnertime, or it can be served solo with a light salad any time of day.

Roast Veal Tenderloin with Root Vegetable Hash. Recipe on p.63

Jeffrey Piccirillo

THE GROVE PARK INN RESORT

Here, romance and four-star sophistication extend to its feature restaurant as well. At Horizons Restaurant, executive chef Jeffrey Piccirillo and his culinary staff offer "innovative classic cuisine" in a romantic dining room with splendid views of the mountains. Imaginative dishes such as Sweet Potato and Jalapeño Pepper Soup combine favorite southern ingredients with flavors from other regions of the U.S. Couples dining at The Grove Park Inn Resort enjoy romantic touches like fresh flowers and crisp white linen tablecloths. Fresh ingredients and beautiful presentations are the hallmark of Horizons' signature dishes.

At The Grove Park Inn Resort, a dedicated culinary team ensures excellence every day of the week. Jeffrey Piccirillo is a Certified Working Chef (CWC), a Certified Food & Beverage Executive (CFBE), and a member of the American Hotel and Motel Association.

Tasso Ham and Boursin Cheese Frittata with Georgia Peach Compote

Makes 2 servings

Pastry Shell
2 cups all-purpose flour
1/2 tsp. salt
2/3 cup shortening*
4 Tbs. cold water

* Made using half butter and half shortening

Frittata
2 oz. Tasso ham, julienned
2 oz. Boursin cheese, softened
4 oz. liquid eggs product
salt and white pepper to taste

Fresh Georgia Peach Compote
2 ripe Georgia peaches**
1/8 cup brown sugar
1/2 tsp. allspice
2 oz. Peach Schnapps
2 oz. red wine

** Peel and cut in a small dice

Asst. banquet chef Dennis Trantham won the "I Love Eggs" recipe contest with this innovative frittata. Get the freshest, juiciest peaches available for the chutney-style compote.

Method for Pastry: Sift flour with salt; then, cut in shortening and butter mixture. Mix in water gradually until the mixture resembles course crumbs. Transfer to a floured board, roll out pastry and cut into 5" circles. Press the pastry circles into tart pans and pre-bake (bake blind) them for 10 minutes at 375°.

Method for Frittata: Sauté ham in 1 oz. butter over medium-high heat. Add eggs seasoned with salt and pepper to make the frittata. Chill for 30 minutes in the refrigerator. Once chilled, shape the frittata and cut out to fit shells. Add cheese and gratinée (brown) briefly under the broiler.

Method for Peach Compote: Reduce the wine to 1/2 over high heat. Add peaches, brown sugar, allspice, salt, and white pepper. Stew over medium heat for 6-8 minutes, or until the fruit is translucent. When cooked and reduced by about 1/2 again, add in the Peach Schnapps. Simmer until the mixture reaches a thick consistency. Chill until ready to serve. Serve along with the Tasso Ham and Boursin Cheese Frittata.

Presentation: Serve the frittata with seasonal vegetables and edible flowers on the plate. Offer the peach compote separately, or place a portion on the plate next to frittata. Lay whole stems of chives across the frittata to finish the dish.

Pinenut and Almond Breast of Chicken with Pineapple Relish, Fried Boursin Polenta, and Grilled Squash

Makes 4 servings

Nut-crusted Chicken
(4) 6 oz. chicken breast fillets (boneless and skinless)
1/2 cup flour
3 eggs, lightly beaten (egg wash)
8 oz. pinenuts
8 oz. sliced almonds
8 oz. seasoned bread crumbs

Pineapple Salsa
1 fresh pineapple*
1/2 red bell pepper*
1/2 green bell pepper*
1/2 yellow bell pepper*
1 small red onion
1 jalapeño pepper, finely diced
1/4 cup cilantro, chopped
1/4 cup orange juice
4 Tbs. lime juice

1/2 tsp. ground cumin
1/4 tsp. each: salt and pepper
*Cut in a 1/4" dice

Boursin Polenta
2 qts. water
1 Tbs. salt
2 oz. butter
3 oz. Boursin cheese
1 lb. yellow cornmeal
1 oz. parmesan cheese, freshly grated

Grilled Marinated Squash
1 whole zucchini*
1 whole yellow squash*
1 whole eggplant*
1 cup Italian dressing
salt and pepper to taste

*Cut on bias into 1/2" slices

Method for Chicken: Dredge chicken breasts in flour. Mix pinenuts, almonds, and bread crumbs together. Dip breasts in egg wash, and then into the nut mixture. Set aside until needed. When everything else is ready, sauté the crusted breasts until golden-brown on both sides.

Method for Salsa: Mix all ingredients and stir to marry the flavors of each.

Method for Boursin Polenta: Place water, salt, butter, and cornmeal in a heavy pot. Heat the mixture, stirring constantly as it thickens. Mix in the cheese while stirring. Cover the pot, and move it to a 350° oven; bake for 25 minutes. Pour the polenta into a greased sheet pan. Allow to cool, and then cut into desired shapes. Just before serving, pan fry until golden-brown on both sides. Sprinkle with the fresh, grated parmesan cheese.

Method for Grilled Squash: Combine all ingredients, and let marinate for 4 hours. Grill and baste with additional marinade.

Presentation: Place chicken breast at 6:00 on the plate. Spoon some pineapple relish on one half of breast. Arrange the squash medley between 12:00 and 3:00. Finally, place the Boursin polenta between 12:00 and 9:00. ✎

Sweet Potato and Jalapeño Pepper Soup

Makes 6 servings

2 Tbs. butter
1 large onion (Peel & cut in a fine dice)
3 medium sweet potatoes (Peel & dice)
6 cups chicken stock
1 jalapeño pepper, thinly sliced
salt and pepper to taste

Garnish
1 cup sour cream
1/2 lime, juice only
2-3 Tbs. fresh cilantro, chopped
1 tsp. lemon rind, grated

Method for Soup: In a stock pot, melt the butter; then, add onions and cook until they turn brown. Add in the sweet potatoes and chicken stock, and season with salt and pepper. Bring to a boil, and simmer partially covered for 30 minutes.

In a small bowl, combine the sour cream, lime juice, and lemon rind together. Reserve this for the soup garnish.

When potatoes are tender, strain the soup mixture (reserving the liquid) and purée the potatoes in a food processor. Blend the purée and liquid back together in the stock pot. Add heavy cream and sliced jalapeño pepper; cook for 10 minutes. Season to taste.

Presentation: Serve the soup hot in individual bowls. Garnish each with a dollop of sour cream mixture and a sprinkle of chopped cilantro. ✎

Windsor Court Hotel

Southern hospitality blends with European charm in the city that fosters great chefs and world-class cuisine

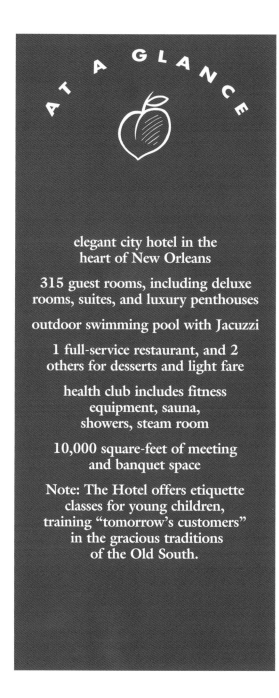

NEW ORLEANS is well-known as a top U.S. city for great food and good times. Located in the heart of the city, the Windsor Court Hotel combines elegant accommodations with gracious hospitality. In fact, it is the only AAA Five Diamond hotel in Louisiana, and the only AAA Five Diamond restaurant in New Orleans. Located near New Orleans' riverfront, the Windsor Court Hotel is part of the Orient-Express Hotel group, owners of some of the most luxurious hotels world-wide. All 315 guest rooms face the Mississippi River or the city of New Orleans. Deluxe guest rooms are appointed with spacious bedrooms and Italian marble bathrooms.

The Hotel's public areas are beautifully decorated with fine furnishings and impressive works of art, including paintings by Gainsborough. But the special touches also extend to guests, who are indulged with nearly any convenience or service imaginable. Travelers who crave champagne and oysters in the wee hours, will feel right at home here—there is access to room service, valet parking, and laundry and dry cleaning services around the clock.

There is so much to do in the city: exploring the riverfront, the French Quarter, or gracious old mansions. After a day spent in town soaking up all of that special bayou culture, slip back into the Hotel for afternoon tea. You will probably be treated to chocolate-dipped strawberries, pecan tarts, assorted cookies, chocolate truffles, tea cakes—and tea, of course!

300 Gravier Street ❧ New Orleans, Louisiana 70130 ❧ (800) 262-2662 or (504) 523-6000

Amelia Island Plantation

Florida's "greenest" resort offers unspoiled beaches, non-stop recreation, and memorable dining

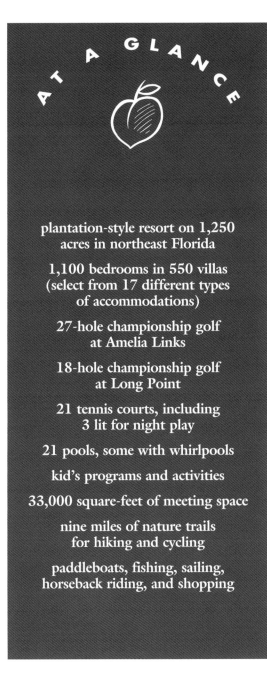

AT A GLANCE

plantation-style resort on 1,250 acres in northeast Florida

1,100 bedrooms in 550 villas (select from 17 different types of accommodations)

27-hole championship golf at Amelia Links

18-hole championship golf at Long Point

21 tennis courts, including 3 lit for night play

21 pools, some with whirlpools

kid's programs and activities

33,000 square-feet of meeting space

nine miles of nature trails for hiking and cycling

paddleboats, fishing, sailing, horseback riding, and shopping

WITH SO much development along both coasts of Florida, Amelia Island Plantation is a refreshing change of pace, with miles of unspoiled beaches and low-rise complexes that blend in with the native marshes, beaches, and forests. It is home to herons, egrets, sea turtles, and deer, and is far from the madding crowds that flock into vacation destinations further south.

Located near Jacksonville in the upper northeast corner of Florida, this 1,250-acre resort pampers guests with fine dining, deluxe accommodations, and world-class golf and tennis. You can select a hotel room at the Inn, or reserve a townhome or villa large enough for the whole family. Rated as one of the nation's best resorts for families, Amelia Island Plantation offers kid's programs for children of all ages. Families enjoy hiking and cycling on paths through the park-like areas of the property where massive live oaks and tidal marshes thrive peaceably under the Florida sun.

Florida's "greenest resort" is one of the top picks in the southeast region for serious tennis and golf. Tennis players can choose from among the Plantation's 21 courts, 19 of which are fast-drying and three have lights for nightime play. The plantation also functions as a golfer's paradise with two courses (27 holes designed by Pete Dye and another 18 by Tom Fazio) scattered across the Plantation, offering views of the woods and ocean in all directions.

The beautiful Golden Isles of southeast Georgia, Fernandina Beach, Florida, and old St. Augustine, Florida are all just a short drive away. ᴖ

P.O. Box 3000 ᴖ Amelia Island, Florida 32035-1307 ᴖ (800)874-6878 or (904)261-6161

The Ritz-Carlton, Amelia

A luxurious island getaway with southern charm and championship golf

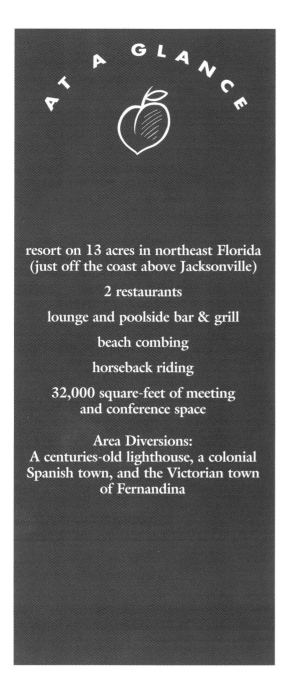

resort on 13 acres in northeast Florida
(just off the coast above Jacksonville)

2 restaurants

lounge and poolside bar & grill

beach combing

horseback riding

32,000 square-feet of meeting
and conference space

Area Diversions:
A centuries-old lighthouse, a colonial
Spanish town, and the Victorian town
of Fernandina

THE RITZ-Carlton, Amelia Island, is only 30 miles and 70 years away from Jacksonville, Florida. Designed to evoke the Golden Age of luxurious oceanfront resorts, this Ritz welcomes guests to a secluded island so unspoiled that you can still ride a horse on the white sand beach. Towering oaks draped with Spanish moss line the entrance drive, which skirts the greens and fairways of an 18-hole championship golf course. You'll arrive at a stately porte cochere with neoclassic columns that leads to a paneled lobby, resplendent with museum-quality art, antiques, Persian carpets, and fresh flowers. Beyond lies a landscaped courtyard, a private beach, and the majestic Atlantic Ocean.

There is a view of the ocean from every one of the Resort's 449 guest rooms. Thoughtful, gracious guest services include high tea and chamber music in the elegant Lobby Lounge, and chef's cuisine "to go" is available from the exclusive Gourmet Shop. Jet skis and ocean kayaks add Nineties flair to traditional sailing, surfing, and deep sea fishing. The Ritz Kids program entertains children from five to twelve with inventive and imaginative activities. And beyond the gates lies a charming Victorian island that begs to be explored.

When night falls, The Ritz-Carlton, Amelia Island slows to a gentler rhythm. You can slip into the Lobby Lounge for live jazz, take a moonlight stroll through the scented gardens, or just relax on your own private balcony to hear the surf ebb and flow, and to watch the stars come out over the Atlantic.

4750 Amelia Island Parkway ☙ Amelia Island, Florida 32034 ☙ (800)241-3333 or (904)277-1100

Jeff Tunks

WINDSOR COURT HOTEL

Jeff Tunks, the Windsor Court Hotel's executive chef, has played a big part in the Grill Room winning numerous culinary awards. "I am committed to finding and cooking only the freshest, seasonal ingredients, adding sublime taste and creative presentation," he says. Tunks' style, an Asian spin on New American Cuisine, has earned much notoriety throughout his 11 years as a culinary professional.

Chinese-Style Smoked Lobster is just one popular dish that typifies chef Tunks' ability to give diners full-flavored foods that are lean and are beautifully presented. In the land of "lagniappe," it takes a lot of effort to earn top honors, and chef Tunks has a knack for creating foods that win people's hearts. Guests may dine with the Hotel's chefs at a seven-to-ten course meal by advance reservation. It promises to be a meal you won't soon forget.

Chinese-Style Smoked Lobster

Pictured on p.77

Makes 2 servings

2 lobsters, 1 1/2 lbs. each
4 cloves garlic
2 tsp. ginger
1 tsp. Vietnamese chili sauce
1 bunch scallions
2 oz. soy sauce
4 oz. olive oil
1 carrot*
2 oz. snowpeas*
1/2 daikon*
1/4 head red cabbage*
2 oz. sesame oil

2 cups fresh spinach, deep-fried
(optional garnish)

* Clean and cut julienne-style

Ingredient Footnote

DAIKON

Daikon is a root vegetable that resembles a large, white carrot. It can be purchased at Asian food stores (or see Resources section). If daikon is unavailable, you may substitute water chestnuts to add crunch to this dish.

Method for Lobsters: Blanch each lobster for 6 minutes in boiling water. Shock in ice water and clean. Using a large knife or cleaver, remove tail and claws from body. Remove the long, loose claw. Leaving the claw meat in shell, cut claw on the bias, using a meat cleaver. Remove the tail meat and cut it once lengthwise, and then cut each long piece across into three medallions. Place the medallions back into shell.

Method for Ginger Paste: In a food processor, place garlic, ginger, chili sauce, and 2 oz. olive oil; purée into a paste.

Method for Vegetables: Using two large pans, add olive oil to one and sesame oil to the other. When the sesame oil gets smoking hot, add the julienne of vegetables and quickly stir-fry. To the smoking hot olive oil pan, add the cut-up lobster and let sit for 1 minute. Add in garlic, ginger paste, and chopped scallions, and sauté for 30 seconds.

Presentation: Place the stir-fried vegetables on a serving plate. Add soy sauce to the lobster in its hot skillet, and then pour lobster over vegetables. Garnish with deep-fried spinach, if desired.

> This Asian dish is easy to prepare.
> The lobster is seared right in its shell,
> keeping the meat succulent.

Steamed Striped Bass with Summer Vegetables

Makes 4 servings

1 boneless striped bass fillet*
2 cups chopped tomatoes, skinned and seeded
1 cup hon she miti mushrooms (or shiitakes)
1 Tbs. ginger, peeled and minced
1 bunch chopped chives
2 oz. soy sauce
1 cup fish fumé (recipe follows)
1 tsp. black sesame seeds
2 oz. butter

* Enough for (4) 7 oz. portions

Fish Fumé
2 oz. olive oil
2 cups fennel, partially cooked and chopped
10 white peppercorns
3 bay leaves
1 sprig fresh thyme
1 lb. fish bones
2 spanish onions, skinned and quartered
3 cloves fresh garlic, crushed
2 cups white wine
1 qt. water
3 oz. lemon juice

Method for Fish Fumé: In a heavy sauce pan, heat 2 oz. olive oil until very hot. Add the next six ingredients and sauté for 2 minutes. Next, add the garlic and continue to cook for 1 minute. Add the white wine, water, and lemon juice, bringing the mixture to a boil. Lower the temperature and allow to simmer for 40 minutes. Strain and let cool at room temperature.

Method for Steamed Bass: In a large sauté pan, add tomato, fennel, mushrooms, ginger, white wine, and 1 cup of the fish fumé. On top of vegetables, place bass skin-side up. Cover and bring to a boil. Then, lower heat and steam fish for 5 minutes, or until it flakes with a fork. Remove fish and vegetables, and set aside. To the pan with vegetables, add soy sauce (low-sodium if you prefer), remaining tomatoes, chives, sesame seeds, and butter; let cook for 2 minutes.

Presentation: Spoon vegetables into a bowl, and place fish on top. Ladle extra liquid over the fish and garnish with the sprig of fennel. 〜

> The bass stays flaky and tender in this dish, a delightful combination of fish with aromatic ingredients.

Curried Crab Cake with Mango, Cucumber, & Lime

Makes 4 servings

Crab Cake
14 oz. crab meat
1 egg
1 lime
10 chives
2 oz. mayonnaise
1/2 cup fresh brioche crumbs
1 tsp. madras curry powder*
4 oz. olive oil
salt and pepper to taste

* Or, use Indian curry powder

Relish
1 mango*
1 large cucumber*
1 1/2 oz. rice wine vinegar
1 lime
1/4 red onion
1/6 bunch cilantro
1 tsp. mint
2 oz. olive oil
salt and pepper to taste

* Peel, seed, and cut into a small dice; chef Tunks uses European hothouse-grown cucumbers for this relish

Sauces and Garnish
1 mango*
1 lime ☞

1 oz. rice wine vinegar
1 oz. olive oil
salt and pepper to taste
lobster coral** (optional garnish)
1 tsp. black sesame seeds (optional)

* Peel and seed
** Lobster coral are the green, fatty eggs; blanch them in hot water (they'll turn bright green) for this recipe

Method for Crab Cakes: Cook and clean meat from fresh crabs or purchase the canned meat itself and pick through for shells. In a mixing bowl, add mayonnaise, egg, juice from one lime, minced chives, curry powder, and salt and pepper to taste; blend well. Fold the mixture into the crabmeat along with half of the fresh brioche crumbs and taste before adjusting seasonings. Form into four crab cakes, each around 3 1/2 to 4 oz. each.

Method for Relish: Place the diced cucumber and mango into a mixing bowl and add minced red onion, chopped cilantro, mint, rice vinegar, juice from the lime, and olive oil; season to taste.

Method for Sauce: Using a blender or food processor, purée the mango pulp along with the rice vinegar, olive oil, and juices from one lime; add salt and pepper to taste.

Presentation: Lightly dust crab cakes with remaining brioche crumbs. Heat olive oil in a sauce pan and lightly brown the cakes on both sides, then place them on a baking sheet. Bake the crab cakes in a 350° oven for 7-10 minutes. Divide room temperature relish onto four plates and place a crab cake on top of relish. Sauce each mound with mango coulis and garnish with lobster coral and black sesame seeds. 🐚

Seared Sashimi of Tuna with Citrus Couscous and Spicy Blood Orange Vinaigrette

Makes 2 servings (appetizer portions)

Sashimi of Tuna
8 oz. #1 grade tuna (cut 1"x1"x6")
1 oz. poppy seeds
1 pinch salt
1 oz. sesame oil

Citrus Couscous
1 3/4 cup couscous
2 cups orange juice
1/2 tsp. orange zest
salt and pepper to taste

Spicy Blood Orange Vinaigrette
2 cups blood orange juice (reduce by 2/3 to equal 1/2 cup orange syrup)
2 chipotle peppers*

2 shallots*
2 cloves garlic**
2 cups olive oil
2 oz. rice wine vinegar

* Mince
** Smash and mince

Brunoise Mirepoix
1/4 cup vegetables, finely diced*
1 Tbs. shallot
1 Tbs. butter
* Combine red bell pepper, zucchini, and yellow squash to equal 1/4 cup total

watercress and mache (optional garnishes)

Method for Sashimi: Roll tuna "log" in poppy seeds and salt. Heat a heavy sauté pan until very hot; add sesame oil and immediately add tuna. (Be careful of flare-up). Cook for 10 seconds on all sides and remove.

Method for Couscous: Place zest and couscous in a heavy casserole dish with lid. Heat orange juice to a boil and pour over couscous mixture. Cover casserole and let stand at room temperature for 20 minutes. Remove lid and flake couscous with a fork. Allow to cool in the refrigerator.

Method for Vinaigrette: Fill a large stainless steel mixing bowl with ice. Nest a smaller bowl in the ice and add blood orange "syrup", rice wine vinegar, garlic, and shallots. Whisk together and slowly add olive oil, whisking continuously. Add chipotle peppers and season with salt and white pepper. ☞

Be sure to use top-quality, fresh tuna for this light appetizer.
The tuna becomes charred outside, but stays velvety and rare inside.

Method for Mirepoix: Cut all vegetables into 1/8" cubes and sauté in butter over medium heat for 2 minutes. Season with salt and white pepper. Fold into citrus couscous.

Presentation: In the center of a serving plate, place a 3" diameter cookie cutter. Spoon room temperature couscous into the form and lightly tamp down with the back of a spoon. Remove cutter. Next, slice tuna 1/4" thick and lay in a circle around the couscous. Place clean sprigs of watercress and mache in center of couscous and lightly spoon vinaigrette around plate. ✍

Chinese-Style Smoked Lobster
Recipe on p.74

Jacky Burette

AMELIA ISLAND PLANTATION

After a busy day on Amelia's links, guests enjoy being treated to imaginative cuisine at the Amelia Inn. Corporate chef Jacky Burette creates wonderful combinations of foods, such as Broiled Rack of Lamb with Wild Mushrooms. Burette insists upon using fresh local and regional ingredients in dishes that never skimp on aroma and taste.

With more than 30 years experience in the food industry, French-born Burette studied classical cuisine and worked as a chef in his homeland, before coming to the U.S. While he has been working for the Plantation, chef Burette has been named to the American Culinary Federation's Resort Food Executive Committee.

At the Amelia Inn, the sensory experience of a meal prepared by chef Burette and his talented staff is made complete with expansive views of the Atlantic Ocean—without a boardwalk, t-shirt shop, or ferris wheel to spoil the view.

Broiled Rack of Lamb with Wild Mushrooms

Makes 4 servings

2-2 1/2 lbs. rack of lamb
2 Tbs. olive oil
1 Tbs. fresh garlic, minced
1 Tbs. cracked black pepper
1 Tbs. shallots, chopped
2 Tbs. fresh thyme, rosemary, and basil (combined)
1 tsp. salt

Wild Mushrooms

1 minced shallot
6 oz. unsalted butter (12 Tbs.)
1/2 lb. fresh shiitake mushrooms
1/2 lb. fresh enoki mushrooms
1/2 lb. fresh oyster mushrooms
salt and pepper to taste

Method for Lamb: Combine all ingredients and rub into lamb. Marinate 8 hours or overnight.

Broil lamb to desired doneness. Remove from broiler and set aside. Sauté shallots in 3 oz. butter for 2-3 minutes (do not brown). Add the mushrooms and sauté over moderate heat for 5 more minutes. Season to taste with salt and pepper. In a small pan, bring the remaining butter to a foam.

Presentation: On warm plates, arrange portions of the mushrooms. Divide lamb into chops and arrange 3 to a plate, over the mushrooms. Spoon foaming butter over the lamb and serve immediately.
NOTE: An assortment of tender, crisp baby vegetables make a tasty accompaniment to the dish.

> This dish combines hearty lamb, wild mushrooms, and flavors typical to the Mediterranean.

Grilled Veal Chops with Balsamic Vinegar

Makes 4 servings

(4) 10 oz. veal chops, well trimmed
salt and fresh ground pepper to taste

Balsamic Vinegar

1 large shallot, minced
4 Tbs. unsalted butter
1/4 cup balsamic vinegar
1/2 cup dry red wine
1/4 cup heavy cream

Method for Veal: Preheat grill. Season chops with salt and pepper and grill for 5-7 minutes on each side, or until veal is just cooked through. While meat is grilling, make the sauce.

Method for Sauce: Sauté shallots in 1 Tbs. butter in an enamel or stainless-steel pan (*You must use a non-reactive sauce pan for this procedure*) for a few minutes over medium heat. Deglaze pan with the vinegar and reduce to 2 Tbs. Add the wine and reduce by 1/2. Add the cream and ☞

continue to reduce, until the sauce lightly coats the back of a spoon. Whisk the remaining butter into the sauce, a little at a time, over low heat. Season with salt and pepper to taste.

Presentation: On warm plates, arrange a bed of sauce. Place chops on top of sauce. Serve with crisp tender baby vegetables, or with fettucine primavera. Other good side dishes include mashed potatoes with garlic, Peruvian (blue) potatoes, or mashed sweet potatoes. ✎

> For a change of pace, you can substitute chicken breasts (with the bone in) for the veal.

Sautéed Red Snapper with Fettuccine Primavera

Makes 4 servings

Snapper & Primavera
(4) 8 oz. red snapper fillets (with skin)
salt and pepper to taste
1 lb. fettuccine
1/2 head cauliflower
1 bunch broccoli
1 carrot
1 zucchini

White Wine Butter Sauce
1 Tbs. butter (don't use margarine)
1 Tbs. heavy cream
1 shallot, minced
3 oz. olive oil
2 oz. white wine
1 Tbs. each: chopped parsley, thyme, & basil

sprigs of parsley & thyme (optional garnish)

Method for Primavera: Prepare fettuccine according to package directions. Drain, rinse with hot water, and set aside. Cut broccoli and cauliflower into florets and julienne the carrot. Blanch in a pot of boiling water until crisp and tender.

Heat the remaining olive oil in a wok over a high burner. Add the cooked fettuccine and blanched vegetables, tossing all until blended.

Method for Snapper & Sauce: Salt and pepper the fish fillets and sauté in 1 oz. olive oil (skin-side first) for 3 minutes on each side. In a small pan, heat white wine and chopped shallots and reduce by 1/2. Add heavy cream and stir, bring to boil, and add butter in small amounts until smooth.

Presentation: Using four warm plates, place pasta on one side and the fish opposite (skin-side up). Top each fillet with the white wine butter sauce. Garnish each dish with sprigs of parsley and thyme. ✎

> Chef Burette advises getting the freshest snapper available from your local fish market, and leaving the skin on for the fullest flavor. And, the primavera is a low-fat version.

Angel Hair Pasta with Shrimp and Sun-Dried Tomato Sauce

Makes 4 servings

1 lb. angel hair pasta
1 lb. shrimp (21-25 count)
2 Tbs. teriyaki sauce
2 oz. shallots, chopped
1/2 cup white wine
2 oz. heavy cream
8 oz. butter
8 plum tomatoes (quartered and dried)

Method for Pasta: Marinate shrimp in teriyaki sauce and a small amount of the shallots for 10 minutes. While the shrimp marinate, cook pasta, drain, and rinse with warm water. Set aside. Thread skewers with six shrimp each and grill.

In a sauce pan over moderate heat, place white wine and 1/2 Tbs. of the shallots, and reduce to 1/4. Add the dried tomatoes and heavy cream, and bring to a boil. Then add the butter in small amounts at a time, until butter is completely melted. Remove the sauce from heat and season with salt and pepper to taste.

Presentation: Arrange pasta on four plates. Remove shrimp from skewers and place on top of pasta. Top each with sauce and garnish with the fresh herbs. ✎

Steven Schaefer

THE RITZ-CARLTON, AMELIA

Dining at The Ritz-Carlton, Amelia Island is a series of delights. The Grill and Bar, with its spectacular ocean view, marries the specialties of a fine English dinner club with Florida's matchless fresh seafood. Steven Schaefer, Executive Chef, and Matthew Medure, Chef of the Grill, offer delicacies like Amelia Island Seafood Risotto, and Spring Onion and Morel Soup with Mussels. The soup goes on the menu in early spring, when the delicate spring onions and heady morel mushrooms are plentiful. The indoor-outdoor café offers a casual terrace setting and a special fitness cuisine in addition to its usual fare.

Executive chef Steven Schaefer is a self-taught, 20-year veteran in the food industry. His focused philosophy is to encourage outstanding work from his 60-strong culinary team as leader, coach, and mentor. "We are a team of craftsmen," he says. "We work our craft with love."

Spring Onion and Morel Soup with Mussels

Makes 6 servings

2 Tbs. olive oil
12 spring onions
1 lb. morel mushrooms, sliced
2 cloves garlic, chopped
salt and pepper to taste
3 dozen mussels
1 cup white wine
1 bunch fennel, sliced
1 qt. fish stock
1 qt. chicken broth
1 bunch Italian parsley, washed and picked
1 Tbs. thyme, chopped

Method for Soup: Sauté spring onions, garlic, and chopped morels in olive oil until caramelized. Simmer mussels and fennel in white wine and stocks for 5-10 minutes until the mussels open. Remove mussels, discard shells and reserve for garnish.

Add remaining stock to onion mixture and simmer for 10 minutes.

Presentation: Ladle servings into soup bowls and garnish each with parsley and thyme.

We use spring onions early in the season because they are so sweet.
The morels add a nice aroma and earthy quality to this soup.

Shrimp and Ginger Mousse on Crostini

Makes 16 servings (appetizer portions)

1 lb. fresh shrimp
(Remove head and tail, devein, and peel)
1 tsp. fresh ginger, chopped
1 tsp. fresh garlic, chopped
2 Tbs. soy sauce
1 Tbs. cilantro, chopped (stems included)
3 egg whites
salt and pepper to taste

1 loaf French bread for crostini
1/4 cup sesame oil

Method for Mousse: Combine first seven ingredients in a food processor, and process until coarsely chopped. Slice French bread into 1/4" slices. Sprinkle slices lightly with sesame oil and toast on one side until golden. Turn bread over and mound shrimp mixture onto each crostini. Bake in a 350°oven for 3 minutes.

Presentation: Assemble crostinis on an hors d'oeuvres platter, and garnish with fresh chives, cilantro, and edible flowers (or slices of red onion or scallions).

Amelia Island Seafood Risotto

Makes 8 servings

2 Tbs. olive oil
1 Tbs. garlic, chopped
1 cup spring Vidalia onions, chopped*
12 oz. arborio rice
1 pint mushrooms (stemmed, but left whole)
8 oz. white wine, divided
1 cup corn, kernels only
1 qt. fish stock or clam juice, divided
1/2 lb. Mayport shrimp**
16 mussels, in shells
1 pint oysters, shucked

1 lb. bay scallops, shelled
2 Tbs. parmigiano-reggiano cheese
1/4 cup parsley, chopped
salt and pepper to taste

* See Resources section, or substitute another mild onion
** Peel, devein, and chop

Garnish
tomato concasse (peel, seed, and dice fresh tomatoes)
fresh parsley, finely chopped

Method for Risotto: Sauté garlic, spring onions, and mushroom caps in the 2 Tbs. olive oil. Remove mushrooms caps and reserve for use as garnish. Next, add risotto to pan and stir to coat all of the rice with oil. Add 4 oz. of the wine and simmer over medium heat until the liquid is absorbed. Then add 1 cup of the fish stock and continue cooking until liquid is absorbed. Add corn and another cup of fish stock and repeat same process. Add in shrimp and fish stock; cook until liquid is again absorbed. When the risotto is soft and easy to chew, add the parmigiano.

Meanwhile, steam the mussels with remaining fish stock (should be 1 cup) and 4 oz. of wine until the mussels open. Remove mussels from their shells and add to the risotto. Steam the fresh oysters separately and set aside.

Strain the steaming liquid and use it to lightly poach the scallops. Reserve scallops for garnish. Add strained liquid to the risotto. Adjust seasoning with salt and pepper to taste.

Presentation: This risotto can be molded in an oiled ramekin and served unmolded on a soup plate, or simply spooned onto the soup plate. Garnish with scallops, steamed oysters, fresh parsley, and tomato concasse before serving. ✆

About this Dish
You may substitute seafood or fish of your choice in any combination to total approximately 2 pounds for this recipe.

Sole Paupiettes with Spinach

Makes 4 servings

(4) 4 oz. fillets of sole
1 lb. fresh spinach*
1 shallot, chopped
1 clove garlic, chopped
2 Tbs. olive oil
1/4 cup white wine
1/4 cup yogurt
salt and pepper to taste
* Wash thoroughly and remove stems
4 toothpicks
whole lemon to finish

Method for Sole Paupiettes: Sauté shallots and garlic in oil until transparent, and then add spinach. Deglaze with wine and cook until almost dry. Add in yogurt, salt, and pepper to taste. Allow mixture to cool.

Lay fillets on plastic wrap and top with spinach mixture. Roll each in cylindrical shape and secure with a toothpick. Bake fillets in a 350° oven for 6 minutes.

Presentation: Place one stuffed fillet on each serving plate. (Stand each paupiette on end, with a toothpick securing it.) Squeeze a little fresh lemon juice onto each one, and finish by garnishing with parsley. ✆

> The paupiettes are light and easy to prepare. Substitute other fillings when you need a change of pace.

Squab Breast in Braised Artichoke with Drambuie®-Flambéd Yams

Makes 4 servings

4 squab breasts (see Resources section)
4 large artichokes*
12 chanterelle mushrooms, peeled
2 shallots, chopped
1 garlic clove, chopped
3 cups chicken stock
2 yams

1 Tbs. butter
1 Tbs. honey
1 oz. Drambuie
salt and pepper to taste

* Remove the heart and choke; save the hulled out artichoke halves for garnish

DRAMBUIE® CANDIED PECAN GARNISH
1/4 cup Drambuie
1/4 cup pecan halves

Method for Garnish: Reduce Drambuie by 50% in a non-stick pan over medium heat (cooking out the alcohol). Add pecan halves and stir. Transfer to a buttered baking sheet and allow to harden at room temperature.

Method for Squab: Bake the yams (whole) at 350° for approximately 45 minutes until done. Debone the squab and season with salt, pepper, and olive oil and reserve. Chop remaining bones and sear in hot sauce pan. Add shallots and garlic and cook for 2 minutes. Add chicken stock, artichokes, and chanterelles; simmer for 10 minutes. Remove artichokes and chanterelles, and continue simmering sauce for another 10 minutes. Strain sauce and reserve.

Final Baking & Presentation: Lay squab breast in each artichoke and place on a sheet pan; bake at 350° for 10 minutes. Remove skin from yams and place them in a bowl. Mash the cooked yams into a purée. In hot sauté pan, add butter, honey, yams, and salt and pepper to taste. Next, add Drambuie® and flame.

Mound yams on a serving plate and top with baked artichokes and squab. Drizzle sauce around plate and garnish with mushrooms and candied pecan halves. Drambuie® liqueur, 40% alc./vol., Hiram Walker & Sons, Inc. Southfield, MI. ✍

> We made this for a Feast on the Beach in Miami, sponsored by Hiram Walker.
> This is a nice fall dish; the squab stays savory, while the liqueur-soaked yams add sweetness.

Halibut in Ramp Broth with Rosemary

Makes 4 servings

(4) 6 oz. fillets of halibut
1 Tbs. olive oil
2 Tbs. parsley, chopped
2 cups fish broth (make or see Resources section)
1 lb. spinach, picked
2 lbs. fresh baby artichokes
2 cups enoki mushrooms
12 ramps*
4 sprigs fresh rosemary
salt and pepper

* See Resources section, or substitute another strong onion if ramps are unavailable

Method for Halibut & Broth: Rub halibut with olive oil, salt, pepper, and chopped parsley. Put in pan and sauté herb-side down for 1 minute. Turn fillets, add broth and poach over medium heat for 2 minutes. Remove fish and keep warm.

Add peeled artichokes and ramps; simmer for 5 minutes. Add spinach, enoki, and salt and pepper to taste. Return fish to broth and reheat for 1 minute.

Presentation: Spoon vegetable mixture onto soup plates, pour broth over, and lay fish on top. Garnish with sprigs of rosemary. ✍

*The Links at
Amelia Island
Plantation*

The Boca Raton Resort & Club

A Florida Gold Coast getaway for haute cuisine and for frolicking under the sun

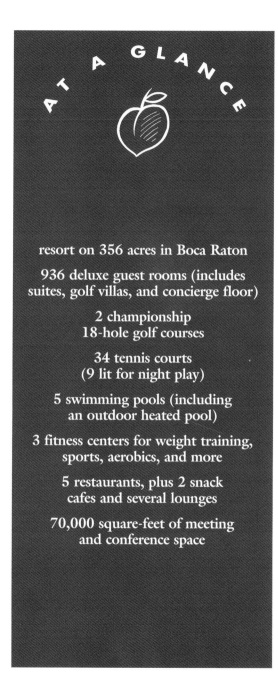

RESEMBLING A moorish palace dotted with stately palms and glistening under the Florida sun, The Boca Raton Resort & Club has everything you need to enjoy a week or two at Florida's playground for the rich and famous—the Gold Coast. Located in southern Palm Beach County, the Resort is easily accessible: Palm Beach Airport is 28 miles north, Fort Lauderdale International Airport is 24 miles south, and Miami International Airport lies 45 miles to the south.

A large Spanish Mediterranean structure built in 1926 called the Cloister functions as the heart of the Resort. Its architecture includes hidden gardens, archways, barrel tile roofs, ornate columns and fountains, and mosaics. Guests may choose to stay at the Cloister or in the modern tower, a 26-story high-rise that offers impressive views of the Intracoastal Waterway and the Atlantic Ocean. There are still more rooms in three other sections: Palm Court Club, Boca Beach Club, and the Golf Villas (for sportsmen who want to sleep close to the first tee).

Few other resorts offer recreational facilities on par with The Boca Raton Resort & Club, dubbed the "elegant place to play." In addition to a half-mile beach with water sports, the Resort includes two 18-hole championship golf courses, 34 tennis courts, five pools, an indoor basketball court, four indoor racquetball courts, and a 25-slip marina. And, it has been rated as one of the nations' "top 10 tennis resorts."

Whether you wish to do everything or do nothing at all, The Boca Raton Resort & Club is simply a wonderful place to stay.

50 East Camino Real ✷ *Boca Raton, Florida 33431-0825* ✷ *(407)447-3038*

The Ritz-Carlton, Naples

Eco-tourism combines with southern hospitality
at this five-star destination

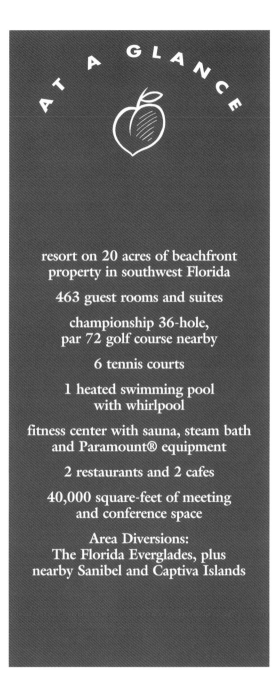

resort on 20 acres of beachfront property in southwest Florida

463 guest rooms and suites

championship 36-hole, par 72 golf course nearby

6 tennis courts

1 heated swimming pool with whirlpool

fitness center with sauna, steam bath and Paramount® equipment

2 restaurants and 2 cafes

40,000 square-feet of meeting and conference space

Area Diversions:
The Florida Everglades, plus nearby Sanibel and Captiva Islands

ONE OF only five U.S. resorts to earn a Mobil Five-Star and the AAA Five-Diamond Award, The Ritz-Carlton Naples offers luxurious accommodations and a wealth of activities for all ages on Florida's southwest coast. During 1994-1995, the resort's 463 guests rooms received major refurbishments in honor of the property's tenth anniversary. The Mediterranean architecture blends in beautifully with this property's beachfront location. With formal gardens and manicured courtyards, this resort exudes southern gentility.

The Ritz-Carlton's promoters encourage travelers to, "Use our property as a base camp, while exploring the Everglades and its environs, one of America's last great wilderness frontiers." They even offer a nature excursion weekend package that includes accommodations for three nights, breakfasts for two, and an Everglades survival bag filled with things that any modern-day scout might need. Custom-designed itineraries can also be arranged to take advantage of the Majestic Everglades cruise through Ten Thousand Islands, a gateway into the Everglades National Park.

Less adventurous souls can enjoy all of the fun at the resort—beachcombing, tennis, golf (not on the grounds, but at several nearby links), swimming, and more. With all of these pleasureable pursuits, it comes as no surprise that this impressive getaway continues to earn high marks.

280 Vanderbilt Beach Road ❧ Naples, Florida 33963 ❧ (800)241-3333 or (813)598-3300

Hyatt Regency Grand Cypress Resort

Central Florida's best bet features water sports and an Equestrian Center

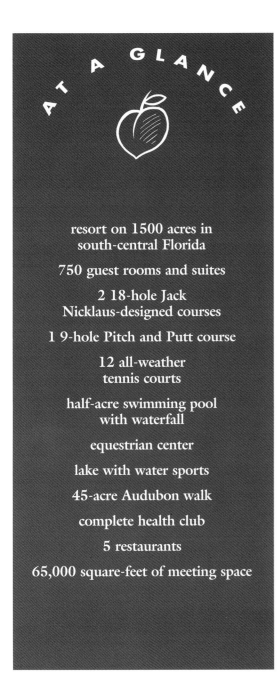

AT A GLANCE

resort on 1500 acres in
south-central Florida

750 guest rooms and suites

2 18-hole Jack
Nicklaus-designed courses

1 9-hole Pitch and Putt course

12 all-weather
tennis courts

half-acre swimming pool
with waterfall

equestrian center

lake with water sports

45-acre Audubon walk

complete health club

5 restaurants

65,000 square-feet of meeting space

SINCE THE Hyatt flagship opened a luxurious resort in central Florida 12 years ago, travelers have been flocking to it as a base for business in Orlando, to visit Mickey's kingdom, or simply to enjoy the resort itself under the warm Florida sun. The Hyatt's rooms have undergone complete refurbishments with a recent 7.5 million-dollar renovation to all 750 guest rooms and suites, outfitting them with new armoires, tables, chairs, and nightstands. New fabrics in a tropical motif, and coordinated carpets and wallcoverings have also been installed in each room.

The Resort has a half-acre, free-form swimming pool—one of the largest in the world—with a grotto food bar, 12 cascading waterfalls, and waterslides to amuse the kids. Parents and children can venture out in sailboats and other pleasure craft on the Hyatt's 21-acre lake. But the fun doesn't stop there. The Resort offers tennis and golf for players of all levels, and a complete health club which is housed in a grotto area under the swimming pool. While tennis, golf, and swimming are found at most resorts, this one also has a full Equestrian Center, with instruction in dressage and jumping. And, joggers can take advantage of the Resort's three- and four-mile jogging trails.

Return to the beautiful atrium hub of this Resort and venture in to any of several fine restaurants, where you can enjoy some of the finest cuisine the region has to offer. Go as healthy as you wish, by sampling the chef's spa selections, or go all out—the choice is yours.

1 Grand Cypress Boulevard ᘓ Orlando, Florida 32819 ᘓ (800)233-1234 or (407)239-1234

Brian O'Neil

BOCA RATON RESORT & CLUB

Feeding the rich and famous can be a daunting task. But because executive chef Brian O'Neil has a keen eye for fresh native Floridian ingredients and a devout attention to detail, preparing fine foods for the Boca Raton Resort's sophisticated travelers becomes a breeze. "We work with many specialized, or cottage purveyors to buy products like fresh truffles, edible squash blossoms, or fresh axis venison," says O'Neil, who also works with fresh herbs grown by staff horticulturists. Prior to joining The Boca Raton Resort & Club, he worked at the Towne Club/Pacific Street Grill in Dallas, Texas, and at the Mandalay Four Seasons Hotel in Irving, Texas. Before that, O'Neil trained at the Mirabeau and Hotel de Paris in Monte Carlo.

Perhaps the Resort's slogan should be altered to the "elegant place to dine and play."

Steamed Chicken and Vegetable Dumplings with Miso Dipping Sauce

Makes 4 appetizer servings (20 dumplings)

Steamed Dumplings

1 lb. ground chicken
1 bunch fresh scallions
1 carrot
soy sauce to taste
1 bunch cilantro
5 cloves garlic
small piece of fresh ginger
1 stalk celery
3 oz. water chestnuts
1 Tbs. red curry paste
20 won ton wrappers
salt and pepper to taste

Miso Dipping Sauce

3 oz. miso
1 oz. rice wine vinegar
1 oz. sugar
1 oz. soy sauce
ginger and garlic (1 Tbs. each, finely minced together)
1/2 bunch cilantro

Method for Dipping Sauce: Heat all ingredients in a small pot and bring to boil. Then, reduce heat and simmer for 5 minutes. Remove from heat and allow to cool.

Method for Dumplings: Process all ingredients (except ground chicken) until finely chopped. Add in the ground chicken and mix thoroughly. Season with salt and pepper.

Holding a won ton wrapper in palm of hand, place a Tbs. of mixture in the middle. Brush edges with water and pinch closed. Place in a steamer basket and steam until cooked through.

Presentation: Arrange the dumplings on a serving platter. Serve with miso dipping sauce.

This recipe consists of little chicken beggar's purses that are steamed in a bamboo steamer. It's great fun to offer at parties.

Bruschetta with Grilled Vegetables

Makes 4 servings

Tomato Mixture

10 medium plum tomatoes (skinned, seeded and chopped)
2 garlic cloves
2 Tbs. olive oil
1 tsp. salt
1 tsp. balsamic vinegar
1/2 loaf of French baguette or crusty
Italian bread
1/2 bunch of fresh basil (reserve 4 sprigs)
fresh black pepper to taste

Grilled Vegetables

1 medium zucchini
2 small yellow squash
1 yellow bell pepper
1 red bell pepper
4 Tbs. olive oil
1/2 medium eggplant
salt and ground black pepper to taste

Salad Garnish

1 head of red oak leaf lettuce
1/2 head of frisee lettuce
8 fresh chives

**Method for Tomato Mixture &
Vegetables:** Prepare and mix together all of the
first list of ingredients, except bread. Slice vegetables on the bias, and season with olive oil, salt and
pepper. Then grill the vegetables until soft.

Method for Bruschetta & Garnish: Wash,
clean and trim the lettuce leaves. Cut bread in
diagonal slices, brush with olive oil, and toast
them in the oven or grill them briefly. Top each
piece of bread with tomato mixture.

---

*Presentation: Arrange bruschetta on plates or in
a basket. Placed the grilled vegetables atop the leaf
lettuce. Garnish with chopped or whole chives and
serve immediately.* ◖◕

> The vegetables in this dish are light and flavorful. You can use just about any kind of bread, and
> you can vary the oils and toppings used, too. Serve this as a great-tasting appetizer.

Vietnamese Spring Rolls with Sesame Vinaigrette

Makes 4 appetizer servings

Sesame Vinaigrette

2 Tbs. rice wine vinegar
2 Tbs. soy sauce
2 Tbs. lemon juice
2 Tbs. ginger
2 Tbs. garlic
1/2 tsp. red chili flakes
1/2 tsp. five spice powder
sesame and vegetable oils (combine and
use 1/4 cup)

Spring Rolls

8 spring roll skins
1/2 lb. lean ground pork
1/4 lb. shrimp, chopped
1 package cellophane noodles*
6 oz. napa cabbage, shredded
3 oz. carrots, finely grated
1 onion, minced
6 cloves garlic
2 tsp. ginger
2 whole eggs
sesame oil to taste
salt and pepper to taste

* Soak in cold water for 5 minutes, and
then cut into 1" pieces

Method for Vinaigrette: Finely mince the
garlic and ginger, and add rest of ingredients.
Set aside until needed. ☞

Method for Spring Rolls: Sauté ground pork and then remove from pan. Add onion, garlic, ginger, and shrimp; sauté until fragrant. Place in mixing bowl and add vegetables, noodles, and eggs. Season with salt, pepper, and sesame oil.

Place mixture in egg roll wrappers, brush edges with egg wash, and roll up. Deep fry each roll at 250° until golden and crispy.

Presentation: Arrange spring rolls on a serving platter. Serve with sesame vinaigrette.

I use plenty of garlic and ginger in these rolls for punch. There are lots of Asian and Mediterranean influences in our cuisine.

Cold Ginger-Marinated Chicken Breast with Soba Noodles and Cilantro Oil

Makes 4 servings

4 chicken breasts
4 cups buckwheat soba noodles*

* Blanch in boiling water for 4-5 minutes

Marinade
4 tsp. ginger, minced
4 tsp. soy sauce

Method for Chicken: Blend all ingredients listed under marinade. Reserve 5 Tbs. of the marinade and set aside. With the remainder, marinate the raw chicken for 2 hours.

Method for Cilantro Oil: Process the fresh cilantro in a food processor until finely minced. Add oil and store in a jar or glass bottle at room temperature until needed.

1/2 cup rice wine vinegar
1 1/2 cups vegetable oil
1 cup pears, diced

Cilantro Oil
1 cup fresh cilantro
1 1/2 cups olive oil

Final Cooking & Presentation: Meanwhile, grill chicken until done and chill them completely. Toss soba noodles with 5 Tbs. of the marinade mixture.

Place seasoned soba noodles in center of each plate. Drizzle cilantro oil around the perimeter of plates. Slice each chicken breast and fan the slices around noodles. Garnish as desired and enjoy!

Everyone love Asian foods because they are so healthy and full of robust flavors. This dish is relatively light, in keeping with our overall concept for food.

Ingredient Footnote
SOBA NOODLES
Your local Asian food grocer offers a wondrous assortment of noodles, such as cellophane, rice, bean thread, and soba noodles, to use in hot and cold Oriental dishes. The soba noodles called for in this recipe are especially tender, like pasta, and are often used in cold salads dressed with oil or peanut sauce. See Resources section for other purveyors of quality Asian foods.

Marinated Grilled Swordfish with Yellow Tomato Salsa

Makes 4 servings

Swordfish
(4) 5 oz. swordfish steaks
6 tsp. olive oil
4 sprigs of thyme, picked
salt and cracked black pepper to taste

Salsa
2 large yellow beefsteak tomatoes*

1 yellow bell pepper*
1/2 oz. onion, finely diced
1/4 tsp. garlic, minced
1/4 bunch cilantro, minced
1 lemon, juice only

* Remove skin and seeds; cut in a fine dice

Method for Salsa & Swordfish: Dice tomatoes and peppers and drain in a chinois for 2-3 minutes. Add remaining ingredients. Adjust seasoning, and allow to sit 2 hours in the refrigerator before serving for flavors to fully blend. Grill swordfish to desired doneness (medium-rare is best).

Presentation: Top each swordfish steak with a portion of salsa. Garnish with fresh thyme and serve. ᐁᐊ

> This is one of chef O'Neil's low-calorie recipes; each serving contains 293.5 calories and 14 grams of fat. This dish is very native Floridian … [taking bounty] fresh from the ocean to the table very quickly. The salsa is robust and flavorful, making a nice counterpoint to the swordfish.

Mille-Feuille of Salmon with Chervil

Makes 4 servings

(4) 5 oz. salmon fillets
(4) 2 oz. squares of puff pastry
1 shallot
1 pint whipping cream
1/4 lb. whole butter
1 cup clarified butter (for cooking salmon)

1 cup white wine
fresh chervil
1/2 lemon, juice only
salt and pepper to taste
1 pinch cayenne pepper
☞

Method for Salmon: Cook the puff pastry very thin and crisp. Set aside. Chop shallots and add to saucepan with the white wine; cook until reduced by 1/2. Add cream and continue to cook until reduced by 1/2 again. Finish by adding the lemon juice and cayenne pepper.

Slice the salmon fillets on the diagonal into very thin pieces and season them with salt and pepper. (You will want to stack same-size pieces of salmon and puff pastry during the final presentation.) Sauté on each side for approximately 30 seconds.

Presentation: Place sauce on each serving plate. Layer on salmon and puff pastry and serve. ᐁᐊ

> This entrée is very simple, yet has a lot of elegance in its simplicity. Chef O'Neil notes that the salmon should be very quickly sautéed, with the puff pastry ready and warm for the last step.

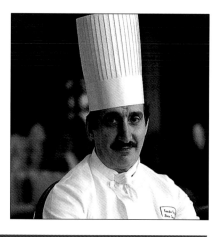

Pierre Dousson

RITZ-CARLTON, NAPLES

Guests staying at this lavish Ritz-Carlton may choose the Dining Room for Continental and French specialties, or the Grill Room, for steaks and seafood in an English club setting.

At the helm of this gastronomic success is executive chef Pierre Dousson, who spends his days creating and preparing foods that are classic and healthy. The menu is infused with Mediterranean accents, and the innovative dishes are prepared under the guidance of chef Dousson and his expert culinary staff. The chef's preference for fresh Florida seafood combined with unusual seasonings, fruits, and vegetables—such as Grilled Tournedos of Swordfish with Black Beans and Atemoya Vinaigrette—gives diners full-flavored entrées that are relatively low in fat. Dousson's secret to success is this: "Keep quality consistent, and make sure that the food is as appealing to the eye as it is to the palate."

Grilled Tournedos of Swordfish, Black Beans, and Atemoya Vinaigrette

Makes 4 servings

Swordfish & Black Beans
(8) 3 oz. tournedos of swordfish, cut round
3/4 lb. black beans*
2 cups chicken stock
1/4 cup carrot**
1/4 cup onion**
1/4 cup celery**
1/4 cup bacon**
1/4 cup canola oil
1 bay leaf
pinch of thyme
pinch of cumin
salt and pepper to taste

* Soak dried beans in tap water overnight before using
** Cut in a dice

Atemoya Vinaigrette
1/2 cup atemoya, diced
1/4 cup sherry vinegar
3/4 cup grape seed oil
1 tsp. tarragon, chopped
salt and pepper to taste
several sprigs of fresh chervil (optional garnish)

Method for Swordfish: Season swordfish with salt and pepper and grill to desired temperature (grilling on both sides).

Method for Beans: In 2 oz. canola oil, sauté carrots, celery, onion, and bacon for 5 minutes. Drain water from black beans and add the soaked beans to vegetables. Add chicken stock and seasonings and cook for 1 hour.

Method for Vinaigrette: Place a pinch of salt and pepper in a bowl, and add sherry vinegar. Whip in the grape seed oil very slowly. Add chopped tarragon and diced atemoya.

Presentation: Place black bean mixture on top of each plate, then place 2 of the tournedos of swordfish on top of beans. Place atemoya vinaigrette around bean mixture. Garnish each tournedo with fresh chervil sprigs.

> **This is a great example of our culinary style; it combines Florida cuisine with a southwestern "twist."**

Soft Shell Crab Appetizer

Makes 4 servings (appetizer portions)

Soft Shell Crabs
(8) 2 oz. soft shell crabs
1/2 cup flour
1/2 cup cornmeal
3 eggs, lightly beaten (egg wash)
1/4 cup olive oil

Caper White Wine Sauce
1/2 cup capers
1/2 cup lemon juice
1 cup dry white wine
salt and pepper
1 cup whole butter, softened

Croutons
8 slices French bread*
1/2 cup extra virgin olive oil

* Cut in 1" thick slices

Basil Tomato Relish
4 large ripe tomatoes
12 leaves fresh basil
1/2 cup olive oil
4 cloves garlic, minced
salt and pepper

Method for Crabs & Sauce: Bread soft crabs with flour, egg wash, and then cornmeal (in that order) and sauté in the olive oil until crisp. Remove from pan. Next, deglaze pan with wine, and add the lemon juice, capers, salt, and pepper; reduce mixture until almost dry. Blend in the softened whole butter until it is melted.

Method for Croutons: Dip bread slices in olive oil and toast in a 300° oven until crisp (takes about 4 minutes if the oven is preheated).

Method for Relish: Remove seeds from tomato and cut into a dice. Add chopped basil, olive oil, and garlic. Season to taste with salt and pepper. Mix and chill.

Presentation: Top croutons with the tomato relish and place on plate; then place a soft crab next to the crouton. (Serve 2 crabs per person). Pour sauce over crab and serve. ✆

> Homemade croutons and crispy, sautéed crabs lend the crunch to this appetizer, while the sauce and relish add bold flavors.

Sautéed Red Snapper in Sweet Potato Slices with Mamey Sauce

Makes 4 servings

(4) 6 oz. snapper fillets
4 whole sweet potatoes, sliced lengthwise very thin
1 Tbs. cilantro*
1/2 cup olive oil
4 chayote squash, peeled and sliced
1 Tbs. garlic*
2 tsp. shallot*
2 cups orange juice
2 mamey fruits, peeled and puréed
1/2 tsp. curry powder
1 cup heavy cream
1 tsp. Italian parsley*
3/4 cup white rum
small bunch Italian parsley
salt and black pepper to taste

* Chop

> Exotic mamey fruit lends a mildly sweet taste to the red snapper in this delightful creation.

Method for Snapper: Season snapper with salt and pepper. Season both sides of fish with chopped cilantro. Wrap the snapper in sweet potato slices, completely encasing each fillet. Bake snapper in a 350° oven for 15-20 minutes. ☞

Method for Sauce: In 2 oz. of olive oil, sauté half of the shallots and the puréed mamey fruit for 1 minute over high heat. Add rum and cook for 2 more minutes. Add orange juice and reduce by 2/3 volume, or until mixture is syrupy. Then add heavy cream and cook for 1 more minute on a high burner. Add salt and pepper to taste.

Method for Squash: In the other 2 oz. of olive oil, sauté chayote squash with chopped garlic, parsley, and remaining chopped shallots. For final seasoning, add curry powder.

Presentation: Place chayote squash mixture in center of plate with snapper fillet on top. Ladle sauce around squash. Garnish with full leaves of Italian parsley all around plate. ◠

Ingredient Footnote
MAMEY
The exotic mamey fruit is grown in sub-tropical regions, such as Florida, and is harvested during the summer. It lends a wonderfully sweet taste to salads, sauces, and more. You can test for ripeness by gently touching its flesh, as you would a mango. Purchase mamey fruit at your local gourmet grocer (or see the Resources section for retailers of exotic fruits and vegetables).

Cinnamon Soufflé with Vanilla Sauce

Makes 4 servings

Soufflé
1/3 cup cold butter
1/3 cup bread flour
1 1/3 cups 2% milk
1/3 cup granulated sugar
5 eggs, separated
1 Tbs. cinnamon
pinch cream of tartar

Vanilla Sauce
3/4 cup heavy cream
2 egg yolks
1/8 cup + 2 Tbs. sugar
1 Tbs. vanilla extract (or 1/2 vanilla bean, split)

Method for Sauce: Boil the heavy cream. While cream reaches boiling, mix the yolks and sugar together. Slowly add a small amount of the boiled cream to yolk mixture to temper it. Add entire mixture into the heavy cream, whisking briskly until it coats the back of a wooden spoon. Strain through a fine sieve. Next, stir in vanilla extract.* This sauce can be served cold, warm, or hot. An orange or almond flavored liquor may be added if you wish.

   * If using vanilla bean, add it to the cream when boiling. When the sauce is strained, scrape the bean to get all of the flavor.

Method for Soufflé: Blend butter and flour together, forming a smooth paste. Meanwhile,

boil the 2% milk. Add paste to boiling milk and stir until smooth; next, beat in egg yolks, sugar, and cinnamon. Allow mixture to cool to room temperature.

   Whip egg white and cream of tartar until a soft peak is formed. Fold egg whites into the base mixture. Ladle 6 oz. of the mixture into buttered (and collared) soufflé cups, and bake at 450° for 15 minutes.

Presentation: As with any soufflé, you want to serve this immediately after baking. If desired, carefully prick the top of soufflé and pour in some sauce, or offer the sauce on the side. ◠

The Ritz-Carlton's cinnamon soufflé is an elegant finale to a fine dinner, especially during the winter months. You can make one large soufflé, or four individual ones.

Kenneth Juran

HYATT REGENCY GRAND CYPRESS

The Hyatt Regency Grand Cypress is renowned for its award-winning cuisine. In the various restaurants scattered throughout the Resort, executive chef Kenneth Juran gives Hyatt guests full flavor without lots of fat in the Hyatt's Cuisine Naturelle selections, developed with the help of nutritionist Pamela Smith of Orlando. Juran's Niçoise Pesto-Coated Tournedo of Salmon and Sturgeon has Mediterranean overtones, while some of his other creations have Oriental influences.

Chef Juran has worked in the food and beverage industry for more than 22 years. A graduate of the Culinary Institute of America in 1977 and the Greenbrier Hotel Culinary Program in 1979, Juran continues to explore new directions in the culinary arts by developing dishes that "enhance the foods' natural flavors with light infusions and fresh herbs."

Potato and Black Truffle-Crusted Scallops

Makes 4 servings

Crusted Scallops

20 large sea scallops
20 slices of cooked black truffle
1 cup (8 oz.) lobster mushrooms
4 whole artichoke*
4 tsp. shallots, diced
1/2 cup (4 oz.) whole butter
1 cup (8 oz.) potato strands**
4 cups peanut oil
1 cup (8 oz.) tomato vinaigrette (recipe follows)
salt and pepper to taste

* Cooked and cut into sixths with stem on
** Grate on a mandolin or cut into straws; crisp them in hot peanut oil and finish in the oven

Tomato Vinaigrette

2 vine-ripened tomatoes*
4 oz. olive oil
1 1/2 oz. fresh lemon juice
1 tsp. fresh shallots, chopped
1/4 tsp. fresh garlic, chopped
1 tsp. combined: basil, Italian parsley, oregano
salt and pepper to taste

* Peel, seed, and cut into a medium dice

Method for Scallops: Make slit in each scallop horizontally and insert truffle slice; season with salt and pepper. Wrap each scallop in potato strands and fry in hot peanut oil for 1 minute. Finish in oven set at 350° for 3 minutes. Sauté lobster mushrooms and steamed artichokes in shallots and whole butter until done; set aside.

Method for Tomato Vinaigrette: To the diced tomatoes, add the lemon juice, olive oil, shallots, garlic, and roughly chopped herbs. Season with kosher salt and white pepper.

Presentation: Place warm artichokes and lobster mushrooms in the center of each serving plate. Place 2 oz. tomato vinaigrette around perimeter; arrange the five scallops around the outer edge of plate.

The crisp potatoes and moist scallops are flavored with essence of truffle in this contemporary main course—what a contrast of textures and flavors!

Lobster and Napa Cabbage Spring Roll

Makes 4 servings (appetizer portions)

4 lobster spring rolls (recipe follows)
2 oz. crisp, fried carrot strands
12 large shrimp*
8 oz. Thai carrot broth (recipe follows)
6 oz. tamarind glaze (recipe follows)
4 tsp. olive oil
salt and pepper to taste

* Wash, peel, and de-vein

Lobster Spring Roll
12 oz. fresh lobster meat
20 oz. napa cabbage
2 tsp. ginger
2 tsp. garlic
Thai fish sauce
1 tsp. wasabi powder
4 tsp. diced shallots
4 Tbs. olive oil
rice paper (reconstituted in warm water)

Tamarind Glaze
16 oz. tamarind pulp (see Resources section)
16 oz. tomato paste
4 Tbs. cognac
8 whole shallots, sliced
4 scallions, white only
4 Tbs. honey

Thai Carrot Broth
12 oz. carrot juice
3 oz. white wine
3 oz. lobster stock (or clam juice)
3 oz. heavy cream
1/2 oz. galanga root
1 bay leaf
3 white peppercorns
1 shallot, diced
1 Tbs. butter
1 Tbs. soy sauce

Method for Spring Rolls: Sauté ginger, shallots, garlic and napa cabbage; deglaze with Thai fish sauce, then add wasabi. Stir to incorporate. Add cooked lobster meat, just enough to warm throughout. Season with salt and pepper. Place lobster mixture on the reconstituted rice paper and roll as tightly as possible. Sauté the lobster rolls in olive oil until brown.

Method for Shrimp: Season shrimp and brown on both sides in olive oil; coat with tamarind glaze and place under broiler to glaze.

Method for Tamarind Glaze: Mix all ingredients thoroughly in food processor.

Method for Broth: Reduce white wine, shallots, peppercorns, bay leaf, and galanga by 2/3. Add lobster stock or clam juice and reduce by 2/3. Add heavy cream; reduce until thick. Add carrot juice and reduce to a thin sauce consistency. Remove from heat. Whip in butter in small pieces. Season to taste with fish sauce, salt and pepper. Strain through sieve and blend once again before using.

Presentation: Place 2 oz. of carrot broth around perimeter of plate. Cut spring rolls on the bias, and stand them up in center. Lean the shrimp on spring roll and garnish with carrot crisps. ✎

Ingredient Footnote

GALANGA ROOT
Galanga is the root of an herb grown i n Thailand. It has an earthy taste like ginger, and is used in many Asian and Thai dished. Purchase galanga from your local gourmet or Asian grocer, or see Resources section.

TAMARIND
Tamarind in a South American pod that yields pulp used in cooking. The tart, flavorful pulp is scraped from inside the pod. Purchase tamarind from your local gourmet grocer, or see Resources section.

> This California-style spring roll is loaded with fresh lobster and crispy napa cabbage, while the tamarind glaze adds "Floribbean" flair. Because the roll is not fried, it stays light and healthy.

Niçoise Pesto-Coated Tournedo of Salmon and Sturgeon

Makes 4 servings

16 oz. fillet of salmon
16 oz. fillet of sturgeon
4 portions of zucchini roulade
4 oz. niçoise olive crust (recipe follows)
8 oz. yellow tomato aioli (recipe follows)
1 tsp. olive oil
salt and pepper to taste

Niçoise Olive and Parmesan Crust

32 oz. fresh white bread crumbs
4 oz. whole butter
8 oz. niçoise olives, chopped
4 oz. parmesan cheese
2 tsp. garlic, finely diced
4 Tbs. Italian parsley, chopped
4 tsp. chives
4 tsp. chervil

Zucchini, Tomato, and Feta Roulade

4 whole zucchini (slice thin — lengthwise)
2 Tbs. olive oil
8 whole tomatoes (peel, seed & cut in a dice)
4 oz. croissant bread crumbs
2 tsp. garlic, freshly chopped
4 oz. feta cheese
salt and pepper to taste

Yellow Tomato Aioli

16 yellow tomatoes (cut in half & remove seeds)
4 cloves of garlic, chopped
4 oz. truffle oil
10 oz. olive oil
4 tsp. chervil, chopped
4 oz. fresh lemon juice
4 egg yolk
salt and pepper to taste

Method for Fish Tournedos: Roll salmon and sturgeon fillets together into round tournedos and tie; season and sear. Spread the sides with olive and parmesan crust, and bake in oven for 13 minutes at 425°.

Method for Niçoise Crust: Remove crust from white bread and chop in food processor. Add all remaining ingredients and mix together.

Method for Roulade: Toss zucchini with olive oil, salt and pepper. Grill lightly and set aside. Sauté tomato with garlic, and season with salt and pepper; cook for 3-4 minutes. Put in strainer and reserve liquid. Reduce when cool. Fold back into tomatoes. Layer the zucchini on wax paper and sprinkle with croissant crumbs. Put tomato and crumbled feta on bottom 2/3 of a zucchini slice, and roll into a roulade. Cut on the bias into 2" pieces.

Method for Aioli: Purée yellow tomato, garlic, and egg yolk in food processor slowly and add truffle oil, olive oil, lemon juice, salt and pepper to form a light dressing.

Presentation: Heat zucchini roulade in oven until warm. Cover the bottom of a serving plate with yellow tomato aioli and place sturgeon and salmon in center of plate; arrange zucchini roulade around the tournedos. When sliced through, the fish tournedos reveal orange and white, like the Chinese yin/yang.

HYATT REGENCY GRAND CYPRESS

chapter 3

Northern California

Napa Valley

Meadowood

Auberge du Soleil

San Francisco & Monterey

Campton Place Hotel

Quail Lodge Resort

The Lodge at Pebble Beach

Northern

The cuisine here is often second to none. Many great American and international chefs look to California for its cutting-edge cuisine and contemporary interpretations of classic foods. Northern California's four- and five-star cuisine reflects the many cultures and lifestyles of the region. It is artsy, bold, and full of imagination. Chefs of the region take advantage of the area's natural resources, including fresh Pacific seafood; the wines and champagnes bottled here; and ripe avocados and citrus fruits. For many California chefs, Mediterranean and Pacific Rim dishes are in high demand among locals and visitors who enjoy international foods.

Four of the properties presented here are luxurious playgrounds for active travelers—two are located in California's verdant Napa Valley, and the other two are on the Monterey Peninsula. In St. Helena, Meadowood combines a gracious country estate and country club, all rolled into one. Meadowood's chef de cuisine, Roy Breiman, combines the flavors of Provençal with classic ingredients. Auberge du Soleil is another top property in wine country. With its dramatic location on a sunlit olive grove and Tuscan architecture, Auberge brings a touch of the southern Mediterranean to Napa Valley. The Inn's Napa-Mediterranean style carries through to delight-

California

ful meals, headed by executive chef Andrew Sutton.

In the Union Square neighborhood of downtown San Francisco, Campton Place Hotel offers many of the guest services and special touches that are practiced by the better hotels of Europe. Executive chef Todd Humphries works his culinary magic behind the scenes with a contemporary menu spiked with Middle Eastern and Indian influences. California's coastal highway leads north to Monterey, a dramatic peninsula that juts out into the Pacific Ocean. The area is a golfer's paradise, with several world-renowned courses. Quail Lodge Resort & Golf Club, with country-style cottages and 245 landscaped acres, is a converted dairy farm. The Lodge's executive chef, Robert Williamson, is known for his use of fresh herbs and edible blossoms. On the southern coast of the Peninsula, The Lodge at Pebble Beach offers luxurious accommodations, championship golf, and memorable cuisine. The Lodge's culinary staff is headed by Beat Giger, who favors fresh seafood entrées with light, citrusy sauces.

California dining can be a very personal and memorable experience. Sit at your favorite sidewalk café in wine country and savor the finest food and drink of the area. Enjoy a four-star dinner at Monterey, while waves crash over a rocky coastline in the distance. Or, feast on sourdough bread in the Golden Gate City. Here, splendid food and scenery go hand-in-hand.

Meadowood

This luxurious wine-country getaway is also
an unforgettable dining experience

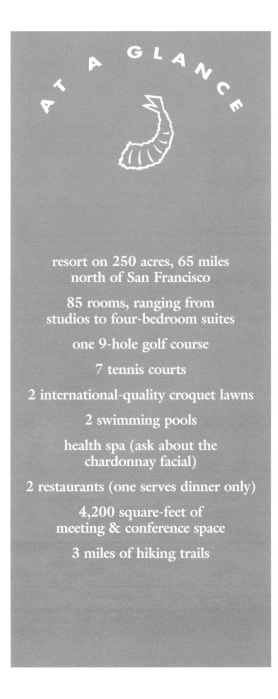

DURING THE annual Napa Valley Wine Auction, Meadowood is the top pick for accommodations among gourmands who flock to California's wine country for the celebrated three-day benefit. The weekend includes lavish dinner parties held under white pavilions on the Meadowood golf course for a few thousand guests. Meadowood's chef de cuisine, Roy Breiman, has the daunting task of coordinating this function, right down to the last fresh lobster and bottle of Merlot.

A member of Small Luxury Hotels and Relais & Chateaux, Meadowood is a wonderful hybrid of country club and resort, all rolled into one. The architecture is traditional New England in style, with classic touches throughout the lobby—wainscotting, watercolor prints, and antiques—creating an elegant country decor. Rooms in the Hideaway Lodges (wonderful little cottages) are spacious and beautifully appointed with beamed cathedral ceilings, window seats, remote control skylights, and king- and queen-size beds.

The hotel is situated upon its own private compound (256 acres in all) within California's Napa Valley, and is surrounded my massive oak trees and the lush fairways of a nine-hole golf course. Like any country estate, Meadowood offers an array of activities, including golf, tennis, swimming, croquet, and hiking. Once you tire of those pastimes, wander down to the luxurious Health Spa for a workout, to take part in an aqua-aerobics class, or to try a chardonnay facial. The pleasures are many at this beautiful retreat. ✆

900 Meadowood Lane ✆ St. Helena, California 94574 ✆ (800)458-8080 or (707)963-3646

Auberge du Soleil

The "inn of the sun" offers extraordinary views
and outstanding cuisine in California's Napa Valley

WITH ITS elegant country inn situated upon a 33-acre olive grove, Auberge du Soleil brings a touch of the Mediterranean to Napa Valley. In fact, developer Claude Rouas built the Auberge in the style of southern France's country inns. European influence is prominent in the Inn's guest rooms: special appointments such as shutters, French doors, working fireplaces, and terra cotta tile floors are reminiscent of Tuscan villas. And, just in case a guest might forget where he is, the refrigerator is stocked with local wines and cheeses.

From the main house, the resort meanders through informal gardens down a slope. A permanent sculpture garden may be viewed from its own half-mile nature path that cuts through an olive grove. Venture past the generous-size swimming pool, and you'll find a series of sun-and earth-colored buildings housing the Inn's 48 guest suites, each with a private terrace offering views of the wine country. The suites range in size from one- to three-bedrooms, making this an ideal choice for couples or for larger families. Bathrooms are big and luxurious, with separate showers, large tubs—some with jacuzzis, double sinks, and thick terry robes.

The Inn's thoughtful staff makes every guest feel welcome. Says owner/developer Claude Rouas, "We try to give people what they want so they can hang up their troubles at the door: memorable cuisine, simple but luxurious surroundings, and service beyond question."

P.O. Drawer B ✺ 180 Rutherford Hill Road ✺ Rutherford, California 94573
(800)348-5406 or (707)963-1211

Roy Breiman

MEADOWOOD

The enjoyment of food and wine is a top priority throughout the Napa Valley, and Meadowood's cuisine competes with the best in the area. Trained in Provence, Roy Breiman blends French country cooking with the natural bounty of California's wine country. Smart combinations of flavors and textures crop up in Breiman's many preparations, including Seared Ahi with Lemon and Coriander Seed.

Chef Breiman's commitment to outstanding presentations makes each dish a work of art. Esquire magazine named Breiman as one of the nation's "eight chefs to keep your eye on."

And Meadowood's resident wine tutor, John Thoreen, is a former vintner and wine writer who routinely wins acclaim for his devotion to educating the public about wines of the region. Many of Thoreen's programs, including wine-tasting games, cooking classes, and vineyard picnics make a weekend at Meadowood a memorable experience.

Seared Ahi with Lemon and Coriander Seed

Makes 4 servings

Ahi
8 oz. ahi (sushi grade)
2 Tbs. ground coriander seeds
2 Tbs. chopped fresh lemon zest
1 Tbs. white peppercorns

Tomato Fondue
3 whole tomatoes (peeled, seeded, and chopped)
1 shallot, chopped
1 garlic clove, chopped
1 Tbs. fresh thyme, chopped
2 oz. + 2 oz. olive oil*
1 tsp. tomato paste
salt and pepper to taste

* 2 oz. for tomatoes and 2 oz. for cooking Ahi

Spinach & Cooked Bacon
6 oz. spinach leaves, picked and washed
1 garlic clove, chopped
2 oz. smoked bacon, thinly sliced
1 Tbs. butter
salt and pepper to taste

Vinaigrette
6 cloves roasted garlic, chopped
1/2 tsp. sugar
1 bunch chives, chopped
1 shallot, chopped
3 oz. olive oil (plus 1/2 tsp. for cooking garlic)
1 oz. balsamic vinegar
salt and pepper to taste

Method for Ahi & Crust: Cut ahi into triangles approximately 1-1/2" across. Season with salt and set aside for final preparation. In a small bowl, combine coriander seeds, fresh lemon zest, and white pepper, mixing thoroughly. Set aside for final preparation.

Method for Tomato Fondue: Blanch, peel, seed, and chop three tomatoes and place them in a medium sauté pan. Add 2 Tbs. olive oil, chopped tomato, shallots, garlic, thyme, and tomato paste. Cook the mixture over medium-high heat for about 15-20 minutes, or until reduced by 90%. Remove from pan and season with salt and pepper; set aside.

Method for Spinach & Bacon: Heat a large sauté pan over medium-high heat. Add the smoked bacon and cook until golden brown. Then add garlic, spinach, and butter. Continue to cook until spinach starts to wilt. Next, remove from pan and chop spinach finely on a cutting board using a chef's knife. Place into small bowl and set aside until needed.

Method for Vinaigrette: Begin by cleaning garlic cloves for the roasted garlic. Place cloves ☞

This dish is very typical Meadowood cuisine: Provençal flavors, reduced fat, and simply prepared. Chef Breiman serves this dish with tomato fondue, smoked bacon, and a roasted garlic vinaigrette.

in aluminum foil and sprinkle with 1/2 tsp. olive oil and 1/2 tsp. sugar on top. Loosely fold foil at the top, allowing heat to permeate. Place 2 cups of water in an oven-proof pan. Put the wrapped garlic in, and cook at 475° until the garlic is soft. Refill water if necessary. Remove garlic from aluminum and place on cutting board; chop finely.

Combine garlic, shallots, chives, olive oil, salt, pepper, and balsamic vinegar into a small mixing bowl and mix thoroughly. Set aside.

Presentation: Evenly coat each side of ahi with the coriander mixture. Heat a non-stick pan over high heat with 2 oz. olive oil for approximately 2 minutes. Add ahi to the pan, cooking about 30 seconds on each side. Remove from pan and cut into 1/2" slices, keeping slightly warm.

In the center of four 12" plates, place a 3" baker's ring. Add 2 Tbs. of the tomato mixture to the ring, smoothing evenly with the back of a spoon. Place 2 Tbs. of spinach mixture on top of tomato and smooth evenly. Remove baker's ring. Place sliced ahi on top in a pyramid shape. Then place 2 Tbs. of the vinaigrette mixture around each plate. Serve warm.

Rouget Niçoise with Capers, Black Olives, and Tomato Fondue
Pictured on p.204

Makes 4 servings

8 whole rouget, scaled and filleted
1 Tbs. black olives (chopped Niçoise-style)
1 Tbs. capers, chopped
1 shallot, chopped
6 leaves of basil, julienned
2 garlic cloves, finely chopped
1 bunch chives, finely sliced

4 whole tomatoes*
2 oz. olive oil**

* Blanch, peel, seed, and chop finely
** 1 oz. for cooking rouget, 1 oz. for tomatoes

Method for Fish: Heat 1 oz. olive oil in a non-stick pan, and cook the rouget skin-side down for approximately 10 seconds. Remove fish from pan and set aside by placing pieces skin-side down. Put chopped capers and black olives atop four fillets, placing the remaining four fillets (skin-side up) on top.

Method for Tomatoes: Place the remaining olive oil, tomatoes, garlic, and shallots in a saucepan and cook approximately 5-10 minutes over low heat, or until most of the water has cooked out of the tomato. Add basil and chives; remove from the pan and set aside.

Presentation: Place 3-4 Tbs. of cooked tomato inside a 3"x3" circular area on the center of each serving plate. Place fish back into the non-stick pan (or use a baking pan) and finish cooking in a 475° oven for about 3-4 minutes. Set the cooked fish atop tomato fondue. Garnish each serving with parsley sprig, fried basil, or diced tomato (optional). Serve warm.

Mille Feuille of Caramelized Bananas, Black Currants, and Chocolate Chips with Caramel Sauce

Makes 4 servings

6 leaves filo sheets (for layers)
6 oz. + 4 oz. butter*
6 oz. sugar
4 sliced bananas
2 Tbs. dried currants
2 Tbs. chocolate chips

1/2 tsp. ground cinnamon
1/4 cup cream
3 oz. water

* 6 oz. clarified, and 4 oz. whole ☞

Method for Clarified butter: Place 6 oz. butter into a small saucepan and bring to a boil. Turn down heat, and continue to cook, skimming the fat off the top until the butter is clear yellow (takes approximately 20 minutes).

Method for Filo: Brush each filo leaf thoroughly with clarified butter and sprinkle granulated sugar evenly atop each layer, stacking one on top of another. Continue this process until all layers are completed, then cut into 3" squares. Lay filo between two pieces of parchment paper and place on a sheet tray. Lay another sheet tray on top and cook in a 375° oven until golden brown (about 15 minutes). Remove from oven and let cool. Remove from sheet tray and set aside.

Method for Sauce: Combine sugar and water in small saucepan and whisk until dissolved. Bring to a boil until golden brown. Remove from heat and let cool for 5 minutes. Next, add cream and whisk for 30 seconds until well blended. Next, add in 2 oz. of the whole butter, whisking all continuously until well incorporated. Set aside and keep warm.

Method for Bananas: Melt 2 oz. whole butter in a non-stick pan (over medium heat); add bananas, currants, and 1 oz. sugar and cook until golden brown (about 2 minutes). At the last moment, add chocolate chips. Remove from stove and set aside, keeping warm.

Presentation: On a large serving plate, sprinkle ground cinnamon around border. Place 2 Tbs. of banana mixture in the center of each plate. Then place filo layer on top. Add another 2 Tbs. bananas on top of filo again, and finish with one more layer of filo. Pour 3 Tbs. of caramel sauce around the mille feuille, and serve immediately. ❧

Meadowood's Mille Feuille of Caramelized Bananas, Black Currants, and Chocolate Chips with Caramel Sauce

Andrew Sutton

AUBERGE DU SOLEIL

Auberge du Soleil's executive chef Andrew Sutton combines classic cooking with non-traditional flavor combinations and innovative presentations of food. "The challenge is to offer cuisine that is both delicious as well as a cultural taste of the region," says Sutton, a graduate of the Culinary Institute of America (CIA). Earlier in his career, Sutton spent six months on a cookbook tour with chef Dean Fearing of the award-winning Mansión on Turtle Creek in Dallas, Texas. During that time, he learned the dynamics of creating world-class cuisine.

Sutton's imaginative cuisine, coined Napa-Mediterranean by food critics, includes Pan-Seared Diver's Scallops, and a light Golden Gazpacho. And, his Poached Pear Walnut Tart with Maytag Blue Cheese and Port Reduction utilizes the finest products of the region—superbly mellowed cheese and wine.

Pan-Seared Diver's Scallops with Cucumber Whipped Potatoes, Caviar, and Champagne Butter Sauce

Makes 4 servings (appetizer portions)

8-12 large diver sea scallops
(approx. 2-3 oz. per person)
2 cups cucumber whipped potatoes
(see recipe)
6 oz. champagne butter sauce (see recipe)
2 oz. Sevruga caviar (optional)
4 sprigs watercress
1 Tbs. pure olive or canola oil
salt and black pepper

Cucumber Whipped Potatoes

3 russet potatoes*
1/2 English cucumber**
3/4 cup heavy cream, scalded
1/2 tsp. fresh dill, chopped
1 Tbs. butter
1/2 fresh lemon, juice only
salt and pepper to taste

* Peel and cut into 1" wheels
** Cut lengthwise (horiz.), remove seeds, and leave skin on

Champagne Butter Sauce

2 whole shallots
3 oz. dry champagne
5 whole black peppercorns
1/2 bay leaf
1 sprig fresh thyme
2 oz. heavy cream
6 oz. sweet butter (cut into 1" cubes)
salt to taste
2 drops lemon juice

Method for Potatoes: Place potatoes in a sauce pan and cover them with 1" of cold water. Bring to a boil, and then turn down to a simmer, allowing the potatoes to cook until fork-tender (approximately 30 minutes). Drain well and pass potatoes through a ricer. Add scalded cream and butter, using a spoon to fold the ingredients together.

Slice cucumber into half-moons about 1/4" thick. Place cucumber and dill in a blender or food processor and purée. Remove the mixture and squeeze out excess water through a strainer. Add to whipped potatoes. Add in lemon juice, and adjust seasoning with salt and pepper to taste.

Can be made in advance and then warmed in a microwave or oven before serving.

Method for Sauce: Using a stainless steel sauce pan, combine the shallots, thyme, pepper, and 2 1/2 oz. of champagne. Reduce down to 1/4 volume. Add cream and gently simmer until sauce thickens. Turn down to a very low heat and begin whisking in the butter, one cube at a time. Whisk constantly until all butter is melted and incorporated. Remove from heat.

Add lemon juice and salt to taste. Strain sauce through a fine sieve. Keep warm (not hot) until final presentation—sauce should be of a smooth, creamy consistency.

Note: Have cucumber whipped potatoes and ☞

This is an Auberge du Soleil signature item, and is served as an appetizer.

champagne butter sauce ready and warm at this stage.

Method for Scallops: Season scallops with salt and black pepper. Heat a 12" skillet over medium heat and then add oil until skillet just begins to smoke. Add scallops one by one on their flat sides, and sauté for approximately 2 to 2-1/2 minutes or until golden brown. (The cooking time will depend upon the size of scallops.) Remove from heat and drain off any excess oil.

Presentation: Place a large spoonful of cucumber whipped potatoes in the center of each plate. Next, place one or two scallops atop the potatoes. Carefully ladle 1 1/2 oz. of sauce around the potatoes. Place three dollops of caviar in various places on the butter sauce. Garnish with watercress to finish. ✎

Golden Gazpacho

Makes 4-6 servings

5 yellow tomatoes*
3 yellow peppers**
1 English cucumber*
1 onion, chopped
3 garlic cloves, chopped
salt
1 tsp. sherry vinegar
1 serrano chile

* Peel, remove seeds, and chop
** Remove seeds, core, and chop

Method for Gazpacho: Blend all vegetables until smooth with a hand blender or food processor. Strain through a fine china cap. Adjust seasoning with salt and about 1 tsp. of sherry vinegar. Chill until ready to serve. ✎

Tempura Ahi and Salmon Sashimi with Shiitake Mushrooms and Pickled Ginger Vinaigrette

Makes 6 servings

6 oz. #1 grade ahi tuna
6 oz. salmon fillet
1 lb. shiitake mushrooms (stemmed and sliced thinly)
1 bunch green onions
1 Tbs. Japanese sushi spice
1 Tbs. wasabi paste
nori (seaweed sheets)
1 tsp. rice vinegar
1 Tbs. sesame oil
2 cups peanut or canola oil

Tempura Batter
1 oz. all-purpose flour
7 oz. corn starch
2 egg yolks
10 oz. ice water
pinch of salt

Method for Mushroom Stuffing: Sauté mushrooms quickly in a touch (about 1 tsp.) of sesame oil. When tender, season with rice vinegar and black pepper. Set aside and allow to cool.

Method for Batter: Combine flour and corn starch in a mixing bowl. Make a well in the center of the flour mixture. Place egg yolks and half of the water in the well, and combine by hand using a whisk. Add the rest of the water to thin the paste into a light batter. Batter may be prepared one hour ahead of time, but must be kept very cold. If it has been prepared ahead, remove it from the refrigerator and stir it before using.

Chef's Tip: Do not overwork the batter;

Garnish
Small amounts of the following may be used as garnish

enoki mushrooms
daikon sprouts
shiso leaves
black sesame seeds

Pickled Ginger Vinaigrette
1 cup tamari soy sauce
1/4 cup pickled ginger juice
3 scallions, sliced
1 Tbs. ginger, grated
1 tsp. garlic, minced
1 1/2 Tbs. cilantro, chopped
1 Tbs. sesame oil
1 tsp. lemon juice
2 Tbs. pickled ginger, chopped
1 Tbs. sesame seeds, toasted

blend only until smooth.

Method for Vinaigrette: Place together in a mixing bowl: the 3 scallions (sliced very thinly), along with grated ginger, cilantro, and the pickled ginger. Next add in the soy sauce, and the pickled ginger juice (the sweet and sour vinegar that the ginger comes in). Stir in the sesame oil, lemon juice, and toasted sesame seeds. Taste before adjusting seasoning—it should not need salt. Vinaigrette can be made up to 4 hours in advance, and kept chilled in the refrigerator until needed.

Method for the Sushi Rolls: Preheat oil to 375° on range top or in a deep fryer. Cut each fish into strips, and spread one side with a thin layer ☞

of wasabi. Sprinkle with sushi spice. Place a thin layer of mushroom atop the ahi, and then place salmon atop mushroom, creating a "log."

Roll whole log in nori paper, sealing with water. Cut rolls into equal size pieces. Dip each roll into chilled batter. Carefully fry each one until outside is crisp but <u>not</u> golden.

Presentation: Drizzle vinaigrette onto each serving plate. Cut each roll in half to expose the colors of the fish. Garnish with shiso, daikon sprouts, enoki mushrooms, and black sesame seeds.

Mango and Lime Brulée

Makes 4-6 servings (10-15 tarts)

9 whole eggs
9 egg yolks
3/4 cup sugar
7/8 cup (7 oz.) lime juice
7/8 cup (7 oz.) mango purée
1 1/2 cup (12 oz.) soft butter
10-15 pre-baked tart shells

Method for Brulée: Mix yolks, whole eggs, sugar, lime juice, and mango purée in a large mixing bowl. Place over boiling water (double boiler-style) and blend vigorously until mixture becomes very thick.

Remove from heat and mix in the softened butter. Place in a container or fill tart shells, cover, and chill.

Presentation: Just prior to serving, cover top of custard with sugar and burn under a broiler.

Chef Andrew Sutton,
Auberge du Soleil

Campton Place Hotel

Romance, Old-World charm and memorable
cuisine in the heart of San Francisco

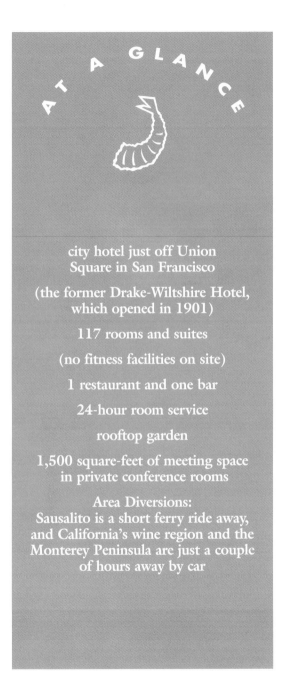

FOR TRAVELERS who insist on great food and romance, Campton Place Hotel is the hands-down choice in San Francisco. Called one of the "Most Romantic Hotels" by *Bon Appetit*, and listed as one of "The Top 25 Restaurants in America" in *Food & Wine* magazine, Campton Place Hotel specializes in cosmopolitan pampering in one of America's loveliest cities. The Hotel offers special getaway packages, with deluxe accommodations, champagne upon arrival, and a rose on your pillow.

The former Drake-Wiltshire Hotel, this property includes two buildings that date back to the turn of the century. In 1981, an 18 million dollar renovation turned this grand old hotel into the luxurious high-rise that it is today. Guests rooms are thoughtfully appointed with oversize beds and down comforters, antique furniture, large desks, and limited-edition artwork. The suites are even more luxurious, with beautifully decorated parlor rooms that make travelers feel like they are staying in a city apartment, rather than in a cramped hotel room. Public areas, including a marbled lobby and a rooftop garden overlooking the city, add to the overall ambience.

The atmosphere of romance carries through to the Hotel's restaurant, with soft peach walls, Wedgwood, cut crystal, and large arrangements of fresh-cut flowers. When it's time to venture out from the Hotel, the city of San Francisco offers an abundance of activities: shopping at Fisherman's Wharf or Ghirardelli Square, riding the cable cars, exploring Chinatown, or browsing the city's many galleries and museums.

340 Stockton Street ❧ San Francisco, California 94108 ❧ (800)235-4300 or (415)781-5555

Quail Lodge Resort

A five-star jewel with lakes, meadows, and lush fairways along the Big Sur coastline

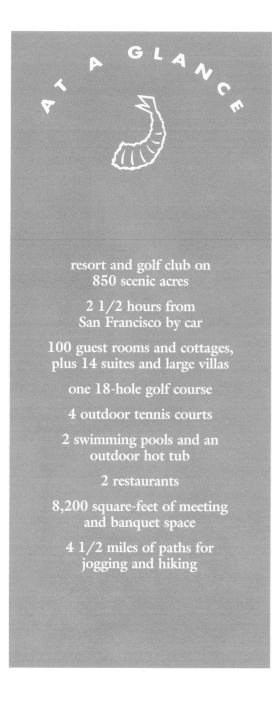

A CONVERTED dairy farm, the Quail Lodge Resort & Golf Club rests upon an oasis of lakes, meadows, and lush fairways, with guest accommodations in country-style cottages scattered throughout the property's 245 landscaped acres. An adjoining nature preserve yields another 600 acres of unspoiled beauty for guests to enjoy. And, true to the resort's name, live quail roam freely around the landscape.

The Resort's consistently high ratings stem from its dedication to excellence in all areas of hospitality, including outstanding guest services, spacious accommodations, and award-winning cuisine. In fact, it is the only property between Los Angeles and San Francisco to receive the coveted Mobil Travel Guide Five Star Award. Quail has earned that prestigious title more than 10 times during a 12-year period, and it is often dubbed a favorite among executives and business leaders.

In addition to the Resort's 18-hole championship golf course, guests enjoy tennis, swimming, and jogging on the many trails that meander around the property's ten sparkling lakes. Just past the rolling hills surrounding the Resort, there is an abundance of activities and sightseeing throughout the Monterey Peninsula. The famed 17-Mile Drive offers spectacular scenery, while Fisherman's Wharf and the Monterey Bay Aquarium provide lots of family entertainment. But one of the best activities here is to take a short drive over to the coast, and watch the waves crash over its rocky shore, looking for the occasional seal or osprey.

The Lodge at Pebble Beach

Spectacular golf and fine dining on the Monterey Peninsula

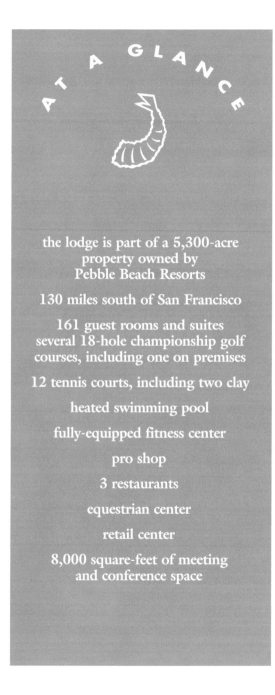

REPRODUCED BY PERMISSION OF PEBBLE BEACH COMPANY

A STAY at The Lodge at Pebble Beach is a golfer's dream vacation. In addition to their own 18-hole course, the Pebble Beach Golf Links, there are other prestigious courses nearby: The Links at Spanish Bay, Old Del Monte Golf Course, and Spyglass Hill Golf Course. In short, golf on the Monterey Peninsula is plentiful, challenging, and always includes breathtaking scenery. The Lodge is situated on the southern coast of California's Monterey Peninsula, and it is accessible from the 17-Mile Drive. It is surrounded by the Del Monte Forest. Because of The Lodge's unique location, it operates a reforestation program, with young Monterey Cypress and Pines, Bishop Pines, and the rare Gowen Cypress trees taking root under the warm California sun.

Active guests are not limited to golf—The Lodge's Beach & Tennis Club has a dozen tennis courts (including two clay courts), a pro shop, heated pool, exercise equipment, and more. The property also operates an equestrian center for riding enthusiasts, and joggers have an abundance of trails at their disposal throughout the Del Monte Forest. Escorted trail rides take guests up into the heart of the Forest.

The Lodge at Pebble Beach has 161 luxury suites and guest rooms, many with balconies overlooking the gardens or the bay. The most luxurious guest room here is not a room at all—it's a private home called "Fairway One," which fronts the golf course and is beautifully furnished.

When the sun sinks below the seaside cliffs, a heavenly meal awaits you at Club XIX or at The Cypress Room.

17-Mile Drive Pebble Beach, California 93953 (800)654-9300 or (408)624-38114

CAMPTON PLACE HOTEL

In the dining room, Campton Place Hotel's tradition of excellence doesn't waiver one bit under the direction of chef Todd Humphries, the former sous-chef of the renowned Lespinasse restaurant in New York's St. Regis Hotel. Humphries' fondness for Middle Eastern and Indian foods—he even roasts and grinds his own spices—has resulted in a lot of subtle but imaginative changes to the Hotel's menu.

"I like to use fresh, local ingredients to create dishes that are simple, straightforward presentations and enhance the food's natural flavors," says Humphries. With that in mind, he creates some extraordinary courses, such as fresh Halibut in Crispy Rice Paper with Brown Basmati Rice, Pickled Mango, and Curried Carrot Sauce; a special garnish of shiitake mushrooms seasoned with ginger and scallions finishes the pungent entrée.

Tuna Tartar with American Caviar and Lotus Root

Makes 4 servings

Pictured on p.101

Tartar

8 oz. sashimi-grade fresh tuna
2 Tbs. extra-virgin olive oil
1 small bunch chives, cut fine
2 oz. American caviar
1/8 tsp. chile oil (to taste)
salt and pepper to taste

Quinoa Salad & Garnishes

1 cup quinoa grain
1/4 cup English cucumber, finely diced
1 small bunch dill, divided into sprigs
8 small yellow cherry tomatoes, quartered
1/2 avocado, diced into 1/4" pieces
2 small radishes, cleaned and sliced paper thin
1 small bunch mint, julienned
3 cups water
1 oz. American caviar (optional garnish)
lemon juice to taste
salt and pepper to taste

Lotus Root Chips

1 large piece lotus root*
3 cups peanut oil

* Purchase from an Asian food store or see Resources section

Cucumber Coulis

1 large English cucumber
3 oz. yogurt
1 1/2 oz. heavy cream
1/4 cup water
1 1/2 oz. crème fraîche (see Chef's Techniques)
lemon, cayenne, salt and pepper

Method for Tartar: With a thin slicing knife, dice tuna into 1/4" pieces. Combine American caviar, chives, and olive oil. Season lightly with chile oil, salt, and pepper. Mix very gently, as not to crush the caviar.

Method for Quinoa: Bring the water to a boil in a quart saucepan. Add the quinoa and cook until tender, approximately 10 minutes. Drain water and chill. In a medium bowl, combine quinoa and half of the diced vegetables*, the mint, and half of the dill. Add olive oil, lemon juice, and season to taste with salt and pepper.

* Remaining vegetables are to be cut in 1/4" dice, and used as garnish

Method for Chips: Peel lotus root and slice across into thin rounds. In a medium sauce pan, bring the oil to about 300°. Fry the lotus root until golden. Remove with a slotted spoon and place onto a paper towel.

Method for Coulis: Peel and seed cucumber and chop roughly. In a blender, purée cucumber and 1/4 cup water; then strain mixture into a bowl. Add the cream, crème fraîche, and yogurt; whisk until thickened. Season to taste with lemon juice, cayenne, and salt and pepper.

Presentation: Place a small amount of the quinoa salad on each plate and top with fried lotus and tuna tartar. Pour cucumber coulis around and garnish with cucumber and tomato (diced), herbs, and American caviar.

Apple Tart with Almonds and Currants

Makes 8 servings

Pastry

1 cup all-purpose flour
4 oz. butter, cut into small cubes
1/8 tsp. salt
1/2 tsp. sugar
1/4 cup ice cold water

Filling

1/4 cup sugar
5 Tbs. butter
1 Tbs. lemon juice
4 lbs. golden delicious apples
1/4 cup almonds, sliced
1/4 cup currants
3/4 cup water

Method for Pastry: Combine flour, salt, and sugar. Mix in butter by hand. Add the water and work dough just until it comes together. Wrap in plastic and let rest.

Method for Filling: Peel and core the apples and cut each in half. In a 12" non-stick pan, combine the sugar, butter, and lemon juice. Let the mixture caramelize over low heat, and then add almonds and continue cooking 10-15 seconds. Remove from heat.

Arrange apples on top of caramel, placing round side down. Next, sprinkle currants on top of apples. Add water and bring mixture to a boil, reducing until water is gone and only sugar and butter remain (mixture will be caramelized at this point).

Remove dough from plastic wrap and roll into 1/8" circle large enough to fit inside of the sauce pan (the pastry is placed across top of pan used for apples). Pierce dough all over with a fork and sprinkle with 1 Tbs. of sugar. Place in a 400° oven for approximately 45 minutes.

Presentation: Let cool and invert onto a serving dish. Serve with whipped cream or ice cream. ✎

> A perfect, easy dessert to make when apples are in season. Serve the tart warm with vanilla ice cream.

Venison with Caramelized Turnips, Chestnuts, and Huckleberries

Makes 4-6 servings

2 lb. trimmed loin of venison
1 pint pearl onions, peeled
1 pint chicken stock
1 lb. huckleberries, puréed
1 lemon, juice only
2 oz. butter
6 purple top turnips (peeled and cut into sixths)

1 lb. chestnuts, roasted and peeled
2 oz. brandy
1 Tbs. black currant jam
1 cup sugar
1 bunch flat parsley, leaves only
salt and pepper to taste ☞

Method for Venison, Vegetables, & Sauce: In a large pot, blanch onions and turnips separately until tender, and then shock in ice water to stop cooking. In another pot, combine chestnuts, half the chicken stock and brandy, simmering chestnuts until tender. Add water if necessary to cover the chestnuts.

Combine huckleberries, jam, and the rest of the chicken stock in a sauce pan and reduce by 1/2 over medium heat. Strain through a fine sieve. Add a little sugar and lemon juice to season sauce. Keep warm.

In a large sauté pan, combine chestnuts, turnips, and onions; add butter and cook for 2-3 minutes. Add sugar and a little water, tossing the pan until the sugar caramelizes and vegetables are evenly glazed.

In another sauté pan, season and sauté the venison in olive oil, browning on all sides. Cook to medium-rare, which should take 5-10 minutes.

Presentation: Slice venison and serve over vegetables. Garnish by sprinkling parsley over; serve the sauce on the side. ✎

QUAIL LODGE

Executive chef Frank R. (Bob) Williamson combines solid culinary skills with artistic freedom behind the scenes at the Quail Lodge Resort & Golf Club. The fresh herbs used in many of the dishes served in The Covey Restaurant are plucked from the chef's own courtyard herb garden, only minutes before the meal is prepared. Chef Williamson also maintains an herb greenhouse, with hardy varieties of tarragon, basil, and chervil growing all year long. Wild field mushrooms and edible flowers that flourish throughout the Carmel Valley are Williamson's other favorite ingredients.

Chef Williamson has worked in the food industry for more than 37 years. "I like presentations that are clean, not overly fussy, and not rigidly geometric," he says. "I select quality ingredients that work well together, and compliment each other in taste and texture."

Spiced Pork Tenderloin with Fresh Fruit Chutney

Makes 4 servings

Tenderloin

1 1/2-2 lb. pork tenderloin
spice blend (see recipe)
3 Tbs. salad oil
fruit chutney (see recipe)

Pork Spice Blend

2 Tbs. peppercorns
2 Tbs. mustard seed
1 1/2 Tbs. cumin seed
1 1/2 Tbs. fennel seed
1 Tbs. caraway seed
salt

Fresh Fruit Chutney
(yields one quart)

5 cups diced peaches (or other soft fruit)
1 medium onion, chopped
2 Tbs. garlic, chopped
1/3 cup candied ginger, chopped
2 cups vinegar
2 cups sugar
1 piece cinnamon stick
3 whole cloves
4 cardamon pods

Method for Tenderloin: Trim fat and sinew from the pork. Roll it in the spices to coat well. Heat oil in a sauté pan. Add pork, and brown on all sides (be careful not to burn the spices). Finish cooking in a 350° oven, approximately 10 minutes, or until meat is firm.

Method for Spices: Toast mustard, cumin, fennel, and carraway seeds in a hot skillet for 2-3 minutes. Grind spices in a coffee or spice mill, pulse grinding in short bursts. Do not grind too fine.

Combine all spices, and add salt (about 1-2 tsp.) to taste.

Method for Chutney: Place all ingredients except fruit in a non-reactive sauce pan. Boil until you have a heavy syrup. Add the peaches and simmer until fruit is soft. For a more traditional "keeping" chutney, boil until it is the fine consistency of jam.

Presentation: Slice the tenderloin thinly and serve with fruit chutney.

Chef Williamson suggests offering this dish as an appetizer or as a main course; its spicy-sweet flavors contrast nicely with the pork.

Chicken Breasts with Prawn Stuffing, Risotto Cakes, and Nasturtium Salad

Makes 6 servings

6 skinless chicken breasts (wing bone on, approximately 6 oz. each)
1 cup-plus cooked prawns, sliced
1/2 tsp. garlic, chopped
1 Tbs. basil, chopped
2 Tbs. green olive, chopped
1/2 cup pine nuts
1/2 cup Japanese bread crumbs
1 egg yolk
1 tsp. lemon juice
salt, pepper, and flour as needed
2-3 Tbs. pine nuts, toasted
1/2 cup chicken stock
1/2 cup cooking oil
nasturtium salad (see recipe)
6 risotto cakes (see recipe)

Nasturtium Salad

6-8 oz. mixed greens
2-3 oz. nasturtium leaves and flowers

1 tsp. dijon mustard
2 tsp. champagne vinegar
3 Tbs. olive oil
salt and pepper to taste

Risotto Cakes

1 cup arborio rice
1 tsp. garlic, chopped
1 Tbs. shallot, chopped
3 cups chicken stock
1 Tbs. olive oil
1 Tbs. clarified butter
salt, pepper, and nutmeg
2 egg yolks
3/4 cup Japanese breadcrumbs
2 Tbs. chives, chopped
2 Tbs. parsley, chopped

Method for Chicken: To make the prawn stuffing, combine shallot, garlic, basil, olives, pine nuts, lemon juice, egg yolk, and bread crumbs in a food processor. Add in the sliced prawns, and season to taste.

Remove the bone and skin from the chicken breasts, and cut a pocket in each filleted breast. Flatten them between two sheets of parchment paper. Place some prawn mixture on each breast, cover it with the fillet, and wrap the two sides over to cover the fillet and stuffing.* Season chicken and dust lightly with flour.

Heat about 2 oz. cooking oil in a heavy sauté pan, and cook the chicken seam-side down for 2-3 minutes over moderate heat. Turn and cook long enough to give the other side a little color, then turn back again and finish cooking in a 375° oven for 10-12 minutes, or until the breasts feel firm.

Remove the chicken and keep warm. Discard the cooking fat, and rinse the pan with chicken stock.

Method for Salad: Blend dressing ingredients together vigorously with a wire whisk. Add the greens and toss.

Method for Risotto Cakes: Gently cook garlic and shallot in the oil and butter for 2-3 minutes. Add the rice and cook it for 2-3 minutes, stirring constantly. Add one cup of the chicken stock. When this has almost boiled away, add another cup of stock. Repeat. When the third cup is almost gone, cover the pan, and let it sit in a warm spot at the back of the stove for 20 minutes or so. ☞

Test the rice—it should be tender. Put the pan back on the heat until it looks quite dry, stirring constantly. Add the egg yolk and season with salt, pepper, and nutmeg. Allow to cool.

Add parsley, rice, and enough bread crumbs (about 1/4 cup) to give the rice mixture a stiff consistency. Divide into six portions and shape each into flat ovals. Cook on a lightly oiled griddle, or in a heavy skillet until golden-brown and heated through.

Presentation: Make nasturtium salad and arrange it on plates. Drizzle the salad with the hot stock. Put a risotto cake in the center of each plate. Slice the chicken and arrange it over the cakes; then sprinkle with toasted pine nuts.

Author's Note

You may take the pounded breast and roll stuffing up inside, sealing up any visible stuffing with the chicken meat. Use toothpicks to secure, if necessary.

> This dish makes a beautiful presentation, with a risotto cake in the middle, the stuffed breast sliced and fanned out, and the colorful nasturtium salad, plucked right from the chef's garden.

Chocolate Mango Frangipane Tart

Makes 10 servings (one 9" tart)

Pastry
1/2 cup unsalted butter
4 1/2 Tbs. sugar
pinch salt
1 egg
1 egg yolk
1 1/2 cups flour

Frangipane
3/4 cup butter*
7/8 cup sugar
3 eggs*

6 Tbs. flour
1 cup hazelnuts, finely chopped

* At room temperature

Other Ingredients
1/3 cup semi-sweet chocolate, finely chopped
2 mangoes (peeled, halved and pitted)
9" tart pan, sprayed with non-stick coating

Method for Pastry: Preheat oven to 400°. Cream butter and sugar together. Add egg and yolk, mixing well. Add flour and salt and mix until it comes together. Roll out and place in sprayed tart pan, then refrigerate.

Method for Frangipane: Cream butter and sugar. Add lightly mixed eggs slowly, one ounce at at time, and set aside. In a separate bowl, blend nuts, flour, and salt together. Fold nut mixture into butter mixture and blend well.

Remove tart shell from the refrigerator and layer chocolate on bottom evenly. Arrange mango slices in a shingle manner. Spread frangipane over the top of the mangoes, using a warm spatula to spread evenly. Bake in oven at 400° for 10 minutes. Reduce oven temperature to 350° and bake for 25 minutes, or until a toothpick comes out clean. Allow to cool.

Presentation: Serve with whipped cream, crème anglaise, or chocolate sorbet.

> Instead of the usual almonds, this frangipane has chopped hazelnuts.
> You may substitute other favorite fruits, such as apricots or pears, for the mangoes.

Beat Giger

THE LODGE AT PEBBLE BEACH

Beat Giger, Executive Chef of The Lodge at Pebble Beach, began his training as a chef in his native Switzerland at the age of 16. Early in his career, Giger worked for several five-star Swiss properties, including the Hotel St. Gotthard in Zurich, and the Hotel Mt. Cervin in Zermatt. He later held positions at esteemed properties in South America and Florida before coming to California.

Chef Giger holds certification as a Certified Executive Chef (CEC), and the prestigious American Academy of Chefs (AAC) accreditations. He also holds a board position at the American Institute of Food and Wine, and he is a member of the Chaine de Rotisseurs. Chef Giger is pleased to practice his craft at Pebble Beach, one of the world's loveliest locations. His goal is to "see Pebble Beach become as famous for our exquisite restaurants and wonderful cuisine as our renowned golf courses."

Crab Cakes with Spicy Cajun Mayonnaise

Makes 12 servings (appetizer portions)

Crab Cakes

8 oz. dungeness crab meat, well drained
1/4 cup carrots*
1/4 cup leeks*
1/4 cup bell peppers*
1/4 cup celery*
1 shallot*
1 garlic clove*
1 egg
1 Tbs. mayonnaise
1 cup white bread crumbs
1 Tbs. butter
salt and pepper to taste
1/4 cup canola oil

* Finely dice

Breading

1/4 cup flour
2 eggs*
1/4 cup milk*
1/2 cup white bread crumbs

* Mix well together

Cajun Mayonnaise

1 cup mayonnaise
1 1/2 Tbs. Cajun seasoning
1 Tbs. half and half
1/2 Tbs. lemon, juice only

Method for Crab Cakes: Sauté the carrots, leeks, bell peppers, celery, shallots, and garlic in butter, stirring until all vegetables are cooked al dente. Place in a mixing bowl and allow to cool. Then, add crab meat, egg, mayonnaise, and bread crumbs, mixing until all ingredients are incorporated. Season with salt and pepper to taste. Form into 24 small cakes.

Method for Breading: Dust each crab cake with flour, then dip into egg/milk mixture, and roll in the white bread crumbs. In a large sauté pan, bring the canola oil to a medium heat. Fry the cakes until golden brown on each side. Place on a paper towel to absorb the excess oil.

Method for Mayonnaise: Combine the mayonnaise, Cajun seasoning, lemon juice, and half and half; mix well. Place in a serving dish and hold until needed.

Presentation: *Place dish with cajun mayonnaise in the center of a pretty platter and arrange the crab cakes in even circles around the mayonnaise.*

> This is a well-balanced crab cake served with a Cajun mayonnaise for an unusual taste sensation. The recipe makes 24 small cakes.

Seared Salmon Medallions and Orange-Ginger Salsa on Tossed Greens with Scalloped Potatoes

Makes 4 servings

(8) 3 oz. salmon medallions
12 oz. baby greens (cleaned, washed, and patted dry)
1 shallot
2 oz. red wine vinegar
1 Tbs. dijon mustard
4 oz. extra-virgin olive oil
4 red cherry tomatoes*
4 yellow cherry tomatoes*
scalloped potatoes (see recipe)
8 oz. orange-ginger salsa (see recipe)

* Cut in half

Method for Vinaigrette: Finely dice the shallot and place it in a large salad bowl. Add the red wine vinegar and dijon mustard. Then add 4 oz. of extra-virgin olive oil. Mix thoroughly and season to taste with salt and pepper.

Method for Scalloped Potatoes: Using a Pyrex dish, layer the potatoes evenly and top with seasoned cream. Bake in a 375° oven for 45 minutes or until done. Set aside for 45 minutes.

Method for Orange-Ginger Salsa: Dice tomatoes and place in mixing bowl. Add ginger,

Orange-Ginger Salsa
8 Roma tomatoes, peeled and seeded
1 orange, zest and juice
1 Tbs. fresh ginger, grated
1 Tbs. cilantro, chopped

Scalloped Potatoes
8 medium new potatoes, peeled and thinly sliced
1/2 qt. cream*
1 garlic clove, chopped

*Season with salt and pepper

juice, zest of orange, and cilantro. Season with rice vinegar, sesame oil, salt, and pepper to taste.

Cooking & Presentation: Sear salmon in frying pan until done. Toss salad with vinaigrette and divide evenly on four plates. Place salmon on top of salads. With a 1" round cookie cutter, cut out the scallop potatoes and place evenly around the salad (should be about 16 slices). Top each serving of salmon with orange-ginger salsa and garnish with the cherry tomato halves.

Chef Giger's salmon is California cuisine at its best.
This is a hot and cold salad with a light, citrusy salsa.

Baked Sea Bass in Fresh Herb Crust

Makes 6 servings

(6) 7 oz. fillets of sea bass (Bluenose is preferable)
3 eggs, beaten
1 cup white flour
6 servings sautéed spinach
6 large red potatoes, steamed & quartered

Herb Bread Crumb Mixture
2 cups Panko bread crumbs (or your favorite brand)
1 Tbs. fresh oregano*
1 Tbs. fresh tarragon*
1 Tbs. fresh dill*
1 Tbs. fresh thyme*
1 Tbs. garlic, minced
2 Tbs. parmesan cheese, grated
2 Tbs. olive oil
1 tsp. white pepper, ground
1 Tbs. kosher salt

* Finely chop

Garlic Broth
4 cups fish fumé or clam juice
6 shallots*
2 Tbs. parsley*
3 Tbs. garlic*
2 Tbs. lemon juice
1/4 lb. whole butter
1 cup white wine

* Mince ☞

Method for Bread Crumbs: Mix all ingredients together and set aside until needed.

Method for Broth: Sauté the shallots and garlic in a little butter. Add white wine and lemon juice, and reduce by 2/3. Next, add fish fumé, parsley, and butter, and bring to a boil; then remove from heat.

Method for the Sea Bass: Season the fillets with salt and white pepper and then dredge each in flour. Shake off excess flour, dip fillets in eggs, and press them firmly onto the bread crumb mixture. Place fish on a buttered sheet pan and cook them in a 350° oven for 15-20 minutes, or until done, depending upon the thickness.

Presentation: Remove fish from oven and place atop sautéed spinach in the center of a serving plate. Pour broth around each fillet and a little on top to moisten the crust. Then place four red potato quarters at 12, 3, 6, and 9 o'clock.

The Lodge's sea bass is a light and juicy entrée, accompanied by sautéed spinach and sweet red potatoes.

Cypress Room, The Lodge at Pebble Beach

Potato Lasagna
Recipe on p. 163

Hawaiian Fresh Fruits with
Chocolate Lilikoi Sabayon
Recipe on p.147

chapter 4

The American West

Unspoiled Hawaii

Hyatt Regency Kauai

The Lodge At Koele

Manele Bay Resort

Oregon & Utah

Heathman Hotel

Salishan Lodge

Stein Eriksen Lodge

BEFORE MY FIRST VISIT TO HAWAII, I WAS FORE-WARNED: "THE FOOD IS LESS THAN WONDERFUL THERE, AND THE BEST PINEAPPLES ARE SHIPPED TO THE MAINLAND." MY ADVISORS WERE WRONG; THE CUISINE I DISCOVERED IN HAWAII WAS NOTHING SHORT OF FABULOUS. THE VERY FRESHEST FISH AND RIPE, TROPICAL FRUITS ARE JUST A FEW ITEMS THAT ARE PREPARED IN FLAWLESS FASHION UNDER THE DIRECTION OF HAWAII'S FOUR- AND FIVE-STAR CHEFS.

The American

Two favorite destinations are covered in this chapter—unspoiled Hawaii and the American West. Three top-rated properties in the Hawaiian Islands (one on Kauai, the Garden Isle, and two on quaint Lana'i) present their luxurious facilities and their chefs' favorite recipes. This chapter also features two beautiful properties in Oregon: one is located in the heart of Portland, a city devoted to culture, and the other is perched up over the Pacific Ocean. A heavenly ski resort in Utah is also presented.

A blend of contemporary design and the romance of old Hawaii, the Hyatt Regency Kauai offers something for every-one. Executive chef David Boucher makes the Hyatt experi-ence complete with his imaginative island cuisine.

While the Manele Bay Hotel and the Lodge at Koele are both owned by the Dole Food Company, they are worlds apart. Manele Bay Hotel is located on the beach, surrounded by acres of tropical gardens brimming with hibiscus and bougainvillea. By contrast, The Lodge at Koele is located on the island's inte-rior, and has an upcountry style, with timbers, fireplaces, and wide porches. Both properties practice award-winning cuisine: at Manele, chef Philippe Padovani whips up imaginative dish-es with the island's bountiful seafood and tropical fruits. Edwin

HYATT REGENCY KAUAI RESORT & SPA

West

Goto, executive chef at the Lodge, also utilizes Lana'i's own resources, including wild venison, fresh seafood, and exotic fruits.

All of these properties share a passion for innovative cuisine that changes with the seasons, and that celebrates the natural resources. The pace is quick at Portland's top property, The Heathman Hotel, which shares a complex with the city's performing Arts Center. Executive Chef Philippe Boulot matches the mood set by the Center, providing diners with artistic entrées.

At Salishan, a woodsy retreat overlooking Oregon's Gleneden Beach, chef Rob Pounding treats guests to creative meals utilizing Pacific Northwest seafood and produce. In Utah's Deer Valley,

Stein Eriksen Lodge offers splended mountain scenery, year-round sports, and memorable meals orchestrated by executive chef Mikel Trapp. Luscious desserts served at the Lodge, including Trapp's Mixed Berry Crème Brulée, are favorites of champion skier Stein Eriksen.

These chefs provide lots of wonderful options for dinner parties of any size. Try chef Padovani's Hawaiian Fresh Fruits with Chocolate Lilikoi Sabayon, which can be prepared in a double-boiler and then served in a fondue pot. The following recipes feature imaginative combinations of flavors, and inventive marriages of ingredients—in short, masterful foods by some top names in the industry. ✿

Hyatt Regency Kauai

This tropical paradise blends modern amenities
with plantation charm

resort hotel on 50 oceanfront acres in the Poipu Beach District, Kauai

(20 minutes from Lihue Airport)

600 guest rooms, including 41 luxurious suites and the Regency Club concierge level

25,000 square-foot spa facility with 2 whirlpools and 2 jacuzzis

massages, facials, herbal wraps

25-yard lap pool

3 restaurants

24,381 square-feet of meeting and banquet space (plus another 68,000 on the beautiful grounds)

THE ROMANCE of old Hawaii is still alive on Kauai, the Garden Isle. The Hyatt Regency Kauai Resort and Spa is truly a tropical paradise, with an abundance of open spaces where nature prevails. Here, Hyatt guests are surrounded by 50 acres of lush tropical beauty, including koi-stocked lagoons and waterfalls. Located on Keoneloa Bay, this contemporary Resort is both elegant and informal.

To capture the natural beauty of the area along with a classic Hawaiian charm, the 1990 Hyatt Regency Kauai drew upon the traditions of classical Hawaiian architecture, with a design that won the Award of Excellence from the Honolulu Chapter of the American Institute of Architects (AIA). The design evokes plantation-era Hawaii through the use of wide overhanging roofs, many lanais (porches), and walls that fold away. And, the buildings rise only as high as the coconut palms.

Each of the Resort's 600 rooms gives guests a spectacular ocean, garden, lagoon, or mountain view. The ANARA Health and Fitness Spa moves many facilities out-of-doors, including the luxurious lava rock shower garden. Many of the Resort's special banquets and parties are held on the beautiful grounds, in three different tropical gardens, beachside, or on the 4,000-square foot private pool deck. Finally, the three main restaurants take advantage of the views—one of them allows diners to enjoy their meals while watching tropical fish swim by in the surrounding freshwater lagoon.

1571 Poipu Road ❧ Koloa, Kauai 96756 ❧ (808)742-1234

Lodge at Koele

A splendid "upcountry resort" in the heart of Hawaii's unspoiled Lana'i

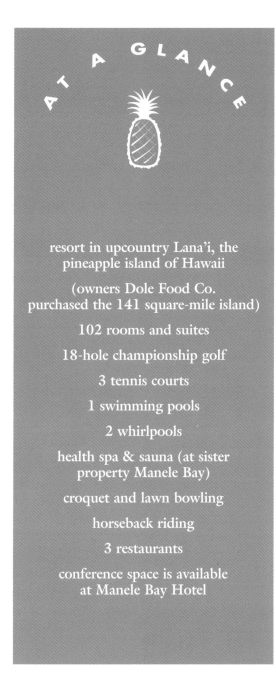

"LANA'I IS a place where wild turkeys and axis deer roam freely, where aromatic forests are filled with rare plants and flowers, where tales of Hawaiian gods and kings live on . . . , where the pace is relaxed and the smiles are always friendly," says entrepreneur David H. Murdock when asked to describe life around the Lodge. There has been so much attention to detail here that the young Lodge at Koele is ranked among the best resorts in the world.

This is a different kind of Hawaii.

Developers carved a plantation out of Lana'i's interior, and created a relaxed, country estate for guests to play at while enjoying the island's sunny, balmy days. Guest rooms continue the plantation style, with ceiling fans, carved four-poster beds, wicker sidechairs, and cheerful fabrics.

Perhaps one of the best activities here is to explore the many desolate beaches, since Lana'i has only 2,800 year-round residents. Besides beachcombing, there is a magnificent, challenging golf course designed by Greg Norman and Ted Robinson, nestled between the island's rolling hills and steep valley gorges. Avid golfers can also practice putting on Koele's 18-hole Executive Putting Course, which is shaded by large banyan trees. There is also tennis, swimming, croquet, and hiking to do at (or near) the Lodge.

During the Lodge's Visiting Artist Program, guests meet renowned authors, chefs, and entertainers. With the resort's unlimited activities and Lana'i's natural beauty, this destination grows in popularity each year.

P.O. Box 310, Lana'i City ✆ Lana'i, Hawaii 96763 ✆ (800)321-4666 or (808)565-7300

Manele Bay Hotel

Elegant dining and spectacular ocean
views on Lana'i's sleepy coastline

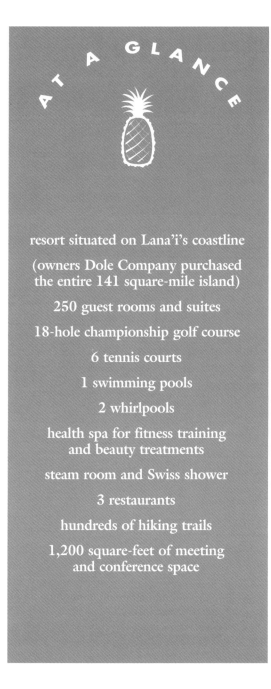

AT A GLANCE

resort situated on Lana'i's coastline
(owners Dole Company purchased
the entire 141 square-mile island)

250 guest rooms and suites

18-hole championship golf course

6 tennis courts

1 swimming pools

2 whirlpools

health spa for fitness training
and beauty treatments

steam room and Swiss shower

3 restaurants

hundreds of hiking trails

1,200 square-feet of meeting
and conference space

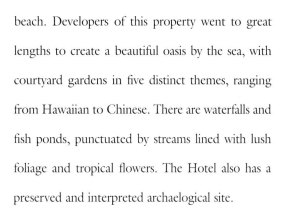

SISTER TO the Lodge at Koele, Manele Bay Hotel offers guests a dramatic beachfront location, with sweeping views of the ocean and the white-sand beach. Developers of this property went to great lengths to create a beautiful oasis by the sea, with courtyard gardens in five distinct themes, ranging from Hawaiian to Chinese. There are waterfalls and fish ponds, punctuated by streams lined with lush foliage and tropical flowers. The Hotel also has a preserved and interpreted archaelogical site.

The Manele Bay Hotel's guest rooms feature large bathrooms, art and antiques, and luxurious fabrics and furnishings. Many of the rooms also have commanding views of the Pacific Ocean. Guests may reserve beach front suites or garden villas that hug the hillside and provide views of Hulopo'e Bay.

Sportsmen enjoy the Hotel's 18 holes of championship golf, designed by touring pro Jack Nicklaus, plus they may venture up to Koele for more rounds of golf (called The Experience at Koele) in a mountainous setting. There is so much to do in this peaceful little corner of Hawaii's pineapple island—swimming, tennis, cycling, horseback riding, jeep touring, snorkeling, and sailing. If only there were more hours in the day!

Lana'i itself is worth much exploration. The island is only 141 square-miles, and is 18 miles long and 13 miles wide. Many visitors enjoy sailing the island's coastline to watch for Spinner dolphins and secluded caves, or exploring the high country on horseback. Lana'i is dotted with coconut groves, open meadows, pine forests, and glistening coastlines—an ideal destination for travelers who want to "get away from it all." ✇

P.O. Box 310, Lana'i City ✇ *Lana'i, Hawaii 96763* ✇ *(800)321-4666 or (808)565-7700*

David Boucher

H Y A T T   R E G E N C Y   K A U A I

At the Hyatt Regency Kauai Resort & Spa, diners enjoy a masterful interpretation of contemporary Hawaiian cuisine that relies upon fresh local foods: Kauai onions and sweet corn, Chinese noodles from the Kauai Noodle Factory, island-grown fruit, and fish from the Pacific waters.

Executive chef David Boucher calls the cuisine "a celebration of Hawaiian ingredients, methods, and recipes, presented with a Nineties flair." He adds, "Our resort has always offered guests country or home-style cooking . . . Now we have added to this the flavors of new and old Hawaii, with all the richness of our diverse culture."

Before his present position, Boucher was executive sous chef at the Hyatt Mauai and at the Hyatt Regency Waikoloa on the Big Island of Hawaii. In 1985, he opened the Kauai Hilton as executive chef.

Chicken Breast Luau with Mango Papaya Relish

Makes 4 servings

Chicken Breasts

(2) 10 oz. boneless, skinless chicken breasts (wing on)
12 oz. fresh taro leaves (or spinach)*
4 oz. raw butternut squash, julienned
1/2 medium onion, chopped
1 oz. safflower oil
1 oz. coconut milk
salt and pepper to taste

* See Resources section

Mango Papaya Relish

1 ripe papaya*
2 ripe mangoes*
1/2 red bell pepper**
1/4 medium red onion**
8 sprigs cilantro
1/2 lemon
2 limes

* Cut in 1/2" dice
** Cut in 1/4" dice

Method for Chicken: Split the whole chicken breast, trim off fat, and French wing the bone by chopping the wing tip at the knuckle. Place breasts between two pieces of plastic wrap and pound thin, taking care not to break through the meat. Place taro leaves in a steamer and steam for 4 minutes; then drain them well.

In a skillet, heat oil and sauté taro, onion, and butternut squash over medium heat, until onions are translucent. *(Note: if substituting spinach for the taro, sauté only, and do not steam it first.)* Season with salt and pepper, and allow mixture to cool to room temperature. Divide vegetable mixture into four parts, placing each portion on a half breast. Roll the breasts, and fasten at bottom with toothpicks. Season top of chicken with salt and pepper, and steam for 5 minutes.

Method for Relish: Coarsely chop the cilantro and place all ingredients together in a mixing bowl. Squeeze the lemon and lime juices over mixture and season to taste with salt and pepper. Chill in the refrigerator overnight for best results.

> This is a modern interpretation of an ancient Hawaiian dish—serve it with the chef's fresh mango papaya relish.

Charred Ahi with Papaya and Pineapple Relish

Makes 4 servings

Ahi

28 oz. ahi tuna*
8 oz. papaya relish (see recipe)
1 oz. sunflower sprouts (optional garnish)
4 oz. blackening seasoning
salt and pepper to taste
4 oz. soy sauce
8 oz. soft butter

* Cut the fillets into 2"x2"x6" chunks

Papaya & Pineapple Relish

2 papayas*
2/3 whole pineapple*
1 red bell pepper**
1/2 red onion**
1/2 bunch cilantro, minced
2 lemons, juice only
4 limes, juice only
salt and pepper to taste

* Dice into large pieces
** Dice into medium pieces

Method for Ahi: Heat a cast-iron or other heavy duty skillet over medium-high heat for 5 minutes. Sprinkle blackened seasoning on ahi. Melt butter in the skillet, and sear ahi in it on all four sides, approximately 30 seconds per side. Set aside to cool.

Method for Papaya Relish: Mix all ingredients, and add salt and pepper to taste.

Presentation: Slice the rectangular pieces of tuna into 1/4" pieces and arrange (fan out) on a serving platter with sunflower sprouts and papaya relish; serve with soy sauce on the side.

Chef Boucher offers this dish for the novice sashimi eater, since the tuna is served charred rather than raw. The entire presentation is light and flavorful, with a relish of fresh Hawaiian papaya and pineapple.

Seared Ahi Poke

Makes 4 servings

Ahi Poke

1 lb. ahi
3/4 cup Kauai (or Maui) onion, sliced
1/2 cup ogo
2/3 cup sunflower sprouts
4 Tbs. green onions
Japanese pepper flakes, to taste
Hawaiian salt (or kosher salt) to taste
2 tsp. sesame oil
4 oz. low-sodium soy sauce

Garnish (optional)

kukui nut, sprinkle
4 ti leaves
4 tamare crabs

Method for Ahi: Season ahi with Hawaiian salt, and then sear very quickly on all sides. Cut into a 1/2" dice. Mix all remaining ingredients together (except ti leaf, kukui nut, and tamare crab) in a mixing bowl.

Presentation: Form ti leaf into a cone, and place it on a serving platter. Arrange the ahi poke spilling out of the ti leaf cone. Garnish with the sprinkle of kukui nut and the tamare crab.

Poke is a favorite dish among natives on Kauai and on Nihau, its small neighbor island. The tamare crab and other garnishes are optional.

Rolled Ono with Anahola Granola and Corn-Tomatillo Relish

Makes 4 servings

Rolled Ono

3 3/4 lbs. fresh ono fillets
8 oz. tropical granola
1 large Kauai onion, finely diced
1 sunrise papaya, skinned and diced
8 sprigs lemon basil, slivered
1 Tbs. soft ginger*
2 cloves fresh garlic*
1/2 red bell pepper*
1 tsp. Hawaiian salt
2 oz. butter

* Mince

Corn-Tomatillo Relish

2 ears fresh sweet corn*

5 oz. fresh tomatillos, puréed (see Resources section)
1 large Kauai sweet onion**
2 cloves fresh garlic**
1/4 cup rice wine vinegar
1/2 cup chicken stock
1 Tbs. corn starch paste
1 oz. butter
1 Tbs. opal basil, slivered
1 Tbs. fresh dill**
1/2 tsp. Thai yellow curry paste
1 tsp. Hawaiian salt

* Cook and cut from the cob
** Mince

Method for Stuffing: Grind tropical granola in a food processor until it is ground, resembling course bread crumbs, and set aside.

Meanwhile, sauté onions, garlic, and bell peppers in butter until translucent. Mix all ingredients (except fish) together in a mixing bowl until well combined, and then refrigerate this stuffing until needed.

Method for Rolled Ono: Split ono down the center, removing the blood line, and then slice the half fillet on the bias into two 3 oz. portions. Lay each piece of fish, one at a time, on a large piece of plastic wrap, folding the wrap over the fish. Gently pound each piece of fish until it is about 3/8" thick.

Method for Tomatillos: Purée tomatillos in a blender on high speed and then set aside. Sauté onions and garlic in butter until translucent, and then put aside. Bring chicken stock to a boil, mix in curry paste, and thicken with cornstarch. Then mix all ingredients together and adjust seasoning.

_____

Cooking & Presentation: *Place about 2 Tbs. of the granola stuffing on the center of each fillet and roll up. Place the rolls in a Chinese steamer basket to steam for approximately 5 minutes. You may serve the ono as is, or slice through each piece, and then fan out slices on the serving plates. Garnish with sprigs of lemon basil and wedges of fresh papaya, if desired.* ✿

Ingredient Footnote

KAUAI ONIONS
If Kauai sweet onions are unavailable, you may substitute Vidalia or another very sweet, mild onion.

Chef Boucher uses 100% Hawaiian-grown foods in this entrée, a blend of island and southwestern American flavors. Use your own favorite resources for the fresh herbs, fish, and produce needed to create this dish.

Edwin Goto

LODGE AT KOELE

The Lodge's upcountry Hawaiian theme is carried through to its innovative menus by chef Edwin Goto and his talented culinary staff. Chef Goto's cuisine is considered "rustic American" but it is also a very mature, sophisticated approach to cooking. "I work closely with the local farmers who grow much of our specialty produce. I cook using fish from local waters, venison from Lana'i forests, and vegetables from local gardens," says Goto. He adds, "The quality of ingredients is unparalled, and my job is to let those ingredients shine."

In this section, Chef Goto shares some of his favorite dishes, including Roast Venison Loin with Fried and Sweet Mashed Potatoes, and Red Pear Napoleon with Anise Sauce. It's an upcountry Hawaiian feast!

Summer Tomato Soup with Pulled Sourdough Croutons and Basil Pesto

Makes 6 servings

Tomato Soup

8 medium tomatoes
1 medium onion, diced
2 garlic cloves, minced
5 cups hot chicken stock
1/8 cup tomato paste
1 Tbs. kosher salt
1/2 Tbs. black pepper, ground
1/4 cup Italian parsley*
1/2 Tbs. thyme**
3/4 Tbs. rosemary**
1/2 Tbs. oregano*
1 Tbs. sugar
1/4 tsp. chile pepper flakes
1/8 cup olive oil

* Chop coursely
** Cut in a fine mince

Sourdough Croutons

3 Tbs. olive oil
2 tsp. garlic cloves, minced
salt and pepper to taste
1 lb. sourdough bread

Basil Pesto

2 cups fresh basil, tightly packed
2 tsp. garlic, finely chopped
2 Tbs. pine nuts, toasted
salt to taste
1/2 tsp. ground black pepper
1 cup mild olive oil
1/2 cup parmesan cheese, freshly grated

Method for Croutons: With your hands, pull the loaf apart to approximately 1/2-1" chunks. Mix the olive oil, garlic, salt, and pepper together. Toss the sourdough bread chunks with the olive oil mixture. Place the bread on a sheet pan and bake in a 300° oven for 20 minutes, or until the croutons are golden-brown and hard.

Method for Pesto: Place the basil, garlic, pine nuts, and pepper in a blender and process until combined. Add about half the oil and purée, then add the remaining oil and blend to a thick purée. There should be tiny pieces of basil left in the purée. Add the cheese and salt to taste. Process until blended. Refrigerate if making ahead.

Method for Soup: Score the tomatoes, and blanch them in boiling water. Then place them in ice water and peel immediately. Cut the tomatoes in half and squeeze out the seeds (straining the liquid and discarding the seeds). Place the liquid in a sauce pan and reduce until it becomes a thick purée. In a large pot, sauté the onion and garlic; reduce heat and add the tomato paste. Cook tomato paste, onion, and garlic for 5 minutes on a low simmer. Then add hot chicken stock to the tomato mixture and cook for 20 minutes. Add all the herbs and the sugar. Mix well, and season with salt and pepper. Simmer for an additional 10 minutes.

Presentation: Place a portion of pesto in serving bowls first, and then ladle in soup and scatter croutons on top to finish.

Pan-Roasted Duck with Lemon Spaetzle

Pictured on p.131

Makes 4 servings

Duck
2 ducks, 5 lbs. each
6 Tbs. kosher salt
2 Tbs. ground black pepper
10 pcs. bay leaves, lightly crushed
2 Tbs. thyme

Lemon Spaetzle
2 eggs
1 1/2 oz. milk
3 oz. flour
salt and pepper to taste
pinch of nutmeg
1 tsp. lemon zest (one lemon)

Method for Duck: Using a boning knife, remove legs (thigh with drumstick attached) and breast pieces from the duck carcass. Remove wing tips, reserving them and backs for stock. Trim loose flaps of skin from duck and pull all loose fat from cavity; reserve. Season duck pieces with salt, black pepper, thyme, and bay leaves. Lay out on kitchen towels, cover, and refrigerate overnight.

Meanwhile, cut reserved skin and fat into small pieces and render out fat. To render fat: place duck skin and fat in a deep oven-proof bowl, and bake in a 300° oven for about an hour, or until bits of skin have floated to the surface. Strain and reserve the fat for the next day.

The following day, rinse the seasoning off the duck under cold water. Allow the pieces to dry. Heat a heavy pot over medium heat. Add duck pieces to pot, skin-side down, and brown duck evenly. Once the duck is completely browned, add rendered fat into pot, completely covering duck. If there isn't enough fat to cover duck, olive oil may be added. Simmer duck for approximately 1 hour and 15 minutes.

Method for Lemon Spaetzle: Combine the eggs, milk, and seasonings in a large bowl and mix well. Work in the flour by hand and let the dough rest for 10 minutes. Season a pot of boiling water with salt. Place a perforated pan over boiling water and push spaetzle dough through the holes with a rubber spatula. Gently stir spaetzle and remove each as it floats up to the surface. Plunge in ice water to prevent spaetzle from cooking further. Reserve for later use.

Presentation: Butter the hot spaetzle and season with salt and pepper to taste. Serve with the duck breast leaned over the leg. Use seasonal fresh vegetables of your choice as a side dish. ✍

About this Dish

To check for doneness, the meat should be easily pierced with a wooden toothpick.

> **This rustic preparation of duck and the traditional spaetzle (with a 'twist') is a Lodge favorite.**

Roast Venison Loin with Fried and Mashed Sweet Potatoes

Makes 4 servings

Venison
2 lbs. venison loin
salad oil
salt and pepper

Port Wine Sauce
4 figs, diced
1 cup port wine
1 1/2 cups veal demi
few drops of lemon juice

Mashed Potatoes
4 sweet potatoes (medium size)
1/2-3/4 cup hot milk
5 Tbs. butter
salt and pepper to taste

Fried Sweet Potatoes
1 sweet potato
vegetable oil
salt

Method for Venison: Preheat oven to 400°. Place a heavy skillet on high heat and add just enough of the salad oil to coat the bottom of the pan. While the pan is heating, season the venison loin with salt and pepper. When the pan is hot, sear the venison on all sides. Transfer to the oven and roast for approximately 10 minutes (medium-rare), ☞

or until desired doneness. Remove venison from the oven and allow to sit for 5 minutes before slicing.

Method for Port Wine Sauce: Add diced figs to the pan and cook over low heat until soft. Add port wine and reduce in volume by 3/4. Add veal demi and simmer until it has reduced by 1/2. Season to taste with salt, pepper, and a few drops of lemon juice. Keep the sauce hot until needed.

Method for Mashed Sweet Potatoes: Peel the potatoes and cut three of them into quarters. (Reserve the fourth potato for frying.) Transfer them to a pot and cover with cold water. Bring to a boil and simmer gently for 20-30 minutes. Drain into a colander and then return the warm potatoes back to the pot. With the potatoes on very low heat, slowly add the hot milk while mashing the potatoes with a fork or a potato masher. Transfer to a warm bowl and whisk in butter until light and fluffy. Season to taste with salt and pepper.

Method for Fried Sweet Potatoes: Heat the vegetable oil in a pot very slowly to 375°. Slice the remaining potato as thinly as possible. Soak slices in cold water for 15 minutes, changing the water twice. Drain the water and dry the potato slices well. When the oil is ready, add the potato slices, one by one, turning frequently. Cook until golden and turn out onto paper towels. Season with salt.

Presentation: Fan slices of the venison next to a dollop of potatoes on each serving plate. Ladle the port wine sauce over the sliced venison. Garnish the mashed potatoes with the sweet potato chips and serve. ✍

Red Pear Napoleon with Anise Sauce

Pictured on p.201

Makes 3 servings

Puff Pastry
1/2 lb. puff pastry

Anise Syrup
1 cup water
1 cup sugar
5 pcs. whole star anise
1 vanilla bean*

* Split and scrape

Pear Sauce
3 ripe pears*
1 Tbs. butter
1 1/2 cups heavy cream**

* Peel, core, and slice
** Use to make 2 cups of whipped cream

Method for Puff Pastry: Roll puff pastry as thin as possible into a 12" x 16" rectangle. Place dough between two sheet pans, and bake at 375° until golden brown (about 10 minutes). Set aside until cool. Cut (12) 3" x 4" squares. Set aside until ready to use.

Method for Anise Syrup: Combine all ingredients in a sauce pan. Bring the mixture to a boil and cook until sugar has dissolved. Remove from heat, strain, and set aside.

Method for Pear Sauce: Cook the pears in butter until golden-brown. Add the remaining anise syrup and stir until pears are coated. Set aside.

Assembly & Presentation: Ladle pear sauce onto the bottom of the dessert plate. Place one puff pastry square down on top of the sauce. Spoon some of the pear filling onto the puff pastry. Spoon whipped cream on top of filling. Add another puff pastry square, a layer of pears, and another layer of whipped cream. Dust the top layer of puff pastry with confectioner's sugar, and the napoleon is ready to serve. Repeat same steps to finish the remaining three napoleons. ✍

Inspired by the cool winter months here, the warm pear napoleon may be enjoyed fireside by guests staying at the Lodge.

Philippe Padovani

MANELE BAY RESORT

At the Manele Bay Hotel's restaurants, French-born Philippe Padovani blends his classic European training with trends and traditions of Hawaiian cuisine. "I am a big fan of Hawaiian chocolate and of the wonderful exotic fruits grown here," says Padovani, who uses them to perfection.

Chef Padovani became intrigued with the Hawaiian Islands while acting as a consulting chef to Oahu's Halekulani Hotel. At that time, he worked as executive chef of the award-winning Restaurant La Tour Rose in Lyon, France. He later became corporate chef at Halekulani, and then served as executive chef of the Ritz-Carlton, Mauna Lani.

Padovani is a member of the Hawaii Regional Chefs' Group, a network of 12 island-based chefs who create award-winning cuisine. He has also prepared foods for international competitions.

Sautéed Onaga with Creamy Curry Sauce *Pictured on p.203*

Makes 4 servings

Sautéed Onaga

2 lbs. onaga (filleted and backbone removed)*
1/4 cup olive oil
salt and pepper to taste

* You may substitute sea bass or John Dory scallops

Creamy Curry Sauce

2 tsp. clarified butter
1/2 cup onions*
1 tsp. garlic*
1/4 cup celery*
1 tsp. green chile*
1 tsp. red chile pepper*
1 tsp. ginger*
1 tsp. tumeric powder
2 tsp. curry powder
1 tsp. coriander powder
1 tsp. garam masala**
1/4 cup fish stock or clam juice
1/2 cup tomatoes***
1 cup cream
2 Tbs. cilantro* (optional garnish)
few drops lemon juice (optional garnish)

* Chop finely
** An Indian spice blend available from gourmet grocers, or see Resources section
*** Blanch, peel, and chop finely

NOTE: Prepare sauce first and then sauté fish just before serving.

Method for Onaga: Cut fish into 8 oz. pieces. Season both sides of the fillets with salt and pepper. Preheat frying pan with olive oil and cook the fillets, from 3-5 minutes.

Method for Sauce: In a sauce pan, sweat garlic and ginger in butter. Add onions, celery, and chile; sweat. Add tumeric, curry powder, coriander, and garam masala. Pour in clam juice and bring to a simmer; next, add tomatoes. Reduce to a syrup, then pour in cream and bring to a boil. Season to taste, and remove from heat when cooked. Garnish with cilantro and lemon juice to finish. Set aside.

Presentation: Preheat four dinner plates. Pour equal amounts of sauce on each plate. Place the fillet in the center of each plate and serve immediately. This dish may be served with lemon grass steamed rice and/or sugar snap peas.

This is a north Indian-style curry with tomatoes and celery in the sauce. Serve the tasty onaga (which is similar to sea bass) with hot basmati rice on the side.

Fresh Kona Oysters with Hawaiian Mignonette

Makes 4 servings

Oysters Mignonette

24 pcs. Kona oysters (shucked without the nerve)*
1/4 cup shallots**
1/3 cup pickled ginger**
1/4 cup seaweed (red ogo)**
1/2 cup rice wine vinegar
1/2 cup mirin
1 Tbs. lemon juice
2 Tbs. cilantro**
salt and white pepper to taste

Method for Mignonette: Mix all chopped ingredients in a mixing bowl and add in liquids and herbs with a whisk. Season to taste and set aside.

Presentation: Chill four dinner plates, and line the bottoms with crushed ice or rock salt. Arrange

* Or, substitute other fresh, high-quality oysters from the Pacific Ocean
** Chop finely

Garnish

whole ogo (seaweed) or parsley for decoration*
crushed ice or rock salt

* Purchase from an Asian grocer or see Resources section; you may substitute dried seaweed if necessary

six oysters per plate, then pour 1 Tbs. of Hawaiian mignonette over each oyster. Garnish with a sprig of ogo or parsley in the center for decor. Serve (chilled) immediately. 🖎

Chef Padovani's oysters mignonette is a light appetizer or lunch entrée with some of the very best flavors of the Pacific Rim, including ginger, ogo, and mirin.

Hawaiian Fresh Fruits with Chocolate Lilikoi Sabayon

Pictured on p.129

Makes 4 servings

Sabayon

1/4 cup sugar
6 egg yolks
1/4 cup lilikoi (passion fruit)*
1/4 cup water
2 oz. Hawaiian Vintage Chocolate, melted**

* See Resources section
** See Resources section; or, substitute Valrhona chocolate

Hawaiian Fresh Fruits

2 papayas*
2 mangoes, peeled and seeded*
12 strawberries**
4 sprigs of fresh mint leaves (optional)

* Select ripe & not overly fibrous fruits
** Wash, remove stems, and slice

Method for Fruit Compote: Peel the papaya, prepare into melon balls, and set aside. Take one half of mango and finely slice lengthwise. Then take one 12" plate and start making the design with the mango into a triangle, leaving the center empty. Next, add the sliced strawberries inside the triangle in one layer. Place the melon balls of papaya in the center (atop the berries). Repeat this for the rest of the plates. ☞

Method for Sabayon: Melt the chocolate in a medium-size bowl over a double boiler. When melted, turn off heat. In a separate bowl, cream the egg yolks and sugar well, but do not beat them. Place the bowl in a hot water bath, taking great care that the bottom of the bowl containing the egg and sugar mixture does not touch the hot bottom of the pan beneath.

Pour the lilikoi and water into the bowl of egg yolks and sugar, stirring continuously. The hot water bath should not come to a boil again but be kept just below the simmering point. Now beat the mixture energetically with a balloon whisk (or with an hand-held electric mixer) until it froths and has doubled in volume. (It should form a ribbon at this point.) Pour chocolate into sabayon and mix together.

Presentation: Serve sabayon with Hawaiian fruit compote. Garnish with sprigs of mint.

If papaya and mangoes are unavailable, you may substitute your favorite fresh fruits, such as bananas, berries, etc. in this wonderful fondue-style dessert.

Maine Lobster on Arugula and Mango Salad, with Brunoise of Vegetable Vinaigrette

Makes 4 servings (appetizer portions)

Lobster
2 Maine lobsters, 1 1/2 lb. each*
1 Tbs. rock salt

* You may substitute other shellfish

Sherry Vinaigrette
1 tsp. dijon mustard
1 Tbs. sherry vinegar
4 Tbs. olive oil
1 screw top jar (optional)
dash of salt and pepper

Arugula & Mango Salad
1 lb. arugula salad (cleaned, washed, and dried)
1 Haden mango (peeled, seeded, julienned)
several sprigs fresh cilantro (garnish)

Vegetable Vinaigrette
2 Tbs. carrot*
2 Tbs. zucchini*
1 Tbs. red pepper, peeled*
1 tsp. shallots**
1 pinch garlic**
1 tsp. cilantro stems
1 Tbs. olive oil
1 oz. white wine vinegar
1 oz. chicken stock
1 oz. red vinegar
white pepper to taste
fine herbs***

* Cut in a brunoise
** Chop finely
*** 1 Tbs. each—chervil, tarragon, parsley, and chives; finely chopped

Method for Vegetable Vinaigrette: Sauté carrots, garlic, shallots, red peppers, and cilantro stems in olive oil. Add zucchini, white wine, and reduce by 1/2. Add chicken stock and reduce by 1/2. Season with salt and pepper, and remove from heat. Sprinkle in the fine herbs and set aside.

Method for Sherry Vinaigrette: In a screw-top jar, combine all ingredients. Cover jar tightly and shake vigorously for 20 seconds.

Method for Lobster: Poach the lobsters in salted boiling water for 8-10 minutes. Remove lobsters from boiling water and let them cool down. Remove heads, peel tails, and break claws to remove meat. Slice each tail into two lengthwise pieces and slice diagonally into six pieces each. Set aside.

Presentation: Chill four dinner plates. In a large bowl, toss arugula, and sherry vinaigrette together; season to taste. Place salad in equal amounts in the center of each plate. Fan the julienne of mango on top of the salad and arrange lobster slices, with the knuckle and claw around the edge of plate. To finish, sprinkle the vegetable vinaigrette over the lobster.

*Desserts are heavenly
at Stein Eriksen Lodge*

The Heathman Hotel

Next to Portland's Performing Arts Center,
The Heathman Hotel earns its own standing ovation

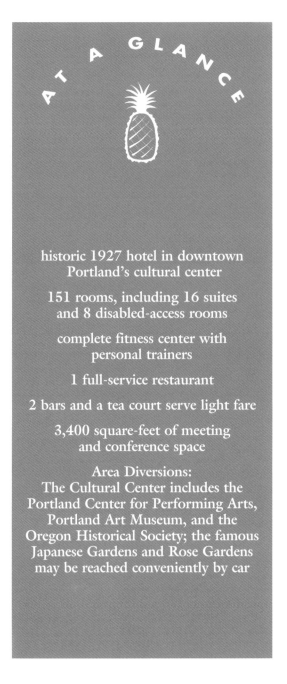

THE HEATHMAN Hotel is dedicated to the arts—not only the arts of gracious hospitality and world-class cuisine, but also to music, painting, and theater. The Heathman, which opened in 1927 and was completely redesigned in 1984, is bound by bricks and mortar to Portland's Center for Performing Arts, and is steps away from Oregon's art museums and cultural centers. In fact, concert-goers visit the Hotel's mezzanine for refreshments during intermissions, and many guests have a view of the concert hall lobby's large (55' x 86') Heathman-commissioned mural. Without a doubt, many artists and performers choose The Heathman for their stays in Portland.

Weekend package deals at The Heathman Hotel are designed for romance— some include horse-drawn carriage rides through the city, breakfast in bed, and elegant dinners for two. And, through their "Support the Arts Even in Your Sleep^{SM}" program, the Hotel's managers donate a percentage of all package rates to Portland's art scene.

The art theme is prominent throughout The Heathman Hotel's public and private areas: rotating exhibits from local galleries grace the mezzanine, and each guest room has an original work of contemporary art. But The Heathman's most outstanding feature is its dedicated staff, who bring the fine art of pleasing guests to its highest level. Whether it's adding an on-call list of experienced personal trainers to the Hotel's fitness center, or encouraging a talented young chef to combine his Paris training with Oregon's own culinary traditions, The Heathman brings excellence to every guest's stay. ❧

Salishan Lodge

Unspoiled northwest scenery and haute cuisine are standard fare at this peaceful, romantic retreat

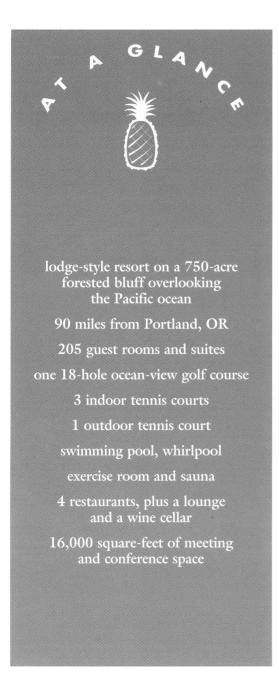

AT A GLANCE

lodge-style resort on a 750-acre forested bluff overlooking the Pacific ocean

90 miles from Portland, OR

205 guest rooms and suites

one 18-hole ocean-view golf course

3 indoor tennis courts

1 outdoor tennis court

swimming pool, whirlpool

exercise room and sauna

4 restaurants, plus a lounge and a wine cellar

16,000 square-feet of meeting and conference space

SALISHAN LODGE, perched above the breathtaking Oregon coastline, provides upscale lodging that enables guests to commune with nature while enjoying the finest foods and wines the region has to offer. But Salishan is really more of a resort than a lodge. It has an 18-hole golf course, four restaurants, indoor tennis, swimming pool, and a fitness facility. Nature buffs enjoy the lodge's tangled network of jogging and hiking trails that connect Salishan to the forest and the sea. Nestled along the Salishan Peninsula, there are three miles of secluded beaches to explore, using a botanical guide and trail map provided by the lodge.

Named after the northwest Indians who occupied the region 3,000 years ago, the Salishan Lodge itself is constructed of wood and stone in an informal Japanese style, with walkways and bridges connecting the guest rooms to the main lodge. Many guest rooms are appointed with stone fireplaces and impressive views from wide windows. The accommodations are conducive to settling in near a crackling fire with a glass of the region's Pinot Noir or a hearty Cabernet. In fact, the Lodge has its own resident sommelier, Phil DeVito, who assists guests in choosing a wine from Salishan's vast cellar of more than 875 selections.

Salishan Lodge's kitchen staff is led by executive chef Robert Pounding, who creates inventive foods that reflect the property's bucolic setting. He explains, "Many of our dishes have subtle Oriental overtones, which symbolize the serenity and traditional spirit of the Lodge."

Highway 101 ᦦ Gleneden Beach, Oregon 97388 ᦦ (800)452-2300 or (503)764-3600

Stein Eriksen Lodge

A luxurious, alpine-style ski resort offers year-round recreation and international dining

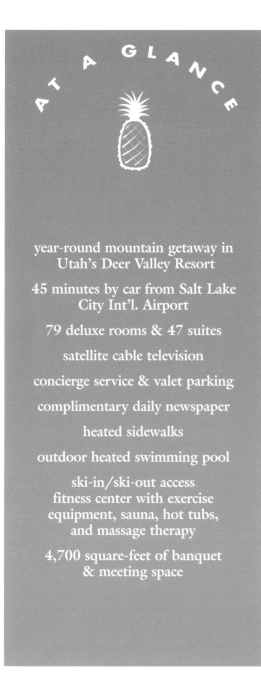

TO FIND the ultimate ski-season getaway, just ask Olympic skier Stein Eriksen. He will gladly recommend his namesake, the Stein Eriksen Lodge, nestled into the side of Bald Mountain at an 8,200' elevation in the Silver Lake area of Deer Valley, Utah. A 1952 Olympic Gold Medalist, Eriksen lent his expertise to this remarkable property, which is fashioned after some of the lovely rustic lodges scattered throughout Eriksen's homeland, Norway.

Since it opened 14 years ago, the Lodge has earned numerous accolades, including being honored as one of the top resorts in the world.

Rooms at the Lodge feature many comforts to return to after a day spent on the slopes—Scandinavian comporters, soft terry robes, and large bathrooms with whirlpool tubs. The suites give travelers even more luxury: large stone fireplaces, spacious living areas, fully-equipped kitchens appointed with hand-painted tiles, and balconies with window seats. The heated outdoor pool may be enjoyed year-round, and is surrounded by spectacular mountain scenery. A fully-equipped fitness room provides guests with a place to get a workout, or to rest in a whirlpool tub after a day spent on the slopes.

During the spring and summer seasons, the mountains are covered with wildflowers, and families can explore the area's many trails and mountain bike routes. The summer season is also when the Lodge offers special packages designed for romance and pleasure-filled days. ✍

Philippe Boulot

THE HEATHMAN HOTEL

The Heathman Hotel's executive chef, Philippe Boulot, is a rising star who believes in "freshness, flavor, and truthful presentations on every plate." Boulot's culinary roots go back to his family farm in Normandy, France, where he helped his grandmother make butter and cheese, and prepare meals with harvest from the garden. As a young apprentice to Parisian chefs Joel Robuchon and Alain Senderens in their well-known restaurants (including Maxim's), and by training at the Jean Drouant Hotel School, Boulot gained experience in creating world-class cuisine. He has since worked at some of the world's finest hotels in Paris, London, San Francisco, New York, and now in Oregon.

Today, chef Boulot's culinary style draws upon his international training—to prepare foods that are refined, yet unpretentious and light-hearted.

Foie Gras Napoleon with Oregon Truffle Whipped Potatoes Balsamic Glaze, and Parsley Essence

Makes 4 servings (appetizer portions)

Foie Gras & Whipped Potatoes

1 lb. foie gras
3 Idaho potatoes*
1/2 cup half and half
1/2 cup butter, softened
4 oz. truffles, minced
salt and pepper to taste

* Peel and cut into large 2" pieces

Potato Galettes & Balsamic Glaze

2 Idaho potatoes, peeled
clarified butter
salt and pepper
1 cup balsamic vinegar
1 Tbs. corn starch

Parsley Essence

1 bunch parsley*
olive oil
salt and pepper

* Use leaves and small stems only

This is a Heathman signature appetizer; a rich indulgence worth every calorie.

Ingredient Footnote

The truffled potato purée should still have some body.

Method for Truffled Potatoes: Cover the potatoes with water and boil until soft, but not mushy. Strain and run through a food mill while still hot. Heat the cream to boiling over a high burner, and whip into cooked potatoes along with soft butter and truffles. Season to taste with salt and pepper.

Method for Potato Galettes and Glaze: Julienne the potatoes to match stick size using a hand grater or mandolin. Toss in a bowl with clarified butter, salt, and pepper. On a sheet tray lined with parchment paper, press the potatoes to form a flat, cohesive circle of about 3" in diameter. (They should resemble little round pancakes.) Bake until golden brown. Seal tight and hold at room temperature until needed.

For glaze, reduce the vinegar in a saucepan by 1/3 on a medium burner. Thicken slightly with a slurry of cornstarch dissolved in water.

Method for Parsley Essence & Foie Gras: In a blender or food processor, mix the parsley leaves with enough oil to create a purée; season to taste. Slice foie gras into 3/4" medallions. Season well with salt and freshly ground black pepper. Grill to medium-rare on the cooler portion of the grill.

Presentation: Using squirt bottles, make a criss-cross pattern of the balsamic glaze and parsley essence on the serving plate. In the center, place a heaping tablespoon of the whipped potatoes followed by a potato galette, pressed gently into the purée. Continue with another spoon of potatoes, one foie gras, and a galette. Repeat the process once again.

Roasted Red King Salmon with Pesto Crust, Napoleon of Wilted Spinach with Oven-Dried Tomatoes, and Red Onion Relish

Pictured on p.200

Makes 8 servings

(8) 7 oz. salmon fillets

Wilted Spinach

3 lbs. spinach
1 shallot, chopped
1/4 cup olive oil

Pesto Crust

1/2 cup fresh basil
1/2 cup white bread crumbs
1/4 cup pine nuts
1/4 cup parmesan, grated
2 cloves garlic
1/4 cup bacon, ground
1/4 cup olive oil

Red Onion Relish

1/4 cup olive oil
3 red onions, diced
1/2 cup lemon juice
1 tsp. ginger*
1 tsp. garlic*
2 tsp. red chile garlic paste
2 tsp. capers
2 Tbs. soy sauce
1 tsp. scallions, thinly sliced
1 tsp. parsley**
1 tsp. cilantro**

* Mince
** Chop

Method for Spinach and for Pesto Crust: Heat olive oil in pan. Add shallots and shake for one minute. Next, toss in the fresh spinach and season with salt and pepper.

For the pesto crust, combine all ingredients except the olive oil in a food processor. Slowly add oil to the mix while processor is on. Add salt and pepper to taste.

Method for Relish: Sweat red onions in olive oil over medium heat. Add garlic and ginger, cooking briefly. Deglaze the pan with lemon juice, cooking until most of the moisture has evaporated. Add the remaining ingredients, adjust seasonings, then immediately pour out onto a sheet tray and chill. (Note: The color should be bright red.)

Finish & Presentation: Press pesto crust onto salmon fillets, making the crust about 1/8" thick. Sear the fish, crust-side down in a dry non-stick frying pan. Turn the fillets and finish cooking in an oven heated to 350°.

Build the napoleon using 1 Tbs. spinach first, then a tomato slice (lightly pressing it down). Place another Tbs. spinach on and continue the process, until you have three layers of each. Spoon red onion relish onto each serving plate, and then place salmon atop the relish.

Chef's Secret

MAKE YOUR OWN GOURMET DRIED TOMATOES

4 Beefsteak tomatoes
1 tsp. coriander
1 tsp. cumin
1 tsp. black pepper
1 tsp. salt
1 tsp. garlic
1/4 cup extra-virgin olive oil

Preheat oven to 200°. Combine spices, salt, and pepper in a bowl. Slice tomatoes 1/4" thick, and place them on an olive oil-coated, parchment-lined sheet tray. Brush tomatoes with olive oil and sprinkle spice mixture evenly over tomato slices. Dry tomatoes in the oven (process should take 2-3 hours). Slices may be stored on paper towels in an air-tight container. Place the container outside in a cool place.

> A Northwestern favorite—king salmon with a bold, crunchy pesto crust. Make this entrée in the summer, when fresh basil is plentiful.

About this Dish

The oven-dried tomatoes, pesto crust, and red onion relish can be made in advance and stored accordingly.

Wild Mushroom Cannelloni

Makes 8 servings

3 lbs. high-quality wild mushrooms*
1/2 cup shallots, chopped
2 tsp. tarragon, chopped
2 tsp. basil
2 tsp. parsley
1 cup goat cheese, softened
30 won ton wrappers
2 lbs. arugula, washed and picked
2 cups chicken jus (reduced stock)
1 cup parmesan, grated
1/2 cup butter

* **Chanterelles, morels, or boletus varieties work well**

Method for Cannelloni: Sweat shallots and mushrooms in pan over moderate heat until all liquid is absorbed. Add herbs, salt, and freshly ground pepper to taste; allow to cool. Pulse the mixture in a food processor, leaving coarse. Blend in the goat cheese.

Blanch the won ton wrappers by plunging them into boiling water, and then into ice water. Lay the wrappers flat on a damp towel and then place mushroom mixture on the lower third. Roll up wrappers into cylinders, tucking in the ends. Sprinkle each with parmesan and dabs of butter. Bake on a cookie sheet in a 350° oven for 5-7 minutes. Serve on top of the arugula (which will wilt a bit from the warm cannelloni) with chicken jus.

Baked Stuffed Mini Pumpkins

Makes 8 servings

Pumpkins & Spiced Crisp

8 miniature pumpkins
3/4 cup brown sugar
3/4 cup white sugar
1 1/2 Tbs. cinnamon
1 Tbs. nutmeg
dash (1/8 oz.) cardamon
1 7/8 cup flour
1 lb. + 4 oz. butter, softened
1 cup oats

Filling

5-6 apples*
5-6 pears*
1/8 cup corn starch
3/4 cup brown sugar
6 oz. melted butter

* Chef Boulot uses sparta apples and bartlett or bosc pears; peel, seed, and chop the fruit

Method for the Topping: Using a mixer with paddle attachment, mix the first 6 ingredients until well combined. With mixer running, add softened butter a little at a time until incorporated. Add oats and mix until just combined. Topping may be stored in refrigerator; simply bring it to room-temperature before using.

Method for Filling: Toss the pears and apples with the corn starch, brown sugar, and butter until well-coated. Place in a 9"x13" baking dish, and cover top of fruit completely with the crisp topping. Bake in a 375° oven until well-browned (about 1 1/2 hours); then cool completely.

Cooking & Presentation: Wash pumpkins with cold water to remove any dirt. Bake the pumpkins in a 400° oven for approximately 20 minutes, or until about 2/3 done. When cool, cut off top around stem*, saving the lid, and scoop seeds out, leaving the pumpkin meat intact.

Using a spoon, cut the crisp into circles small enough to fit inside the pumpkins, making sure the topping stays on top. Just before serving, reheat in a 375° oven for approximately 15-20 minutes, or until heated through. Serve with vanilla ice cream.

This dessert makes a grand finale to a hearty autumn meal. An apple-pear crisp is placed into the baked mini pumpkins, making a beautiful presentation on the dinner table.

Author's Note

*The larger the lid, the easier it is to fit crisp in without breaking it.

Rob Pounding

SALISHAN LODGE

Salishan's executive chef, Robert (Rob) Pounding, is a former New Yorker who trained at the Culinary Institute of America (CIA). Today, Pounding transforms the Lodge's laid-back attitude into a culinary powerhouse with his innovative use of native northwestern ingredients. Local fisherman catch fish, mussels, and oysters to the chef's specifications, and a local gardener grows fresh produce especially for Pounding and his meticulous staff.

A barbecue with chef Pounding is an event you won't forget. During the holiday season, he often prepares whole Albacore tuna outdoors on a smoking alder plank and serves it with a savory oyster bread pudding. As the flames rise up inside the planks, the tuna becomes seared and smoked in a campfire culinary extravaganza. It is imaginative tricks like this that earn Pounding and Salishan much attention from food critics across the nation.

Grilled Hot Smoked Sablefish with Rustic Bread Salad

Makes 8 servings (appetizer portions)

1 side hard smoked sablefish (divide into 4 oz. portions)
1 loaf Tuscan wheat bread, cubed
2 cups wild foraged mushrooms*
2 lemons, zested and juiced
1 1/2 cups extra-virgin olive oil
1 tsp. garlic, minced
1 bunch chives**
1 small bunch of arugula
salt and freshly cracked black pepper to taste

* Chanterelle, hedgehog, cauliflower, lobster, or oyster mushrooms
** Snip into 1" lengths

Method for Sablefish: Using a barbecue grill or smoker, smoke the sablefish to desired doneness. Next, grill the fish approximately 2-3 minutes skin-side down, or you may put them skin-side up under a broiler.

Heat olive oil until medium-hot, and add garlic and mushrooms. Cook for one minute and add to cubed bread. Toss together with lemon zest, juice, and chives. Season and refrigerate until needed.

Presentation: Toss the arugula leaves with the room-temperature bread salad. Arrange on plates beside the smoked sablefish, garnish with more chives, and serve imediately. ⟆

Fresh Albacore Tuna Roasted on a Smoking Alder Plank

Makes 6 servings

1 boneless centercut albacore tuna loin (1.5-2 lb.)
3 oz. prosciutto, sliced very thin
3 leaves fresh sage
1/2 tsp. fresh thyme
1/2 tsp. fresh marjoram
1/2 tsp. black pepper
1 tsp. kosher salt
2 Tbs. extra-virgin olive oil
2 Tbs. shallots, chopped
4 oz. Pinot Gris wine

6 oz. rich chicken or fish broth
1 alder plank 1/2"x8"x16" *
6 cups marinated vegetables**
1 cup fall mushrooms (chanterelle, lobster, etc.)
4 Yukon gold potatoes, blanched

* Or you may use another hardwood, such as birch, cedar, or aspen
** Eggplant, squash, sweet pepper, & onion ☞

Method for Vegetables: Marinate vegetables (eggplant, squash, sweet pepper, and onion) in a basic vinaigrette of 3 parts olive oil and 1 part vinegar, seasoned with chopped fresh marjoram, thyme, garlic, salt, and black pepper, for 2 hours.

Method for Tuna: Heat oven to 500°. Season tuna loin with kosher salt, black pepper, chopped herbs and whole sage leaves, and wrap all in prosciutto. Tie the tuna roast with twine, and rub lightly with olive oil. When the plank begins to give off a smoky aroma, place the vegetables and tuna directly on the surface and roast at high heat until medium (should take 10-15 minutes).

While the fish and vegetables are in the oven, prepare the sauce by sautéing shallots in olive oil until caramelized; add the mushrooms and cook briefly. Add the wine and continue cooking to reduce the mixture by 1/2. Then add the stock, herbs to taste, and reduce slightly.

Presentation: When the tuna is done, let it rest for 5 minutes, then slice and serve family-style with the vegetables and a savory oyster bread pudding, plus the mushroom sauce.

This is an interesting northwestern substitute for the traditional holiday meal—different, but still full of comfortable, traditional warm flavors associated with Thanksgiving and Christmas.

Pacific Abalone with Flowering Asian Greens, Grilled Jasmine Rice Cakes, and Thai Lemon Grass Aioli

Makes 8 servings

16 abalone steaks*
2 pounds choi sum or baby bok choy greens
1 tsp. bottled Chinese oyster sauce
2 cups egg batter (made with underbeaten raw eggs)
seasoned flour
2 Tbs. clarified butter (for grilling)

* 1 1/2 oz. each; sliced thin and pounded

Thai Lemon Grass Aioli

homemade aioli (see recipe)
1/3 cup white onion, chopped fine
2 Tbs. cilantro stems*
2 Tbs. lemon grass*
1 Tbs. tumeric
1 Tbs. ginger root*

1 Tbs. cumin
1 Tbs. garlic*
1/2 tsp. red pepper, crushed
1/4 cup water

* Mince

Rice Cakes and Sauce

4 cups jasmine rice
8 cups water
4 oz. aji mirin rice wine
1 bunch spring onions, chopped
2 cups Oregon Riesling wine
1 cup rice wine
1 cup fish jus (see recipe)
1/2 cup lime juice
1 cup whole butter

Method for Abalone & Greens: Steam greens until stalks are tender and season with oyster sauce. Dredge abalone in flour, dip in egg batter, and sauté quickly in the heated butter.

Method for Thai Aioli: Blend all remaining ingredients (in the second section) together in food processor until fairly smooth. Add this mixture to the fresh aioli, and blend all to a creamy consistency.

Method for Rice Cakes: Bring water, rice, and rice wine to boil. Reduce heat to simmer and cook until liquid is gone. Remove from heat. Fold in chopped green onions, and spread rice mixture evenly onto buttered half sheet pan. Cover and refrigerate for approximately 2 hours. Cut into triangles and sauté in a non-stick pan heated with 1-2 Tbs. of butter until crisp.

Reduce Riesling and rice wine over medium heat to one cup. Add fish jus and lime juice. Finish by blending in whole butter. ☞

Presentation: Place abalone on the remaining butter sauce and place lean crisp rice cakes on greens. Paint each plate with Thai lemon grass aioli.

Homemade Aioli

2 cloves of garlic, mashed
3 egg yolks
1 cup extra-virgin olive oil
1 Tbs. boiling water
2 Tbs. lemon juice

Blend garlic, egg yolks, and water in a food processor. With the processor running, pour in oil to a desirable thickness. Add a little salt if needed. When the mixture is thick, add 1 Tbs. of the lemon juice, then more oil, and then the remaining lemon juice. Blend thoroughly once more.

The Salishan's Pacific abalone combines some very exciting Asian tastes and textures.

How to Make Fish Jus

1/2-3/4 lb. fresh halibut, whole
1 whole onion*
2 carrots*
salt and pepper to taste

* Peel and cut into small pieces

Add the above ingredients to 1 qt. of water in a stock pot. Bring to a boil, and then reduce to a simmer until you have a nicely flavored broth. You may remove the fish and vegetables before using this as a stock, if you prefer. Freeze or refrigerate the remaining fish jus for later use.

Natural Oregon Calves' Liver with Sweet Onions, Roasted Hood River Apples, and a Smoky Porter Wine Sauce

Makes 4 servings

Calves' Liver & Porter Sauce

(12) 2 oz. calves' liver medallions
24 wedges of red apple (4 large apples)*
16 oz. Portland Porter wine
4 tsp. pancetta, cooked
4 Tbs. tomatoes**
12 oz. veal jus (demi glace)
2-3 Tbs. olive oil

* Peel, core, and cut into wedges
** Cut in a brunoise

Onion Confit

1 medium white onion, julienned
1 medium red onion, julienned
1 tsp. shallots, chopped
1 tsp. garlic, chopped
1 Tbs. olive oil
2 oz. Madeira
6 oz. veal demi glace (see recipe)

Shoestring Potatoes

1 lb. Russet potatoes
seasoning salt to taste
oil for frying

Method for Liver: Lightly dredge the liver medallions in flour lightly seasoned with salt and pepper, and sear in olive oil along with the seasoned apple wedges. Transfer to pie tin and hold in a 350° oven. Sauté tomatoes and deglaze with porter, reducing the liquid as it simmers slowly. Add the veal stock and reduce once again. Finish with a pinch of fresh parsley.

Method for Confit: Sauté onions, garlic, and shallots slowly in olive oil until translucent. Deglaze with Madeira. Add veal stock and reduce until thick. Store in refrigerator until needed. Later, heat an 8 oz. portion to serve with veal medallions.

Method for Potatoes: Peel whole potatoes julienne-style on a mandolin and hold in water until needed. When your main course is ready, fry potatoes in 375° oil until crispy.

Presentation: Drizzle porter lager sauce all around the rims of each plate and place apple wedges around. Lay one liver medallion in center and place 1 oz. of onion confit on top, then another medallion, more confit, and the third medallion. Top with shoestring potatoes.

Chef's Secret

HOW TO MAKE VEAL DEMI GLACE
Simmer veal bones and trimmings with some typical broth vegetables such as carrots, onions, and celery in 1 qt. of water to make a hearty stock that can serve as the basis for various other soups and sauces.

Mikel Trapp

STEIN ERIKSEN LODGE

Stein Eriksen's guests come out of the cold and into the warmth of the Glitretind Restaurant, where executive chef Mikel Trapp offers a myriad of dining options for breakfast, lunch, and dinner. Known for American contemporary cuisine blended with European flair, the Glitretind offers a Skiers' Buffet at lunch time and an elegant dinner menu. Its Sunday Brunch, made festive with live jazz, was voted one of the best in the nation by the Zagat Survey.

Though he received no formal training in the culinary arts, Trapp worked his way up the ranks in the kitchens of resorts and hotels throughout the United States. He has been a chef for 11 years. Chef Trapp's basic philosophy is to "utilize the finest ingredients available, and to craft them into simple, but memorable preparations."

Curried Coconut and Squash Soup with Roasted Corn and Lobster Fritters

Makes 6 servings

Curried Soup

2 lbs. butternut squash
1 medium onion
1 cup sweet corn, cooked
1 carrot
1 cup (8 oz.) coconut milk
24 oz. chicken stock
2 Tbs. curry powder
salt and white pepper to taste

Roasted Corn and Lobster Fritters

1/4 cup all-purpose flour
1/4 tsp. baking soda
1/4 tsp. baking powder
1/4 cup (2 oz.) buttermilk
1 egg yolk
1 egg white
salt and white pepper to taste
3 oz. roasted corn*
3 oz. lobster**
minced chives (optional garnish)
crème fraîche (optional garnish)

* Roast whole cobs in the oven or on a grill, and then cut kernels off
** Steam and cut in a small dice

An autumn soup goes "Caribbean" with the addition of curry and coconut milk. The lobster fritters add an imaginative garnish!

Method for Soup: Preheat oven to 375°. Cut squash in half lengthwise and discard seeds. Cut onions in half. Toss carrots and onions lightly in the salad oil, salt, and pepper. Place on a baking pan and roast in the oven for approximately 20 minutes. Repeat this procedure with the squash and roast for 25-30 minutes.

Scrape the outer skin from carrots and onions and cut into a small dice. Pour 1 Tbs. of salad oil into an 8-qt. pot, and add the carrots, onions, curry powder, salt, and pepper. Sauté the vegetables for 2 minutes over medium heat. Next, add in the chicken stock and coconut milk.

Scoop the flesh from the squash and add it to soup; cook for 10 minutes. Purée the soup and adjust seasonings to taste. Add the cooked sweet corn.

Method for Fritters: Sift flour, baking soda, and baking powder into a mixing bowl. Add egg yolk and buttermilk; mix well. In a separate bowl, beat egg white until stiff peaks form. Fold the egg white into base mixture.

Toss corn and lobster together. Add enough batter to hold ingredients together. Next, pan-fry the fritters (using 1 Tbs. of batter for each) in hot oil or butter.

Presentation: Ladle soup into bowls and top each with a fritter. Garnish each serving with minced chives and crème fraîche (optional).

Potato Lasagna

Pictured on p.128

Makes 6 servings

Lasagna

3 Idaho russet potatoes, peeled
1 Tbs. chives, chopped
8 oz. shiitake mushrooms, sliced*
8 oz. oyster mushrooms*
8 oz. crimini mushrooms*
3 egg whites**
oil or butter for sautéing
salt and pepper to taste

* Wash and pat dry
** Lightly whip

Nage

1 lb. leeks**
1 lb. celery**
1 lb. onions, peeled**
16 oz. Chablis

** Wash and cut in a medium dice

Optional Garnishes

tomato concasse (blanch, peel, seed, and dice tomatoes)
chives, minced

Method for Nage (Sauce): Steam or boil potatoes for approximately 12 minutes; then allow to cool. Add leeks, celery, and onions to stock pot and sauté until translucent; add wine and reduce by 1/2. Next, add enough water to cover vegetables and reduce again by 1/2. Strain the mixture and reserve. Add 4 oz. of nage to a sauté pan and bring to a boil. Remove pan from heat and swirl in 2 Tbs. of butter until emulsified.

Method for Potato Pancakes & Mushrooms: Grate potatoes and toss with egg whites, 1 Tbs. of chopped chives, salt, and pepper. Form the mixture into 2" round pancakes and pan-sear until crisp on both sides. Keep warm until needed. Sauté mushrooms in oil or butter, and season with salt and pepper; keep warm until needed.

Presentation: Place 1 pancake in the center of each serving plate. Top the pancake with 3-4 oz. of the sautéed mushrooms, and place another pancake on top. Drizzle sauce around plate and garnish with tomato concasse and minced chives.

> Gourmet mushroom lovers will enjoy this unusual lasagna.
> The real surprise is that it contains no pasta.

Mixed Berry Crème Brulée

Makes 6 servings

1 qt. (32 oz.) heavy cream
1 vanilla bean, split
3/4 cup sugar
10 large egg yolks
1 pint mixed berries*

* Raspberries, blackberries, and blueberries work well

Method for Brulée: Bring cream and split vanilla bean to a scald. Turn off heat. In a mixing bowl, whisk egg yolks and sugar until pale in color, and sugar is dissolved. Temper cream mixture slowly into the yolks, and then strain mixture through a fine china chinois into a container.

Place (6) 8 oz. soufflé bowls into a 2" deep baking pan. Fill each bowl with 5-6 assorted berries; then pour cream mixture over the berries, filling bowls about 2/3 full. Fill baking pan with hot water halfway up the soufflé bowls. Cover the entire baking pan with foil and poke holes around the edges.

Bake in a 325° oven for approximately 60 minutes, while rotating pan every 20 minutes to ensure even baking. Sprinkle tops with brown sugar and brown briefly under the broiler to caramelize.

Presentation: Place the mini soufflé cups onto serving plates and garnish with a few fresh berries, if desired.

chapter 5
The East & New England

The Cities

Four Seasons Hotel Chicago

The Ritz-Carlton, New York

Four Seasons Hotel, Philadelphia

The Getaways

The Point

The Balsams Grand Resort Hotel

Wheatleigh Hotel

The East &

The major cities along the Eastern Seaboard attract some of the best chefs in the nation: New York, Philadelphia, and Chicago are just a few of the top picks for luxurious hotels and for award-winning cuisine. Many of these hotels are patterned after the fine Old World hotels of Europe, with round-the-clock concierge services, elegant lobbies filled with masterful oil paintings, antique furnishings, and fresh flowers. Add on contemporary amenities, such as state-of-the art health spas and modern business services, and travelers have the best of both worlds.

At the heart of the Windy City, chef Mark Baker pays homage to his New England roots by adding a creamy Nantucket Stew of Lobster and Early Summer Corn to the Four Seasons Hotel Chicago's menu in Seasons Restaurant. At the Ritz-Carlton, New York, executive chef Craig Henne creates magic in the kitchen with winning combinations of ingredients, and Mediterranean-inspired sauces that are high in flavor and low in fat. The tour of cities winds up at the elegant Four Seasons Hotel in Philadelphia, where executive chef Jean-Marie Lacroix delights guests with Mango Soup, and with Lobster Wrapped in Crispy Potatoes with Caviar Sauce.

Many New Yorkers find respite from the pressures of the city by spending a weekend at The Point, an idyllic retreat on a

New England

wooded peninsula on Upper Saranac Lake, New York. The Point provides the best scenery of the Adirondacks, along with award-winning meals served fireside in the lodge. Chef Sam Mahoney applies his knowledge of international cuisine to the classic foods offered at The Point: Poussin with Sweet Corn Fritters and Wild Mushrooms, and the Risotto with Herbs and White Truffle Oil are just a couple of the resort's standout selections.

The Balsams Grand Resort Hotel resembles a Vistorian castle nestled into the woods in New Hampshire's White Mountains. Man-made Lake Gloriette and the mountains surrounding the Resort provide plenty of scenery and year-round recreation. At the helm of the Balsams' culinary staff is executive chef Charles Carroll, who creates updated Yankee classics, such as: Baked Haddock with Finnan Haddie, Molasses-Marinated Scallops, and Asparagus Spears; and New England Bread Pudding.

The third "getaway" is Wheatleigh Hotel, a chateaux-style property in Lenox, Massachusetts, at the gateway to the Berkshire Mountains. The finest accommodations of this summer resort area may be found at Wheatleigh, which backs up to the music festival at Tanglewood. Lesley Iacobacci, the Wheatleigh's pastry chef offers some of her favorite recipes in this section—luscious, decadent desserts that are grand finalés to any meal. ❦

Four Seasons Hotel Chicago

The city's only Mobil Five Star, AAA Five Diamond Hotel

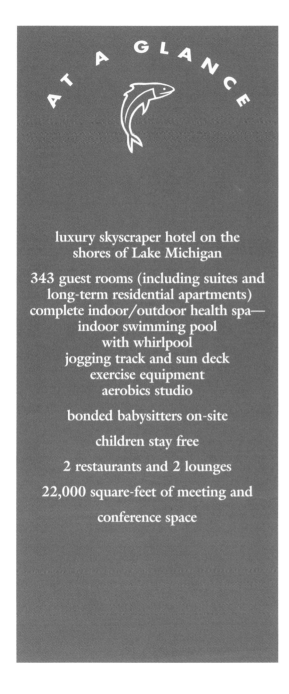

THE BEST way to see Chicago is from the large windows of a towering skyscraper on North Michigan Avenue, at the heart of the city's "magnificent mile." Your unique vantage point happens to be from the Four Seasons Hotel Chicago, an outstanding property with panoramic views of downtown Chicago and of Lake Michigan. Every rooms has a vista, because the Hotel occupies the 30th through 46th floors of 900 North Michigan, a 66-story, 2.7 million-square-foot building that opened in 1989.

Four Seasons Chicago only comes down to earth for its gleaming street-level entrance at 120 East Delaware Place. Everything else about this property flies high, including its facilities, guest services, and thoughtful amenities. It reaches the heights, too, in the impressive list of awards bestowed—a rare success for a Hotel that has been open for less than one decade. In addition to the coveted Five Stars and Five Diamond Awards, the Four Seasons Hotel Chicago was named best hotel in Chicago, and second best in the nation by the 2,600 executives who responded to *Andrew Harper's Hideaway Report's* 14th Annual Reader Poll.

Among its special facilities, the Hotel counts a state-of-the art Business Center with a multi-lingual staff and flexible meeting space. There is also a complete fitness facility with an indoor swimming pool and attached whirlpool, plus saunas, massage and steam rooms. The fitness center has top-of-the-line exercise equipment. An outdoor jogging track enables joggers to take in another glimpse of the Chicago horizon and the city sprawled out below.

120 East Delaware Place ✺ *Chicago, Illinois 60611* ✺ *(312)280-8800*

The Ritz-Carlton, New York

A private oasis that looks out onto Central Park

GUESTS AT New York's elegant Ritz-Carlton in Central Park often feel like they are staying somewhere else, like at a private residence or at their own personal oasis within the Big Apple. As travel writer Linda Packer said in *The New York Times*, "It is nearly impossible to describe the sensation of walking into a hotel in the midst of the most chaotic city in the world, and feeling not just a sense of calm, but welcome."

The building did, in fact, originate as a private home on a grand scale: years ago, it was the residence of a Spanish Consul General. In 1982, it became The Ritz-Carlton, New York. After a multi-million dollar refurbishment in 1993, The Ritz-Carlton received the American Automobile Association's (AAA) coveted Five Diamond award in 1994. Today's guest rooms boast such amenities as two telephones, each with two lines; Italian marble bathrooms, also with telephone; a fully stocked honor bar, plush terry robes, lots of pillows—and, in many cases, a marvelous view of Central Park.

Among the special amenities extended to guests are the Fitness Center with panoramic windows overlooking Central Park; meeting and banquet space that can accommodate anything from a small dinner party for 10 people to a cocktail reception for 200 guests; and a multi-lingual concierge staff known to solve all kinds of problems.

And each weekday morning, guests are treated to a courtesy limousine ride to Wall Street.

112 Central Park South ❧ New York, NY 10019 ❧ (212)757-1900

Four Seasons Hotel, Philadelphia

A grand city hotel with museum-replica furnishings

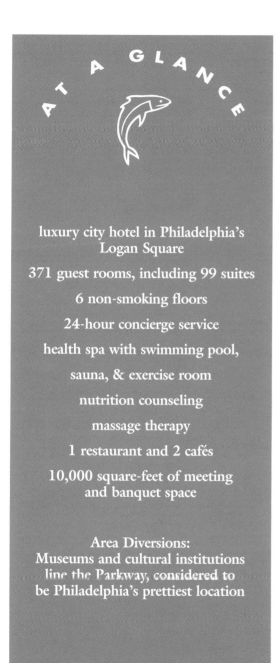

ONE OF Philadelphia's loveliest locations is Benjamin Franklin Parkway, a tree-lined boulevard reminiscent of Paris. Many of the city's museums and cultural institutions line the Parkway, which is also graced by colorful flags, illuminated fountains, and statues. Look again and you will notice the elegant, columned facade of the Four Seasons Hotel, Philadelphia—a Five Diamond winner.

The Hotel's ambience reflects the Federal Period in United States history (1785-1825), when Philadelphia was the center of intellectual and artistic activity. The furniture and decor of this period were beautifully designed, and the pieces created in Philadelphia had a particular flair. The Four Seasons Hotel has specially commissioned furnishings inspired by the collection at the Philadelphia Museum of Art. Interior design in the guest rooms takes its cue from the Federal Period's fabrics of uniform color, while the lobby level has rose-tinted marble, rich blond woods, and fresh flowers.

To these reminders of a gracious past, the Hotel adds contemporary luxury. Among the most popular amenities are the 24-hour concierge service and the fully-equipped health spa. And there are the splendid dining spots: the Fountain Restaurant, named for the Swann Fountain just outside in Logan Square; the Swann Lounge and Café, a sophisticated gathering place for cocktails and for after-theatre drinks; and the Courtyard Café, which offers garden dining in season. ✤

1 Logan Square ✤ Philadelphia, Pennsylvania 19103 ✤ (215)963-1500

Mark Baker

FOUR SEASONS HOTEL, CHICAGO

Nestled inside the Hotel, Seasons Restaurant wins its share of awards, including recent recognition from Condé Nast Traveler *as the third best restaurant in Chicago, rising above many of the city's all-time favorites.*

Executive chef Mark Baker leads a staff of 50 in the creation of inspired contemporary American cuisine, which includes special low-calorie, low-cholesterol dishes for guests who prefer light dining. Chef Baker's light selections include Ravioli of Grilled Garden Vegetables with Fresh Tomato Coulis, and Chilled Golden Gazpacho with Drizzle of Cilantro Cream, which uses only top-quality, farm-fresh ingredients. Baker changes the menu four times a year, in keeping with the Restaurant's seasonal theme. "But in every season, the dishes follow my belief that cooking today should be natural, with emphasis on flavors, textures, and freshness," he explains.

Chilled Golden Gazpacho with Drizzle of Cilantro Cream

Makes 8 servings

2 golden bell peppers
2 yellow tomatoes
1 zucchini
2 carrots
1 red onion
1 cucumber, seeded
1/2 bunch fresh cilantro
1/2 bunch Italian parsley
2 whole jalapeño peppers
salt and pepper to taste
4 oz. sherry wine vinegar

Cilantro Cream (optional garnish)
2 Tbs. crème fraîche
1 Tbs. cilantro purée*
1 Tbs. olive oil

Dried Cucumber Rings
(optional garnish)

Remove hard skins from cucumbers and slice lengthwise 1/8" thick; allow to dry in a food dehydrator

Chef's Secret

HOW TO MAKE A CILANTRO PURÉE
* Made by blending 1/2 bunch of fresh, clean cilantro with a drizzle of olive oil in a food processor; add a touch of garlic and season to taste with salt and pepper.

Method for Gazpacho: Prepare vegetables by cleaning, washing, and seeding them. Cut them into quarters or manageable pieces for grinding. Assemble all ingredients and grind through a medium-fine plate grinder attachment in a grinder or a food processor. Adjust seasonings and flavor with the sherry vinegar; the soup should be a little spicy but not too hot.

Presentation: Ladle soup into chilled bowls and drizzle crème fraîche over each; then top with dried cucumber rings.

Chef Baker suggests serving this light gazpacho in a burgundy glass, as they do in Spain. This is a summertime favorite, when tomatoes and cucumbers are ripe on the vine.

Ravioli of Grilled Garden Vegetables with Fresh Tomato Coulis

Makes 4-5 servings

Vegetable Ravioli

1 package Chinese wonton or gyoza
wrappers
4 slices zucchini*
4 slices eggplant*
2 leeks**
2 yellow beefsteak tomatoes**
fresh thyme flowers
fresh basil, cut julienne
2 shallots, finely chopped
touch of extra-virgin olive oil

* Slice 1/4" thick and grill lightly
** Split in half and grill lightly

Method for Coulis: Blend all in a food
processor, then strain through chinois or strainer.
Refrigerate until needed.

Method for Ravioli: Cut grilled vegetables
into 1/4" dice and combine them in a mixing
bowl. Add fresh herbs, salt, and pepper to taste.
Moisten the mixture (ravioli filling) with a touch
of olive oil and mix well.

Form ravioli by placing a spoonful of filling in
the center of each wonton wrapper. Moisten edges
of wrapper and fold over, sealing tightly. (The ravioli may be prepared ahead and then frozen until
needed.)

Garnish

fresh basil, cut julienne
basil oil (optional; see recipe)*
dried tomato rings (may be made in a
home food dehydrator unit)

Tomato Coulis

6 fresh plum tomatoes, coarsely chopped
2 oz. red wine vinegar
4 oz. virgin olive oil
salt and pepper to taste
2-3 thyme leaves

---

*Cooking & Presentation: When ready to serve,
steam the ravioli in a bamboo steamer for approximately 3 minutes, depending upon whether or not
they are frozen. While the ravioli are cooking,
warm sauce and finish by adjusting seasoning and
whisking in a bit of olive oil.*

*Arrange ravioli on large soup plates and spoon
the sauce around. Sprinkle top with the julienned
basil, dried tomato rings, and dot with basil oil.*

Chef's Secret

HOW TO MAKE BASIL OIL
Fresh basil oil is made by puréeing one
bunch of fresh basil with 8 oz. olive oil
in a blender or food processor for 15
minutes; strain through a cheesecloth to
obtain the vivid-color oil.

Author's Note

If the weather doesn't permit grilling
vegetables, baste them lightly with olive
oil and roast in a 400° oven. Try the
recipe again sometime when you can use
the grill—you may notice that the
grilling process renders sharper flavors.

**This light dish is entirely vegetarian, and
it utilizes a summer crop of vegetables.
It's great as a flavorful appetizer, too.**

Seasons' Open-Faced Vegetarian Burger on Natural Grain Bread

Makes 5 servings

2 cups brown or wahini rice, cooked
1 red bell pepper*
1 leek*
6 shiitake mushroom caps, sliced
8 sun-dried tomatoes, sliced
1 medium zucchini**
1 carrot, peeled**
1 medium red onion*
potato buds or rice flour as needed
fresh thyme

fresh chives, chopped
fresh basil, cut julienne-style
olive oil (as needed)
natural 7 or 10 grain bread as needed
assortment of garden baby lettuces
aged balsamic vinegar

* Cut to a medium dice
** Shred using a hand grater

Method for Burger: Prepare the rice so that it is somewhat overcooked and starchy; let cool to room temperature. Assemble the shredded vegetables and sauté over medium heat in olive oil until vegetables appear to be light-brown and are fairly well-cooked. Add vegetables to rice and mix together thoroughly. Next, add the fresh herbs to the rice/vegetable mixture (using about 1/2 tsp. of each). Adjust seasoning with salt and pepper to taste.

Next, blend in 1/2 cup of the potato buds or rice flour to help bind the mix. Form 3-4" patties, each approximately 3/4" thick and rounded. Place them on a plastic sheet and refrigerate for 1 hour.

Cooking & Presentation: When ready to serve, preheat a non-stick sauté pan and brush the bottom with olive oil; pat burgers on both sides in a bit of potato buds and then place in pan. Allow burgers to brown slowly on both sides over medium heat; this should take approximately 8 minutes. Remove burgers from pan and place on the grain bread (toast the bread if desired).

Serve with a bouquet of the freshest greens you have and some balsamic vinegar, or with your favorite tomato relish.

Unlike many vegetarian selections, chef Baker's mock burger is filling and fabulous.

Traditional New England Lobster Bake

Makes 4 servings

4 whole Maine lobsters
1/2 bushel littleneck clams
1/2 bushel Prince Edward Island mussels
6 ears corn, shucked
12 baby red potatoes
seaweed (optional)
2 garlic cloves
2 thyme branches
8 oz. sea salt or kosher salt
2 Tbs. black peppercorns
1 bottle white wine

Method for Lobster Bake: Thoroughly wash clams and mussels in cold water to remove any sand and grit. Fill a large steaming pasta pot halfway with 3-5 gallons of tap water, and bring to a rapid boil. Add salt, peppercorns, thyme, garlic, and white wine. Then add seaweed and potatoes, and boil for approximately 5 minutes. Next, add the lobster, mussels, clams, and corn.

Cover pot tightly and boil for at least 7 minutes—do not overcook as lobster will become tough. Remove all ingredients from the pot, including seaweed, and arrange on a large platter. Reserve broth to serve on the side.

Presentation: Lemon and drawn butter complement the dish, and lobster bibs may be provided to guests. As a wine recommendation, chef Baker prefers a crisp Sauvignon Blanc with the bake.

Nantucket Stew of Lobster and Early Summer Corn

Makes 4 servings

Nantucket Stew

2 cups lobster corn soup (see recipe)
2 whole Maine lobsters, steamed
1/2 cup fingerling potatoes*
1/2 cup corn kernels
1/2 stick whole butter
1 pinch chives (optional garnish)
1 pinch thyme (optional garnish)

* Cut in quarters and boil until nearly done; substitute red bliss or new potatoes if fingerlings are unavailable (or see Resources section)

Method for Corn Soup: In a large sauce pan over medium heat, sauté bacon with leeks in whole butter until translucent; then add corn. In the same sauce pan, stir in wine, brandy, and cream; then, reduce heat and add lobster stock. Stir mixture and remove from heat just before the boiling point. Purée the mixture in a food processor until very fine, and then add the pinch of thyme. Hold until needed for Nantucket stew.

Lobster Corn Soup

4 cups lobster stock*
2 strips of smoked bacon**
1 cup corn kernels
1 stalk of leek**
1 stick whole butter
1 pinch of thyme
1 cup heavy cream
1 cup white wine
1 cup brandy

* Prepare like chicken stock, but substituting lobster shells
** Cut into small pieces

Method for Stew: Cut steamed lobster into small pieces. Warm pieces of lobster in a soup pot with 1/2 stick of whole butter and the fingerling potatoes.

Presentation: Add the corn soup and corn to the Nantucket stew. Divide stew up into serving bowls and season with thyme and chives.

> **A native New Englander, Chef Baker makes this stew with some of his favorite ingredients—tender lobster and sweet corn.**

About this Dish

The fingerling potato is known for its rich, buttery flavor. It's a long, thin potato. Ask for this flavorful spud at your local gourmet store, or see Resources section.

Szechuan Barbecued Corned Beef Brisket

Makes 6-8 servings

1 whole cooked corned beef brisket (about 2-3 lbs.)
1/2 cup Japanese soy sauce
1 cup mirin
1 cup sake
1 cup honey
Chinese red chile paste or dried chiles, to taste (See Resources section)
1/2 cup grenadine
1/2 bunch fresh cilantro, chopped
1 Tbs. ginger root, grated

Method for Brisket: Trim corned beef of excess fat and split it into the two natural pieces that are separated by a fat vein running through them. Combine all liquid ingredients in a large pot and bring them to a near boil. Then, place corned beef in a deep container and pour the liquid over to cover the beef. Cool to room temperature and refrigerate overnight.

To cook, roast the brisket in an oven heated to 350° on a rack fitted over a drip pan or over a charcoal grill. If grilling, make sure the fire isn't too hot, or the brisket will burn. Grill brisket approximately 45 minutes over moderate coals, basting every 10 minutes or so with the remaining marinade. Remove from heat and slice across the grain into thin slices.

Presentation: Serve the sliced brisket with a flavorful chutney, chilled pasta salad, and grilled vegetables.

When Craig Henne joined The Ritz-Carlton, New York as Executive Chef in 1991, his ultimate goal was to revamp the Hotel's Signature Restaurant. To express the hotel's style, chef Henne and his team chose to feature the elegant cuisine of Northern Italy. A traditional European decor was also installed in warm tones of peach and mauve with working fireplaces, and china designed by Gianni Versace. The new restaurant, named Fantino, opened in March, 1994, and is a favorite of travelers and of native New Yorkers.

Fantino began winning awards at its inception, including its own Five Diamond rating with AAA (separate from the one earned by the Hotel) in 1995. The secret lies in chef Henne's approach to food. "Food should not be overworked," he says. "It should be prepared and served in the simplest of ways, using the freshness of the products and their natural textures and flavors."

Jumbo Lump Crab Cakes with Mustard Sauce

Makes 2 servings

1 lb. jumbo lump crab meat
1 whole egg
8-12 saltine crackers
1 Tbs. parsley, chopped
1 Tbs. Old Bay Seasoning™
1/2 Tbs. dry mustard
1/2 tsp. cayenne pepper
4 oz. butter*
1 medium round cutter
chopped chives (optional garnish)
lobster roe (optional garnish)

* 2 oz. clarified + 2 oz. whole

Mustard Sauce
(yields one quart)
1 qt. fish stock
4 1/4 oz. white wine
1 cup heavy cream (reduce by 1/2)
2 1/2 whole shallots
1-2 whole white peppercorns

1 faggot:
    fresh thyme
    1/2 bay leaf
    1/4 celery stick

1/4 cup pommery (grain) mustard
salt to taste
1 tsp. buerre manie*

* Consists of 1 Tbs. flour blended with 1 Tbs. melted butter

Method for Crab Cakes: Pick out all cartilage in the crab meat, squeezing out all moisture. Crumble saltines and add to crab meat. Add all remaining ingredients and mix well by hand. Adjust portions when necessary. Weigh out balls at 3 1/2 oz. each. Pack each 3 1/2 oz. ball into round cutter, giving it sharp edges. Sauté 2 crab cakes in half clarified butter and half whole butter, basting while they cook. Finish in oven heated to 375° for 5-10 minutes.

Method for Sauce: Reduce fish stock, white wine, peppercorns, and faggot by half; add in heavy cream (which has already been reduced 50% by simmering it on a medium-high burner). Thicken with buerre manie and let cook out. Strain and add pommery mustard. Adjust seasoning to taste.

Presentation: Ladle 2 oz. mustard sauce onto serving plate, covering all. Place crab cakes overlapping in center. Top crab cakes with fried shoestring potatoes (see recipe on p. 161). Garnish plate with finely chopped chives and lobster roe.

This is a simple, understated dish. Chef Henne's mustard sauce is a tangy accent to the mild crab.

Grilled Center Cut Swordfish and Vegetable Marinara, with Balsamic Vinegar and Extra-Virgin Olive Oil

Makes 6 servings

(6) 7oz. center cut swordfish steaks
4 tomatoes
1 bulb fennel
4 stalks celery
2 zucchini
2 red peppers
2 green peppers
2 cucumbers

20 green olives
20 black olives
2 Tbs. capers
olive oil
garlic-scented salt
1 qt. balsamic vinegar
fresh coriander and cilantro (garnishes)

Method for Vegetable Marinara: Peel the tomatoes, peppers, and cucumber; seed and dice all vegetables, and set aside. Blanch vegetables individually and pat dry. Mix vegetables together, and then add olives and capers. Season with olive oil, salt, and freshly ground coriander. The mixture may be refrigerated for up to four days.

Method for Swordfish & Vinegar Reduction: Season swordfish with spice mixture.

Reduce 1 qt. of balsamic vinegar to 8 oz., and remove from pan. Grill the fish, approximately 3 minutes per side.

Presentation: Spoon vegetable marinara over top and sides of swordfish. Drizzle balsamic vinegar and oil over and around fish. Season plate with fresh coriander and finish with a garnish of cilantro. ✺

> A light and healthy swordfish dish that's very popular in The Ritz-Carlton, New York's dining room.

House Smoked Sea Bass with Eggplant, Tuscany White Beans, and Olive Oil *Pictured on p.180*

Makes 4 servings (appetizer portions)

Smoked Bass
10 oz. fillet of fresh sea bass
5 shallots*
3 Tbs. salt
1 Tbs. sugar
1/4 piece of fennel
1 tsp. fennel seeds
1 tsp. whole black pepper
apple wood chips for smoking
2 tsp. Tuscany extra-virgin olive oil

Eggplant & Garnish
2 fresh baby eggplants
1 1/2 cups of yellow frise lettuce
3-4 Tbs. Tuscany extra-virgin olive oil
1 red radish** (optional garnish)
4 Tbs. white Tuscany beans, cooked
juice of one fresh lemon

* Chop finely
** Cut in a fine julienne

Method for Curing the Sea Bass: Mix the salt and sugar together in a bowl and set aside. Place the fillets (skin-side down) in a sheet pan on top of a grill. Mix the salt and ☞

sugar together, and rub 1 1/2 Tbs. on the fillet to cure it. In a separate bowl, mix the finely chopped shallots, fennels, and fennel seeds; cover the fish with this mixture. Sprinkle 1 tsp. of black pepper on top. Let the fish cure for 12 hours, uncovered, at room temperature.

Method for Smoking the Sea Bass: Once the fish has cured, wipe the fillet clean using a paper towel. Smoke the fish over apple wood chips for 4-6 hours. Rub the fillet with Tuscany extra-virgin olive oil, and then refrigerate for 10 hours.

Method for Eggplant & Garnish: Peel the eggplant and slice them on the bias into 1/8" pieces. Sauté eggplant in a non-stick pan—with 2 Tbs. of the Tuscany oil—until golden brown. Remove the eggplant and add a dash of salt.

Toss the frise lettuce lightly with a couple Tbs. of Tuscany olive oil, salt to taste, and a drop of fresh lemon juice.

Presentation: Divide the salad mixture among four 7" serving plates, placing it in the center of each (making a bed of lettuce). Slice the smoked bass of the bias into 1/8" pieces, and place on top of the lettuce, alternating pieces of sea bass and eggplant in a circular pattern. (There should be a space in the center.) Place a small mound of warm Tuscany beans in the center of each plate. Garnish with julienne of radish and a touch more olive oil.

All of the rich flavors of Mediterranean cuisine come together in this creation. Begin making this dish a day ahead, to allow ample time for the curing, smoking, and marinating steps.

House Smoked Sea Bass with Eggplant, Tuscany White Beans, and Olive Oil

Lamb Loin Saltimbocca with Pepper and Carrot Tarts

Makes 2 servings

Pepper and Carrot Tarts

10 oz. puff pastry
butter for form
1 lb. carrots
3 oz. butter
2 Tbs. parsley, chopped
salt & pepper to taste
pinch sugar
6 oz. cream
2 eggs
2 ea.: small red, green, and yellow peppers
butter for form
10 oz. puff pastry
6 egg
3 oz. cream
2 Tbs. browned butter
salt and pepper

Sage Sauce

10-11 lbs. lamb bones and trimmings
1 lb. onions
1/2 lb. carrots
4 oz. celery
2 1/2 Tbs. tomato paste
1/2 Tbs. cracked white peppercorns
2 bay leaves
2-3 thyme sprigs
2-3 rosemary sprigs
1 gallon lamb stock (see Resources section)
1 Tbs. arrowroot
sage butter (see recipe)

Lamb Loin

1 lamb loin (approx. 12 oz., makes 2 6 oz. portions)
2 thin slices parma ham
1 piece caul fat
2 sage leaves

Method for Pastry: Roll puff pastry very thin, and place in four buttered tart pans. Prick puff pastry with fork. Cover with parchment paper and fill with dried beans. Bake at 350° and check after 10 minutes—it should be crisped.

Method for Carrot Filling: Wash and peel carrots; cut 2/3 of them into a fine julienne. Melt butter in pan; sweat the julienned carrots for two minutes. Add chopped parsley, salt, and a pinch of sugar. Divide carrots into four; put into molds. Remaining carrots should be juiced; yields about 1 oz. juice.

Mix juice, cream, and beaten egg. Season with a pinch of salt, sugar and pepper. Pour over carrot mixture. Pour into the pre-baked pastry shells and bake at 350° approximately 12 minutes.

Method for Pepper Filling: Quarter, seed and boil peppers for 5 minutes. Shock (with cold water); peel skin. Cut peppers into diamonds. Butter four flan forms. Roll out puff pastry, prick, and then let chill for 20 minutes. Divide peppers into the four forms. Mix egg, cream, and browned butter; season. Pour over peppers in the pre-baked pastry forms, and bake at 350° for 15 minutes.

Method for Sage Sauce: Chop lamb bones; brown with trimmings. Remove fat.

Meanwhile, clean vegetables and finely chop. Add to bones. Add a splash of red wine and reduce until thick. Add more red wine; repeat two more times. Add rest of red wine, herbs and spices. Pour in stock and enough water to cover bones, and cook for one hour. Strain; reduce to one quart. Thicken with a little arrowroot. Season with salt, pepper, Marseilles wine, and balsamic vinegar. Before service, whip in sage butter.

Method for Lamb Loin: Wrap lamb loin with parma ham. Place a sage leaf on each side, and wrap in caul fat. Salt, pepper, and flour lamb loin. Cook in garlic and olive oil to medium rare, turning frequently. Remove from pan and let rest 2 minutes. Heat vegetable tarts in oven.

Presentation: *Place tart on plate at 12 o'clock. Slice lamb in 1/4 inch slices and fan out beside tart at 4 o'clock and at 8 o'clock. Ladle a small amount of sage butter sauce over the lamb loin.*

> This dish makes a beautiful presentation, with the sliced lamb fanned out next to the vegetable tarts.

Chef's Secret

HOW TO MAKE SAGE BUTTER:
5-6 stalks of fresh sage
1/4 lb. butter
Put sage in a pan with whole butter and bring to a simmer. Remove from heat and use in sauces or store for later use.

Grilled Free-Range Chicken with Tuscany White Beans and Sweet Red Pepper Sauce

Makes 2 servings

2 double breasts from a small free-range chicken (2-3 lb.); or 1 double breast, split, from a large (4-5 lb.) chicken

Tuscany White Beans

12 oz. white beans, soaked for at least 12 hours
1 qt. chicken stock
1 small onion
1 bay leaf
1 thyme sprig
1 garlic clove
3 oz. leeks, cut in diamonds, blanched
salt and pepper

Sweet Red Pepper Sauce

1 oz. olive oil
4 shallots
2 oz. celery
4 red peppers
1 tsp. paprika
20 whole allspice
6 tomatoes
2 thyme sprigs
1 bay leaf
2 garlic cloves
1 cup white wine
1 1/2 qts. chicken stock
1 cup heavy cream
4 oz. cold butter
salt and pepper

Method for Beans: Simmer chicken stock on medium-high heat with diced onion, bay leaf, thyme, and garlic; bring to boil. Add beans and cook until soft. Before serving, add leeks and season to taste.

Method for Pepper Sauce and Chicken: Heat olive oil; sauté shallots until glassy. Add celery, peppers, tomatoes, and seasoning. Deglaze pan with white wine. Add stock and cream; stir and cook 20 minutes over medium-high heat. Strain through a fine chamois. Meanwhile, grill chicken breast.

Presentation: Place cooked beans in center of plate, and top with a chicken breast. Spoon 2 oz. of sauce around edge of plate and serve.

Free-range chicken is grain-fed and free of all of the hormones and chemicals used to "fatten" birds. The white beans and sweet red pepper sauce add plenty of taste and texture.

Dover Sole Fillets with Asparagus Tips and Green Peppercorn Sauce

Makes 2 servings

Sole & Asparagus Tips

8 Dover sole fillets, each cut in half
1/4-1/3 cup flour
salt and pepper
16 green asparagus tips
10 orange segments
12 fresh tarragon leaves (garnish)

Green Peppercorn Sauce

8 oz. orange juice, strained
1 tsp. green peppercorns, crushed
1 oz. butter
2 Tbs. whipped cream

Method for Peppercorn Sauce: Reduce orange juice by 1/2, over medium-high heat, and then add green peppercorns. Remove from heat and add butter. Before serving, fold in whipped cream.

Method for Asparagus: Place asparagus tips in small pan over medium-high heat with 1 oz. water and 1 tsp. each—whole butter and salt. Cook until water has evaporated. (Asparagus should be glazed.)

Method for Sole: Salt, pepper, and flour the Dover sole. Sauté quickly in clarified butter over high heat. Remove from pan.

Presentation: Place Dover sole on plate. Scatter asparagus tips and orange segments over the sole. Cover with green peppercorn sauce, and garnish with tarragon leaves.

FOUR SEASONS, PHILADELPHIA

The Four Seasons Hotel, Philadelphia boasts the only restaurant in the city to be recognized as one of the "Top 25 Restaurants in America" by Food & Wine *magazine. This is the Fountain Restaurant, and it reputation for fine dining is the achievement of Jean-Marie Lacroix, Executive Chef since the hotel's opening in 1983.*

A native of Epinal, in France's Franche-Comte region, chef LaCroix received his formal training at Thonon les Bains on Lake Geneva. He has practiced his craft at fine restaurants and hotels in France, Switzerland, England, Scotland, and Canada.

Chef Lacroix is also known for encouraging young chefs to practice and perfect their skills in the kitchen. Many of his protegés gathered to honor him at a 1992 benefit called "Papa's Feast."

Mango Soup

Makes 4 servings

2 whole ripe mangoes
4 oz. coconut milk
1 lime, juice only
2 Tbs. dark rum

> **Try this light soup as a starter to a summer meal, when mangoes are ripe and plentiful.**

Method for Soup: Carefully halve and remove the stone from the mangoes. Scrape out the mango flesh, leaving shells (skins) intact. Blend mango with the rest of the ingredients, and then pour the mixture back into mango shells.

Presentation: Serve well chilled, accompanied by cookies.

Lobster Wrapped in Crispy Potatoes with Caviar Sauce

Makes 4 servings (appetizer portions)

4 oz. lobster meat, cooked**
2 large Idaho potatoes*
1 tsp. fresh parsley**
1/2 tsp. fresh dill**
1/8 tsp. salt
pinch of pepper
vegetable oil for frying

* Cut julienne-style
** Chop these ingredients

Caviar Sauce

1/4 oz. caviar
2 oz. white wine
1/4 Tbs. shallots
2 oz. butter
1 oz. crème fraîche

Method for Sauce: Sauté shallots in 1/4 oz. of the butter. Add white wine and reduce by 3/4. Whip in remaining butter, 1/2 oz. at a time. Finish the sauce by blending in the crème fraîche, and add in caviar at the last minute.

Method for Lobster: Julienne the two large potatoes and season them with salt, pepper, parsley, and dill. Divide potatoes into four equal piles. Place cooked lobster meat in the center of each potato pile. Next, wrap each pile with plastic wrap, making sure lobster stays centered in each pile, with potatoes completely surrounding it. Freeze until ready to cook.

Cooking & Presentation: Heat vegetable oil to 350° F. Remove the plastic wrap and deep-fat fry the potatoes until golden-brown. Serve with caviar sauce on top or beside the wrapped lobster.

Eggplant Cannelloni with Tomato Coulis

Makes 4 servings

1 large eggplant
1 whole roasted bell pepper
1 cup spinach
1 medium onion*
1 cup mushrooms*
pinch of garlic
pinch of shallots
1/4 cup boursin-style cheese

2 Tbs. parmesan, grated
ground oregano to taste
parsley
salt and pepper to taste
2 cups tomato coulis (see recipe)
olive oil

* Cut in a dice

Method for Eggplant: Slice the eggplant lengthwise, 1/4" thick. Season slices with salt and pepper, and drizzle with oil. Grill or sauté the eggplant until fully cooked, about 5 minutes. Remove and allow to cool.

Method for Cannelloni Filling: Sauté the diced onion in olive oil until transparent; add mushrooms and cook until they become soft. Next, add the garlic and shallots. Finally, add the spinach and season all with salt and pepper. Remove from heat and allow to cool. Once cooled, transfer the onion/mushroom mixture to a bowl. Mix in the oregano, parsley, and peppers. Add boursin cheese (crumbled) and fold in the parmesan.

Lay the pieces of eggplant out flat on a work surface. Place one heaping Tbs. of the vegetable/cheese mixture on one end of each eggplant slice, and roll it upwards, creating a cannelloni effect. Place the eggplant rolls side-by-side in a baking pan. Top with 1 cup of the tomato coulis and cover with foil. Bake in an oven preheated to 350° for 30 minutes.

Presentation: Serve hot with the remaining cup of tomato coulis (heated). Serve with a colorful salad, such as radicchio tossed with a light vinaigrette. ᕗ

Chef's Secret
HOW TO MAKE TOMATO COULIS

This light, refreshing tomato sauce is made by using 5-6 fresh tomatoes (or one large tomato per person). Peel the tomatoes, remove seeds, and whirl them briefly in the food processor. By making your own tomato sauce, you can eliminate high levels of sodium, preservatives, and other additives found in the packaged sauces.

> Vegetarians love this light entrée. Chef Lacroix presents the mock cannelloni with a lightly dressed radicchio salad.

South Street Market,
New York

The Point

Candlelight dinners and a romantic setting on an Adirondack peninsula

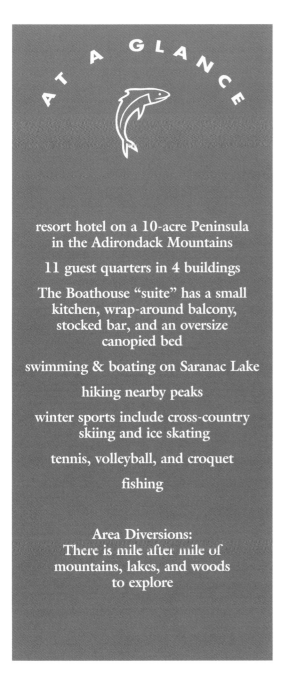

resort hotel on a 10-acre Peninsula
in the Adirondack Mountains

11 guest quarters in 4 buildings

The Boathouse "suite" has a small
kitchen, wrap-around balcony,
stocked bar, and an oversize
canopied bed

swimming & boating on Saranac Lake

hiking nearby peaks

winter sports include cross-country
skiing and ice skating

tennis, volleyball, and croquet

fishing

Area Diversions:
There is mile after mile of
mountains, lakes, and woods
to explore

A VISIT TO The Point on Upper Saranac Lake, New York is like "joining old friends for a house party in the woods," say owners Christie and David Garrett. Situated on an isolated peninsula between lake and woods up in the Adirondack Mountains, The Point is both rustic and luxurious. It has been heralded as a top American resort, including a #1 Resort Hotel in the U.S. by the *Zagat Hotel, Resort, and Spa Survey*, and it is on the National Trust's Historic Hotels of America registry.

Built as a luxurious getaway for William Avery Rockefeller in the 1930's, The Point remains one of the Great Camps built in America. An upscale lodge atmosphere—massive stone fireplaces, museum-replica twig furniture, and timbered walls and cathedral ceilings—is evident throughout the Main Lodge. Guest rooms are housed in the Lodge and three other buildings (Eagle's Nest, Guest House, and the Boat-house) on the wooded peninsula. One of the love-liest accommodations is the spacious suite in the Boathouse, a dwelling that juts out over Upper Saranac Lake. Inside, a white gauze-canopied bed and wide-window views of the lake make the Boathouse a top choice for romance.

Dinners at The Point are the antithesis of the resort's rustic style—they include lavish and elegant courses on a prix fixe menu. During the Christmas season, the enormous Great Hall becomes warm and intimate with candlelit tables; a towering tree decked out with pinecones, red bows, and twinkling lights; and a large stone fireplace kept ablaze. There is so much beauty here that The Point should be experienced more than one season. ❧

Balsams Grand Resort Hotel

Skiing, golf, and grand cuisine in northern New Hampshire's White Mountains

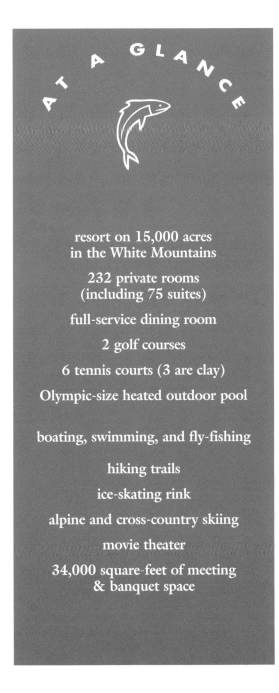

IMAGINE A snow-crowned Victorian castle set in 15,000 acres of pristine wilderness that are yours to explore. Imagine a challenging array of private downhill and cross-country ski trails, where there are no lines and no waiting times. And, in the summer, the crowds are sparse on the Balsams' classic golf course, designed in 1912 by the legendary Donald Ross. Imagine mountain panoramas that sweep across two states and Canada, an elegant ballroom where you can dance away the evening, a frosty fall hayride, or a spirited game of tennis—and you have The Balsams Grand Resort Hotel, built in 1866.

Guests can fill their days with activities ranging from craft and cooking classes to swimming and aerobics. On man-made Lake Gloriette, there is boating, swimming, and fly-fishing for stocked trout. From the Resort, a staff naturalist offers daily guided walks and hikes, picnic tours, and group presentations. Many guests take maps and handbooks to navigate miles of annotated trails.

All meals and activities at The Balsams are covered under a single fee, the all-inclusive American Plan. And at dinnertime, the temptations are many in the columned dining room, where guests sit at the same table throughout their stay. All of the dishes offered at the meal are displayed on a table in the center of the room, so guests can see exactly what the choices are.

Perhaps the tough decisions get easier for Balsams' guests who opt to stay several glorious days and nights. The toughest decision to be made is when to leave!

Dixville Notch, New Hampshire 03576 (800)255-0600 or (603)255-3400

Wheatleigh Hotel

A 16th-Century Italian Renaissance estate in the
Berkshire Mountains of Massachusetts

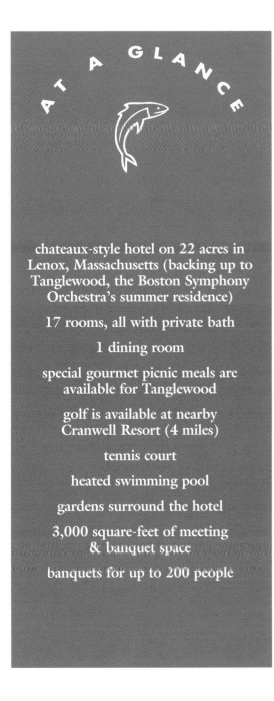

AT A GLANCE

chateaux-style hotel on 22 acres in Lenox, Massachusetts (backing up to Tanglewood, the Boston Symphony Orchestra's summer residence)

17 rooms, all with private bath

1 dining room

special gourmet picnic meals are available for Tanglewood

golf is available at nearby Cranwell Resort (4 miles)

tennis court

heated swimming pool

gardens surround the hotel

3,000 square-feet of meeting & banquet space

banquets for up to 200 people

EVERYTHING IS done on a grand scale in the Berkshire Mountains, a summer playground in western Massachusetts. Wheatleigh continues this tradition by offering guests sophisticated accommodations in a country estate. The 22-acre property in Lenox, Massachusetts, features a 16th-Century Italian Renaissance hotel built in 1893, and is a member of Small Luxury Hotels of the World. Period furnishings throughout the public areas and the guest rooms, and hand-carved Chippendale chairs in the dining room carry through the tradition of European elegance.

Guest accommodations vary from modest to sublime: standard rooms are small (generally 11' x 13'), all have private baths, and some come with queen beds; superior rooms are large, with high ceilings, king beds, and some have fireplaces; deluxe rooms are very spacious, bright rooms with high ceilings, king beds, fireplaces, and the best views of the Berkshires.

The Berkshire Mountains have long been a favorite getaway for New Yorkers and for Bostonians. During the summer, Tanglewood comes alive with the strains of the Boston Symphony, who have been "summering" here for more than five decades. Active guests enjoy swimming in Wheatleigh's secluded garden pool, playing a set of tennis, or playing a round of golf at any of the four courses in the area. A stay at Wheatleigh during the Tanglewood season is not complete without one of the chef's gourmet picnic lunches or suppers—to be enjoyed with a fine champagne, and the celebrated sounds of the BSO.

Hawthorne Road ✆ Lenox, Massachusetts 01240 ✆ (413)637-0610

Sam Mahoney

THE POINT

Executive chef Sam Mahoney is once again working his magic behind the scenes at The Point. Years ago, after he completed an apprenticeship at Le Gavroche, a 3-star restaurant in London, England, Mahoney participated in The Point's chef trainee program. 18 months later, chef Mahoney left the Adirondacks to further his career in southern Japan. .

Next, chef Mahoney returned to Europe, where he went to work for the five-star Grand Hotel in Amsterdam. His Brasserie was a Best of Amsterdam recipient, reflecting Mahoney's innovative style and his ability to make a menu stand out in a city where award-winning cafés and Brasseries line nearly every street.

The motive behind his return to The Point is: "To continue to expand the gastronomic reputation of this intimate, top-end resort."

Poussin with Sweet Corn Fritters and Wild Mushrooms

Makes 4 servings

Poussin
4 whole poussins*

* Select birds about 12 oz. each; remove legs, and debone the breast (keeping it in one piece to give a heart shape)

Fritter Batter
2 egg yolks
2 egg whites
1/4 tsp. salt
1 cup milk
3 Tbs. butter, melted
1 cup flour
2 tsp. baking powder

Sweet Corn
2 cups sweet corn
1 onion
1-2 Tbs. butter
1 tsp. each: thyme and chives
2 tsp. parmesan cheese, grated
pinch of nutmeg
salt and pepper to taste

Savory Sauce
4 cups veal jus
2 cups prepared chicken stock
carcasses of poussin
2 cups red wine
1 carrot*
1/2 onion*
1 stalk celery*
1/2 knob garlic
2 sprigs thyme

* Cut in a dice

Wild Mushrooms
3 oz. girolles
3 oz. trompet de la mort
3 oz. cèpes
3 Tbs. butter
3 oz. shallot
3 oz. garlic

Method for Batter: Mix milk, egg yolks, baking powder, melted butter, salt, and flour into a smooth paste. Beat egg whites until stiff, and then fold them into the batter. Cook the sweet corn. Cook the onion in butter and add the sweet corn and herbs; allow to cool. Mix the batter through the sweet corn and cook in small rings in a pan, like a crèpe.

Method for Sauce: Chop and sauté the carcasses; add the carrot, celery, and onion and cook until lightly brown. Add the red wine and allow to reduce by 2/3. Add the veal juice and simmer for 1 1/2 hours until reduced. Strain and adjust the seasoning.

Method for Mushrooms: Clean all the mushrooms and sauté in 3 Tbs. butter over a hot burner with a little shallot and garlic. Set aside until needed

Presentation: Sauté the legs of poussin and the breasts. Heat the mushrooms and the corn fritter, then place the legs on the corn fritter and the breast on top. Put the mushrooms around the plate and coat with sauce.

Gazpacho Andalouse

Makes 8-10 servings

Garlic Croutons
3-6 garlic cloves
5 slices bread
2/3 oz. oil

Gazpacho
1 lb. tomatoes
1/2 lb. cucumber
3/4 lb. green pimiento
1/3 oz. vinegar
1 Tbs. cumin seeds
1 lb. ice

Garnish
Use 3.5 oz. each of the following:
croutons
onion, finely chopped
cucumber, diced
tomato concasse (remove peel and seeds, and dice fresh tomato)
pimiento, diced

Method for Croutons: Peel and crush the garlic in a basin. Cut the bread into cubes and place with the garlic, mixing well. Add the oil gradually and mix in well. Season with salt and allow to stand for 10 minutes.

Method for Gazpacho: Cut tomatoes into quarters, seed and chop the cucumber, and remove the seeds from pimiento and chop finely. Add all remaining ingredients to the previous mixture, season, and allow to stand for 10 minutes.

Crush the cumin seeds, add them to the mixture and pass it through a fine sieve or mix in a blender. Add ice to chill the soup and bring it to the correct consistency.

Presentation: *Serve the soup well-chilled and garnished with desired amounts of croutons, onion, cucumber, tomato concasse, and pimiento.* 🍲

> **This summer soup goes well with steamed lobster or shrimp for a light lunch or dinner.**

Risotto with Herbs and White Truffle Oil

Makes 4 servings

2 cups arborio rice
8 cups (approx.) chicken stock
2 Tbs. olive oil
1 onion
3 Tbs. fresh parmesan cheese, grated
1 tsp. white truffle oil (optional)*
2 Tbs. butter (optional)
2 Tbs. chopped herbs**

* See Resources section; or purchase from a gourmet grocer
** Combine chives, parsley, tarragon, and chervil

Method for Risotto: Heat the chicken stock until boiling. Cook the onion in olive oil until transparent. Add the rice and cook until coated in the oil. Add about 1 cup of chicken stock (enough just to cover the rice). Allow this to cook slowly until absorbed, then add another ladle of stock, once again just enough to cover the rice and repeat this process until the rice is cooked but not gluey. Add the parmesan cheese, herbs, truffle oil, and butter (if desired). 🍲

Chef's Tip
The secret of a good risotto is not to boil the rice vigorously, and to slowly add the stock in about four or more stages.

Salad of Herring and Gravad Lax

Makes 4 servings (appetizer portions)

Salad

6 oz. gravad lax
6 oz. marinated herring
1 hard boiled egg
1 tsp. dill, chopped
1 whole shallot, chopped

Dijon Mustard Sauce

2 Tbs. dijon
2 Tbs. grainy mustard
3 Tbs. white wine vinegar
1 1/2 cup oil
1 Tbs. dill, chopped
**adjust to taste with sugar and
more vinegar**

Method for Salad: Dice the gravad lax into a 1/4" dice and mix in a bowl with the chopped dill and shallot. Season with a little vinaigrette, salt, and pepper. Cut the marinated herrings into a similar dice, and chop up the onions that come with the herrings. Place a little of the gravad lax mixture in the base of a timbale mold, then place a layer of the herring mixture on top. Finish with the gravad lax. Press lightly and chill for 2 hours.

Presentation: Serve demolded with a little salad of fresh greens and some mustard sauce.

The Point's Salad of Herring and Gravad Lax is a favorite starter course

Charles M. Carroll

BALSAMS GRAND RESORT HOTEL

At The Balsams Grand Resort Hotel, certified executive chef Charles M. Carroll's creations routinely earn high praise. A graduate of the Culinary Institute of America and The Balsams' own apprenticeship program, Carroll says his post is rewarding because of "management's absolute priority on food. American Plan hospitality succeeds as a result of its food." His interpretations of contemporary American regional cuisine follow this credo: "As much as possible, use locally-produced vegetables, herbs, fish, meat, and poultry. Preserve the integrity of the food by relying on the natural flavors and blends of flavors."

This common-sense philosophy guides the making of house specialties, such as Baked Haddock with Finnan Haddie and Molasses-Marinated Scallops, and a traditional Bread Pudding, topped with cinnamon and chopped pecans.

Lobster and Finnan Haddie Chowder, Balsams Style

Pictured on p.165

Makes 8-10 servings

2 bay leaves
1 cooked lobster, meat only*
1 cup smoked cod (leave whole)
1/4 cup green pepper**
1/4 cup pimiento**
1/2 cup onion**
1/2 cup potatoes**
pinch of salt
pinch of pepper
1 Tbs. butter
1 cup water
3 Tbs. fresh or dried parsley (optional garnish)

* Chop tail and claw meat into large pieces; reserve a few pieces for garnish
** Cut in a medium dice

Béchamel Sauce
6 cups milk
3 Tbs. flour
1/2 stick butter

Method for Béchamel: Melt butter over low heat for the béchamel sauce. Add flour to form a roux, and cook over medium heat for 4 minutes. Add milk a little at a time, whisking continually to avoid lumps. Next, add bay leaves, and simmer on low heat for 10 minutes.

Method for Chowder: Melt the butter in a 4 qt. heavy stock pot. Add the diced peppers and onions; sauté until onions are translucent. Add the potatoes, and stir for 1 minute. Add lobster, whole smoked cod and water. Simmer until cod starts to break up and the potatoes are cooked. Strain béchamel liquid into the sauté and stir. Serve immediately.

Presentation: Ladle 8 oz. portions of soup into chowder bowls and garnish with a few pieces of lobster, and/or a sprinkle of parsley.

Chowder, the coastal New England favorite, gets reinvented at
The Balsams with the addition of fresh lobster
and smoked cod (finnan haddie).

Baked Haddock with Lemon Caper Mayonnaise Glaze and Chive Oil

Makes 4 servings

(4) 6 oz. haddock fillets (skin and bones removed)
3/4 cup mayonnaise*
1 1/2 Tbs. capers, chopped
1/2 Tbs. fresh lemon juice
1 tsp. salt

1 tsp. freshly ground black pepper
3/4 cup virgin olive oil
1/2 cup fresh chives, chopped
1 tsp. salt

* Use a high-quality brand with a stiff consistency

Method for Haddock: Mix together the mayonnaise, capers, lemon juice, salt, and pepper. Place haddock, skin-side down, onto a greased baking dish. Spread 3 Tbs. of the mayonnaise mixture on top of each haddock fillet. Bake in a preheated 400° oven for 8 minutes.

Method for Chive Oil: Chop the chives and place into a blender or food processor with the olive oil and salt. Turn blender on and off until chives are completely puréed. Place haddock on a warm plate and drizzle 2 Tbs. of the chive oil around the fish. ✍

This haddock is one of chef Carroll's favorite dishes; it relies on the natural flavors of the products used. The one-step glaze gives the fish a golden-brown color.

About this Dish

Sautéed onions and leeks go well with this entrée.

New England Bread Pudding   *Pictured on p.202*

Makes 12 servings

1 sm. loaf of bread (or 15 slices)
4 large eggs
1 3/4 cups sugar
3 oz. butter, melted
3 cups milk
vanilla, to taste
2 tsp. cinnamon

Method for Bread Pudding: Whip eggs using a mixer set on high speed until light and frothy. Slowly stream in sugar. On medium speed, add in the melted butter. Add milk and vanilla on low speed.

Cut 15 slices of bread into 3/4" cubes. Toast in 350° oven until golden-brown. When cool, place in a 9" x 11" x 2" pan. Sprinkle with cinnamon and chopped pecans. Pour custard over the top. Soak bread for 30 minutes, gently stirring once after 15 minutes. Bake in a hot water bath* for 30 minutes in an oven heated to 350°.   * *Place the pan containing pudding in a larger pan filled with a couple of inches of boiling water.*
✍

Bread pudding is an easy
dessert that is best made
with firm, leftover bread. Serve this warm
dessert when it's chilly outside.

Baked Haddock with Finnan Haddie, Molasses-Marinated Scallops, and Asparagus Spears

Makes 6 servings

Haddock & Breading
(6) 4 oz. fresh haddock fillets
2 cups fresh bread crumbs
1 tsp. salt
1/2 tsp. pepper

Lemon Butter Sauce
1 stick butter, melted*
1 lemon (juice only)*

* Combine and set aside until needed

Marinated Scallops
12 scallops
1/2 cup molasses
1 Tbs. catsup
1 tsp. garlic, chopped
1/2 lemon, juice only
1/2 Tbs. coriander seed
1 Tbs. cilantro or parsley, chopped
1 tsp. salad oil

Method for Haddock: Mix dry ingredients (bread crumbs, salt, and pepper) together. Dip the haddock fillets into melted butter and lemon, and then into dry bread crumbs. Place on pre-greased baking sheet, and bake in a 400° oven for 8-10 minutes.

Method for Scallops: Marinate scallops for 20 minutes; drain well. Preheat a 10" non-stick sauté pan over medium-high heat; add oil and place scallops in. Turn each scallop over individually when golden-brown. (Be careful not to burn marinade—if pan gets too hot, add a few drops of water.)

Presentation: Asparagus spears go well with this entrée. French bread sliced on the bias (sharp angle), toasted, also adds a nice touch.

For this seafood entrée, chef Carroll takes a New England favorite and gives it a contemporary, four-star adaptation with the addition of marinated scallops.

Chef's Secret
You may use finnan haddie recipe or leftover finnan haddie chowder (see recipe) as a sauce for this dish.

Baked Haddock, Balsams style

Lesley Iacobacci

WHEATLEIGH HOTEL

At Wheatleigh, pastry chef Lesley Iacobacci and executive chef Peter Platt combine their talents in the creation of dishes that are nearly too beautiful to eat. Lesley's elegant dinner finalés include Valrhona Guanaja Chocolate Sorbet, and a luscious Red Wine Cherry Compote.

A graduate of the Culinary Institute of America (CIA) in New York's Hyde Park, chef Iacobacci finds the Berkshire Mountains to be the perfect location for her work as a chef. A Chicago native, Platt worked as a chef at Boston's Parker House Hotel, and he has apprenticed with renowned chefs Lydia Shire and Jasper White.

The elegance and graciousness of Wheatleigh's formal dining room is beyond compare. The dining room itself is palatial, with two Waterford crystal chandeliers, carved mouldings, Chippendale chairs, and candlelit tables. And then there's the food—glorious meals fit for royalty.

White Chocolate Mousse

Makes 8 servings

14 oz. white chocolate, chopped
1/4 oz. plain powdered gelatin (about 3/4 pkg.)
2 oz. white creme de cacao liqueur
1 1/4 pints heavy cream
2 large eggs
1 oz. sugar
white chocolate shavings (optional garnish)

> Wheatleigh's mousse is very light, but creamy, too. Chef Iacobacci makes it very silky, with a subtle white chocolate flavor—and guests love it!

Valrhona Guanaja Chocolate Sorbet

Makes 8-10 servings

2 3/4 cups water
1 cup sugar
1/5 cup (about 1.6 oz.) cocoa powder
7 oz. dark, bitter chocolate, chopped*
1 oz. Godiva™ chocolate liqueur

* Lesley uses Valrhona Guanaja chocolate (generally available from coffee shops and gourmet grocers) for best results

Chef's Note

*If mixture is not hot enough to melt chocolate, you should melt the chocolate separately and then add it in.

Method for Mousse: Melt chocolate using a double boiler. Bloom and dissolve gelatin powder in with the creme de cacao. Meanwhile, whip the cream and set aside. Whip eggs and sugar over hot water in a double boiler until the mixture is very thick and forms a ribbon.

Add melted chocolate and dissolved gelatin. Cool over an ice bath, stirring occasionally. Carefully fold in whipped cream and mold as desired.

Presentation: Unmold individual portions of the mousse onto serving plates, and garnish with white chocolate shavings. Serve with red wine cherry compote and chocolate sorbet (both recipes follow), if desired.

Method for Sorbet: Heat water and sugar until sugar dissolves; add cocoa and whisk until smooth. Slowly bring the mixture up to a boil. When it reaches a boil, cover and turn off heat. Allow it to rest, covered for at least 30 minutes. Whisk chopped chocolate into the warm cocoa mixture until completely melted.* Add liqueur.

Strain the mixture and cool over an ice bath. Then, freeze, using a conventional ice cream freezer.

Presentation: Place a scoop of chocolate sorbet into a short glass dessert dish and garnish as desired.

Red Wine Cherry Compote

Makes 6 servings

Red Wine Syrup
1/2 bottle pinot noir
1/2 cup sugar
1/2 vanilla bean
1/2 lime*
1/2 orange*
dash of pepper
2 basil leaves, cut in chiffonade

* Use zest only

Cherries
3/4 lb. fresh sweet cherries

Method for Wine Syrup: Combine all ingredients for the red wine syrup in a saucepan; reduce over medium-high heat until very thick (30-45 minutes). Allow to cool, and remove vanilla bean.

Method for Cherries: Pit cherries by cutting them in half, twisting them open, and removing the pits with needle-nose pliars. This method retains the shape of the cherry halves. Roast cherries in an oven (preferably convection) heated to 375° for 5-6 minutes. Cool slightly.

Presentation: Add desired amount of the red wine syrup to the warm cherries and toss. If desired, allow the compote to cool (over an ice bath and then in the refrigerator) before serving.

For Wheatleigh's Red Wine Cherry Compote, the cherries are roasted, releasing an intense flavor.

Salmon with Pesto Crust,
The Heathman Hotel,
recipe on p.157

*Red Pear Napoleon with
Anise Sauce, The Lodge at
Koele, recipe on p.145*

*New England Bread
Pudding, Balsams
Grand Resort Hotel,
recipe on p.196*

*Sautéed Onaga
with Creamy Curry
Sauce, Manele Bay
Hotel, recipe on p. 146*

Rouget Niçoise with Capers, Black Olives, and Tomato Fondue, Meadowood, recipe on p.109

*Poussin with Sweet Corn Fritters and Wild
Mushrooms, The Point, recipe on p.192*

Resource Section

Contact the following sources, as many of the four-star chefs do, for high-quality recipe ingredients. These vendors of gourmet foods and hard-to-come-by products operate mail-order sales direct to the consumer. Specific items and prices vary greatly, so contact the firms for a catalog or to inquire about the price and availability of a particular food.

BROOKS TROPICALS

Chile Peppers & Southwestern Items

OLD SOUTHWEST TRADING COMPANY
ALBUQUERQUE, NM
(505)831-5144

Chile pepper pods (16 varieties), 17 chile powders, ground annato seed, achiote paste, and specialty beans

This mail-order source for Mexican and southwestern cooking ingredients has been around since 1987. The Boulders' chef Chuck Wiley often gets his chiles and achiote from Old Southwest. Owner Jeff Gerlach is is also selling a steady supply of southwestern beans, including bolita (which were popular before farmers switched to pintos for higher yields), Anasazi, black, pinto, and turtle beans.

DEAN & DELUCA
NEW YORK, NY
(800)221-7714 or (212)431-1691 in New York

More than a dozen chile peppers, corn husks, blue corn meal, chorizo, and gourmet beans

American gourmands have long praised the opening of this spectacular showroom and gourmet market on Broadway in New York. Specialty ingredients needed for southwestern cooking are readily available here, and you don't have to be in the Big Apple to take advantage—their mail order service brings tamale wrappers and hot chiles right to your door.

Exotic Foods

MELISSA'S BY MAIL
LOS ANGELES, CA
(800)588-0151

800+ items, including 88 spices, fresh and dried mushrooms, exotic foods, and specialty items

Melissa's stocks many of the gourmet markets across the nation with unusual foods and spices. If you can't find what you want in the stores, call Melissa's by Mail and ask for a catalog. What's popular these days? Portabella mushrooms and creminis, the Italian brown mushrooms, are in high demand among chefs and consumers alike.

Fish, Meat, & Game Birds

D'ARTAGNAN™
JERSEY CITY, NJ
(800)DARTAGN OR (201)792-0748

Specialty smoked products: tasso and black forest hams, chorizo, andouille sausage, nitrite-free bacon, and smoked poultry; foie gras, patés, and terrines; plus specialty raw meats, poultry, and demi-glaces

When a recipe calls for top-quality duck, capon, pheasant, partridge, or squab, D'Artagnan is the place to call. The company promotes the nutritional benefits of game birds, which are low in fat and cholesterol and high in protein. D'Artagnan is often called upon to supply chefs across the U.S. with offbeat meats, such as buffalo, alligator tail, antelope, and wild boar. Try the French Kiss, a whole prune marinated in Armagnac and stuffed with a mousse of foie gras.

SUMMERFIELD FARM
CULPEPER, VA
(800)898-FARM OR (540)547-9600

A luxurious selection of smoked salmon, dry aged beef, pellet-free game birds, natural veal, Glace de Veau*, lamb, venison, and gourmet sausages

This company boasts, "If you don't have two or three days to simmer Glace de Veau from scratch, try ours!" Glace de Veau is the veal jus called for many times throughout this cookbook, and Summerfield Farms offers one that is completely skimmed of fat. Try Summerfield's fancy sausages, such as veal with sun-dried blueberries and apple lamb with roasted garlic, with your next picnic feast, or to accompany any of the chef's meat or poultry entrées. This is also a quality source for game birds and aged beef.

* A 32 oz. restaurant container of Glace de Veau costs $30, and may be stored frozen for up to a year.

Fruits & Vegetables

FRIEDA'S
LOS ALAMITOS, CALIFORNIA
(800)241-1771

Exotic, fresh fruits and vegetables, specialty foods, and related items

When an exotic becomes mainstream, it can no longer carry the Frieda's label. In fact, Frieda's spokesperson says it was Frieda who introduced the kiwi (and more recently the Asian pear) to the U.S. market. Contact this company for rare squashes, Asian vegetables, and sweetheart potatoes. Frieda's is also a good source for exotic fruits, such as the popular cherimoya with its sweet creamy white pulp, and feijoa, an exotic

SUTTON PLACE GOURMET

from the Peruvian Highlands that has a minty, citrusy taste.

Gourmet Chocolate & Exotic Foods

SUTTON PLACE GOURMET
BETHESDA, MD
(800)3-GOURMET

Valrhona chocolate, lichi nuts, fresh lemon grass, prickly pear cactus leaves, spices, dried beans, and more

These full-scale department stores are fashioned after the great food markets of Europe, such as Fauchon and Harrods. Each Sutton Place Gourmet boasts 15 departments, brimming with meats, poultry, pastries, wines, candies, fresh flowers, and produce. The markets also carry specialty condiments and spices used in international cuisine. They are known for offering the fresh, dried beans of Elizabeth Berry / Galena Canyon that are a favorite of chef Mark Miller.

Thai & Indian Cooking Ingredients

DEAN & DELUCA
NEW YORK, NY
(800)221-7714 OR (212)431-1691
IN NEW YORK

A source for curry paste, masa harina, and the Indian Spice kitchen

Dean & DeLuca features an Indian and Thai cooking section, complete with all of the spices and special ingredients needed to make foods from these lands.

Tropical Foods

MAUI TROPICAL PLANTATIONS
MAUAI, HAWAIIAN ISLANDS
(800)451-6805 OR (808)244-7643
(NO CATALOG)

Available by export to the mainland: pineapple, coconut, Mauai onions, and macadamia nuts

Folks working the gift store of this authentic

PHOTOGRAPHS OF PAPAYA (ABOVE) AND CARAMBOLA (RIGHT) COURTESY OF BROOKS TROPICALS

Taste of the Tropics

BROOKS TROPICALS in Homestead, Florida supplies exotic tropical fruits and vegetables to markets all across the United States. The company harvests and imports more than 40 tropical products, including atemoya, avocado, boniato, calabaza, carambola (star fruit), Key limes, mamey sapote, papaya, and scotch bonnet pepper, on 5,000-plus acres in Florida, the Bahama Islands, and Belize.

Because Brooks Tropicals has no retail division, spokesperson Robin Sprague suggests, "Urge your area specialty food store managers to carry the specific exotics that you like to prepare."

Hawaiian plantation will pack and mail these tropical delights by Federal-Express™ to your door, about two or three business days later. All of the foods listed above are grown on the Plantation, which is 11-years old. Fresh, whole pineapples are sold in single-, two-, or eight-fruit shipments. The motto here is, "If you want something and we don't have it, we will go else where on the island to get it."

Truffles & Wild Mushrooms

URBANI FARMS
LONG ISLAND CITY, NEW YORK
(800)281-2330 OR (718)392-5050

The nations largest importer of truffles; plus truffle butter, flour, and oil; imported caviar; dried exotic mushrooms; fresh wild mushrooms in season

There is no substitute for the rich, exotic flavor of truffles. Urbani Farms sells white and black truffles to chefs and to consumers. They also retail fresh morels and other seasonal favorites. When wild mushrooms are not in season, a number of dried varieties are available.

Index of Foods

Appetizer

Appetizer Pizza	30
Bruschetta with Grilled Vegetables	91
Corn Dough Pizza with Smoked Chicken & Plum Tomatoes	20
Crab Cakes with Spicy Cajun Mayonnaise	125
Foie Gras Napoleon with Oregon Truffle Whipped Potatoes, Balsamic Glaze, & Parsley Essence	156
Fresh Kona Oysters with Hawaiian Mignonette	147
Grilled Hot Smoked Sablefish with Rustic Bread Salad	159
Grilled Vegetables	91
House Smoked Sea Bass with Eggplant, Tuscany White Beans, & Olive Oil	179
Lobster & Napa Cabbage Spring Roll	98
Lobster Wrapped in Crispy Potatoes with Caviar Sauce	183
Maine Lobster on Arugula & Mango Salad with Brunoise of Vegetable Vinaigrette	148
Seared Sashimi of Tuna with Citrus Couscous & Spicy Blood Orange Vinaigrette	76
Shrimp & Ginger Mousse on Crostini	80
Soft Shell Crab Appetizer	95
Steamed Chicken & Vegetable Dumplings with Miso Dipping Sauce	90
Vietnamese Spring Rolls with Sesame Vinaigrette	91

Bean

Stewed Anasazi Beans with Morel Mushrooms	50
Tuscany White Beans	182

Bread

Dutch Oven Green Chile Corn	19
Jalapeño Fry	28
Sunflower & Millet Seed	52

Broth

Fish Fumé	75
Fish Jus	161
Garlic	126
Thai Carrot	98

Compote

Fresh Georgia Peach Compote	66

Confit, Relish, & Chutney

Basil Tomato Relish	95
Corn-Tomatillo Relish	142
Fresh Fruit Chutney	122
Mango Papaya Relish	140
Mango Relish	75
Onion Confit	161
Papaya & Pineapple Relish	141
Red Onion Relish	157

Dairy

Brier Run Chèvre Cheese Soufflé	64
Tasso Ham & Boursin Cheese Frittata with Georgia Peach Compote	66

Dessert

Apple Tart with Almonds & Currants	121
Baked Stuffed Mini Pumpkins	158
Chocolate Macadamia Nut Praline Torte	21
Chocolate Mango Frangipane Tart	124
Cinnamon Soufflé with Vanilla Sauce	96
Hawaiian Fresh Fruits with Chocolate Lilikoi Sabayon	147
Mango and Lime Brûlée	113
Margarita Mousse with Tuile Tacos	39
Mille Feuille of Caramelized Bananas, Black Currants, & Chocolate Chips with Caramel Sauce	109
Mixed Berry Crème Brûlée	163
New England Bread Pudding	196
Red Pear Napoleon with Anise Sauce	145
Red Wine Cherry Compote	199
Rosemary Pinot Noir Sorbet	63
Savorin with Grand Marnier	49
Valrhona Guanaja Chocolate Sorbet	198
White Chocolate Mousse	198

Dip

Cajun Mayonnaise	125

Entrée

Beef and Pork

Pacific Rim Tamales	29
Spiced Pork Tenderloin with Fresh Fruit Chutney	122
Szechuan Barbecued Corned Beef Brisket	177
Tournedos of Beef "Perigourdine"	50

Fish

Baked Haddock with Finnan Haddie, Molasses-Marinated Scallops, & Asparagus Spears	197
Baked Haddock with Lemon Caper Mayonnaise Glaze & Chive Oil	196
Baked Sea Bass in Fresh Herb Crust	126
Baked Swordfish with Ancho Chile Aioli & Cornbread Herb Crust	36
Charred Ahi with Papaya & Pineapple Relish	141
Couscous-Crusted Salmon with Cumin Carrot Sauce	48
Dover Sole Fillets with Asparagus Tips & Green Peppercorn Sauce	182
Fresh Albacore Tuna Roasted on a Smoking Alder Plank	159
Grilled Center Cut Swordfish and Vegetable Marinara, with Balsamic Vinegar & Extra-Virgin Olive Oil	179
Grilled Salmon Medallions & Sea Scallops with Saffron Grits, Wilted Watercress, & Lemon Chive Butter Sauce	62
Grilled Tournedos of Swordfish, Black Beans, & Atemoya Vinaigrette	94
Halibut in Ramp Broth with Rosemary	82
Marinated Grilled Swordfish with Yellow Tomato Salsa	93
Mille-Feuille of Salmon with Chervil	93
Niçoise Pesto-Coated Tournedo of	

Salmon & Sturgeon 99

Roasted Red King Salmon with Pesto Crust, Napoleon of Wilted Spinach with Oven-Dried Tomatoes, & Red Onion Relish 157

Rolled Ono with Anahola Granola & Corn-Tomatillo Relish 142

Rouget Niçoise with Capers, Black Olives, and Tomato Fondue 109

Sautéed Onaga with Creamy Curry Sauce 146

Sautéed Red Snapper in Sweet Potato Slices with Mamey Sauce 95

Sautéed Red Snapper with Fettuccine Primavera 79

Sautéed Striped Sea Bass with a Wild Mushroom Fricassee 42

Seared Ahi Poke 141

Seared Ahi with Lemon & Coriander Seed 108

Seared Salmon Medallions & Orange-Ginder Salsa on Tossed Greens with Scalloped Potatoes 126

Sole Paupiettes with Spinach 81

Steamed Striped Bass with Summer Vegetables 75

Game Bird

Poussin with Sweet Corn Fritters & Wild Mushrooms 192

Skillet-Seared Squab with Apples, Sweet Potato, & Red Onion 19

Squab Breast in Braised Artichoke with Drambuie-Flambéd Yams 82

Tamales of Shredded Wild Turkey, Molé Rojo, & Salsa of Grilled Pineapple & Habanero 25

Whole Roasted Cornish Game Hens with a Supreme Sauce 40

Game Meat

Roast Venison Loin with Fried & Sweet Mashed Potatoes 144

Sautéed Medallions of Venison with Braised Cabbage and a Sun-Dried Cranberry Sauce 41

Venison with Caramelized Turnips, Chestnuts, & Huckleberries 121

Lamb

Lamb Loin Saltimbocca with Pepper & Carrot Tarts 181

Misc.

Pacific Abalone with Flowering Asian Greens, Grilled Jasmine Rice Cakes, & Thai Lemon Grass Aioli 160

Tasso Ham & Boursin Cheese Frittata with Georgia Peach Compote 66

Poultry

Chicken Breast Luau with Mango Papaya Relish 140

Chicken Breast with Prawn Stuffing, Risotto Cakes, & Nasturtium Salad 123

Chicken Divan Crêpes 52

Chicken Piccata 52

Cold Ginger Marinated Chicken Breast with Soba Noodles & Cilantro Oil 92

Grilled Free Range Chicken with Tuscany White Beans & Sweet Red Pepper Sauce 182

Pan-Roasted Duck with Lemon Spaetzle 144

Pinenut & Almond Breast of Chicken with Pineapple Relish, Fried Boursin Polenta, & Grilled Squash 67

Shellfish

Angel Hair Pasta with Shrimp & Sun-Dried Tomato Sauce 79

Baked Haddock with Finnan Haddie, Molasses-Marinated Scallops, & Asparagus Spears 197

Chinese-Style Smoked Lobster 74

Curried Crab Cake with Mango, Cucumber, & Lime 75

Grilled Dungeness Crab & Bay Shrimp Cakes with Fresh Strawberry Salsa 28

Grilled Salmon Medallions & Sea Scallops with Saffron Grits Wilted Watercress, & Lemon Chive Butter Sauce 62

Lobster & Finnan Haddie Chowder, Balsams Style 195

Nantucket Stew of Lobster & Early Summer Corn 177

Pan-Seared Diver's Scallops with Cucumber Whipped Potatoes & Champagne Caviar Sauce 111

Pan-Seared Jumbo Sea Scallops Provençale 41

Potato & Black Truffle-Crusted Scallops 97

Steamed & Seared Scallops with Cilantro Leaves, Tamarind, & Ginger 24

Traditional New England Lobster Bake 176

Jumbo Lump Crab Cakes with Mustard Sauce 178

Veal & Lamb

Broiled Rack of Lamb with Wild Mushrooms 78

Grilled Veal Chops with Balsamic Vinegar 78

Natural Oregon Calves' Liver with Sweet Onions, Roasted Hood River Apples, and a Porter Wine Sauce 161

Rack of Colorado Lamb 37

Roast Veal Tenderloin with Wild Mushroom Crepinette, Root Vegetable & Butternut Squash Hash, & Madeira 63

Vegetarian

Eggplant Cannelloni with Tomato Coulis 184

Ravioli of Grilled Garden Vegetables with Fresh Tomato Coulis 175

Season's Open-Faced Vegetarian Burger on Natural Grain 176

Garnish

Buttermilk-Fried Sweet Onions 24

Cilantro Cream 174

Drambuie Candied Pecan 82

Dried Cucumber Rings 174

Garlic Croutons 193

Lotus Root Chips 120

Roasted Corn & Lobster Fritter 162

Tomato Coulis 175

Jus & Stock

Veal Demi Glace 161

Veal Stock 63

Pasta & Dumpling

Angel Hair Pasta with Shrimp & Sun-Dried Tomato Sauce 79

Lemon Spaetzle 144

Ravioli of Grilled Garden Vegetables with Fresh Tomato Coulis 175

Paté

Wild Mushroom Crepinette 63

Pesto

Cilantro Pesto 20

Potato

Cucumber Whipped Potatoes 111

Fried & Mashed Sweet Potatoes 144

Potato Galettes & Balsamic Glaze 156

Potato Lasagna 163

Scalloped Potatoes 126

Shoestring Potatoes 161

Truffle Whipped Potatoes 156

Rice & Grain

Amelia Island Seafood Risotto 81

Citrus Couscous 76

Creamy Stone Ground Saffron Grits 62

Grilled Jasmine Rice Cakes 160

Quinoa Salad & Garnishes 120

Risotto Cakes 123

Risotto with Herbs & White Truffle Oil 193

Salad

Arugula & Mango 148
Nasturtium 123
Pineapple Banana 51
Radicchio & Butter Lettuce with Orange Vinaigrette 51
Salad of Herring & Gravad Lax 194
Shrimp Salad with Spicy Golden Tomato Vinaigrette 18
Spinach Leaves with Texas Peanut Dressing & Buttermilk-Fried Sweet Onions 24

Salad Dressing

Sherry Vinaigrette 148
Texas Peanut Dressing 24

Salsa

Orange-Ginger Salsa 126
Pineapple Salsa 67
Salsa of Grilled Pineapple 25
Strawberry Salsa 28
Yellow Tomato Salsa 93

Sauce

Ancho Chile Aioli 36
Basil Oil 175
Basil Pesto 143
Bechamel 195
Brown Truffle 50
Caper White Wine 95
Caviar 183
Champagne Butter 111
Crème Fraîche 39
Cucumber Coulis 120
Cumin Carrot 48
Curry 146
Dijon Mustard 194
Green Peppercorn 182
Homemade Aioli 161
Lemon Butter 197
Lemon Chive Butter 62
Madeira 63
Miso Dipping 90
Mustard 178
Nage 163
Parsley Essence 156
Port Wine 144
Porter Wine 161
Sage 181

Sage & Sun-Dried Tomato 37
Sauce Molé Rojo 25
Savory 192
Sun-Dried Cranberry 41
Sweet Red Pepper 182
Tamarind Glaze 98
Thai Lemon Grass Aioli 160
Tomato Coulis 184
White Wine Butter 79
Wild Mushrooms 78
Yellow Tomato Aioli 99

Sauce, Dessert

Anise Syrup 145
Chocolate Lilikoi Sabayon 147
Pear 145
Vanilla 96

Sorbet

Rosemary Pinot Noir Sorbet 63
Valrhona Guanaja Chocolate Sorbet 198

Soufflé

Brier Run Chèvre Cheese Soufflé 64
Cinnamon Soufflé with Vanilla 96

Soup

Baked Onion Soup Yavapai 37
Black Bean Soup with Cilantro Lime Sour Cream 29
Chilled Golden Gazpacho with Drizzle of Cilantro Cream 174
Curried Coconut & Squash Soup with Roasted Corn & Lobster Fritters 162
Gazpacho Andalouse 193
Golden Gazpacho 112
Lobster Corn 177
Lobster & Finnan Haddie Chowder, Balsams Style 195
Mango 183
Painted Desert Corn Chowder 49
Rustic Soup of Butternut Squash, Chile Pasilla, Roasted Garlic, & Pepitas 23
Smoked Corn Chowder 27
Spring Onion & Morel Soup with Mussels 80
Summer Tomato Soup with Pulled Sourdough Croutons & Basil Pesto 143
Sweet Potato & Jalapeño Pepper 67

Sushi, Sashimi, & Tartars

Tempura Ahi & Salmon Sashimi with Shiitake Mushrooms & Pickled Ginger Vinaigrette 112
Tuna Tartar with American Caviar, Lotus Root, Avocado, & Cucumber Coulis 120

Vegetable

Oven-Dried Tomatoes 157
Pepper & Carrot Tarts 181
Root Vegetable & Butternut Squash Hash 63
Spinach & Cooked Bacon 108
Sweet Corn Fritters 192
Tomato Coulis 175
Tomato Fondue 108
Wild Mushroom Cannelloni 158
Wild Mushrooms 192
Wilted Spinach 157
Zucchini, Tomato, & Feta Roulade 99

Vinaigrette

Atemoya Vinaigrette 94
Garlic Vinaigrette 108
Golden Tomato Vinaigrette 18
Orange Vinaigrette 51
Pickled Ginger Vinaigrette 112
Spicy Blood Orange Vinaigrette 76
Vegetable Vinaigrette 148

Index of Chefs, Properties, Regions & Chapters

Amelia Island Plantation (FL)   70
American Southwest   9
Arizona, Central   12
Auberge du Soleil (CA)   106

Baker, Mark   174
Balsams Grand Resort Hotel (NH)   188
Bayou & Northern Florida   68
Boca Raton (FL   84
Boca Raton Resort & Club (FL)   84
Boucher, David   140
Boulders, The (AZ)   12
Boulot, Philippe   156
Breiman, Roy   108
Broadmoor, The (CO)   44
Burette, Jacky   78

California, Northern   102
Campton Place Hotel (CA)   114
Carroll, Charles   195
Chef's Techniques, Glossary of   6
Credits & Acknowledgments   214

Dousson, Pierre   94

East & New England   166
Eastern Mountains   58
Eisenberger, Siegfried   48
Enchantment Resort (AZ)   32

Florida, Central & Southern   84
Florida, Northern   70
Four Seasons, Chicago   168
Four Seasons, Philadelphia   172

Giger, Beat   125
Goto, Edwin   143

Greenbrier, The (WV   58
Grove Park Inn & Country Club   60

Harings, John   40
Hawaiian Island   134
Heathman Hotel, The (OR)   150
Henne, Craig   178
Hill, Jon   27
Hyatt Regency Grand Cypress (FL)   88
Hyatt Regency Kauai (HI)   134
Humphries, Todd   120

Iacobacci, Lesley   198

Juran, Kenneth   97

Kauai (HI)   134

L'Auberge de Sedona   34
Lacroix, Jean-Marie   183
Lana'i (HI)   136
Lodge at Koele, The (HI)   136
Lodge at Pebble Beach, The (CA)   118

Maguire, Kevin   36
Mahoney, Sam   192
Manele Bay Hotel (HI)   138
McGrath, Robert   23
Moleterno, Anthony   51

Napa Valley (CA)   104
Naples (FL)   86

O'Neil, Brian   90
Oregon   150

Padovani, Phillipe   146

Phoenician, The (AZ)   14
Piccirillo, Jeffrey   66
Point, The (NY)   186
Pounding, Rob   159

Quail Lodge Resort (CA)   116

Resource Section   207
Ritz-Carlton, Amelia Island (FL)   72
Ritz-Carlton, Naples (FL)   86
Ritz-Carlton, New York (NY)   170

Salishan Lodge (OR)   152
San Francisco & Monterey (CA)   114
Schaefer, Steven   80
Sedona (AZ)   32
South, The American   56
Stein Eriksen Lodge (UT)   154
Sutton, Andrew   111

Tall Timber (CO)   46
Trapp, Mikel   162
Tunks, Jeff   74

Utah   154

West, The American   132
Wheatleigh (MA)   190
Wigwam, The (AZ)   16
Wiley, Charles   18
Williamson, Robert   122
Windsor Court Hotel (LA)   68
Wong, Robert   62

Credits & Acknowledgments

To the Resort & Hotel Staffs
Many thanks to all staff and management at the properties included in this book—without your patience, advice, and assistance Resort & Hotel Chefs' Top Secrets would not have been possible. We also extend thanks to Sheila Donnelly & Associates, L.M. Communications, The Hallock Agency, Lou Hammond & Associates, and Len Reed for contributing their time and effort to this project.

Photo Credits

Cover Photos
Front cover photo of chef Philippe Boulot, photographed by Jim Lommasson, courtesy of The Heathman Hotel. Front cover photo of Chinese-Style Smoked Lobster, courtesy of Windsor Court Hotel. Back cover photographs: courtesy of The Lodge at Koele (Jeffrey Asher, photographer), Windsor Court Hotel, and The Boulders.

The American Southwest
Sunset cactus photograph, courtesy of Arizona Office of Tourism. Resort and chef photographs provided by The Boulders, The Phoenician, The Wigwam, Enchantment Resort, L'Auberge de Sedona (by Knight/Bilham Photography), The Broadmoor, and Tall Timber. Phoenician chef Robert McGrath's photograph is by Randall Photography. Photo of The Broadmoor's din-

ing room, © 1994 D.A. Beightol.

The American South
Beach photograph is courtesy of Florida Department of Commerce, Division of Tourism. Resort and chef photographs are provided by The Greenbrier (© Dan Dry), Grove Park Inn & Country Club, Windsor Court Hotel, Amelia Island Plantation, The Ritz-Carlton (Amelia), Boca Raton Resort & Club, The Ritz-Carlton (Naples), and the Hyatt Regency Grand Cypress. Amelia Island Plantation's dining room photograph, © Kufner Photography of Miami. Aerial view of Ritz-Carlton (Amelia), © Brantley Photography.

Northern California
San Francisco Convention & Visitors Bureau photograph by Kerrick James. Resort and chef photographs are provided by Meadowood, Auberge du Soleil (by Jerry Alexander Photography), Campton Place Hotel, Quail Lodge, and The Lodge at Pebble Beach (reproduced by Permission of Pebble Beach Company). Photograph of Roy Breiman, by Faith Echtemeyer. Campton food photograph (Tuna Tartar), © Fred Lyon / Todd Humphries photograph, © 1993 Bob Adler.

Hawaii & American West
Resort and chef photographs are provided by Hyatt Regency Kauai, The Lodge at Koele,

Manele Bay Resort, The Heathman Hotel, Salishan Lodge, and Stein Eriksen Lodge. Photograph of chef David Boucher (Hyatt Kauai), © 1990 Stephen Gnazzo. Photograph of chef Edwin Goto (Lodge at Koele) is by Jeffrey Asher / Koele Lodge exterior and formal dining room photographs are by Arnold Savrann / Koele Lodge food photographs are by Jeffrey Asher. Manele Bay Hotel exterior photograph is by Kyle Rothenborg. Photograph of chef Padovani and Manele food photographs are by Jeffrey Asher. Photograph of chef Boulot (Heathman Hotel) is by Jim Lommasson. Salishan Lodge photographs are by C. Bruce Forster, © 1994. Photograph of chef Mikel Trapp (Stein Eriksen Lodge), © 1993 Mark D. Maziarz.

The East & New England
Manhattan skyline and South Street photographs: courtesy of New York State Dept. of Economic Development. Hotel, resort, and chef photographs are provided by Four Seasons Chicago, Ritz-Carlton New York, Four Seasons Philadelphia, The Point, The Balsams Grand Resort Hotel, and Wheatleigh Hotel. The Point food photograph (p. 194), by Gary Clayton-Hall. Balsams Haddock photograph is by Paul Charest, © Morning Lane Photography. Chef Jean Marie Lacroix's portrait is by Richard Bowditch photography.

WHEATLEIGH
HOTEL